STITCHING FREEDOM

A TRUE STORY OF INJUSTICE, DEFIANCE, AND HOPE IN ANGOLA PRISON

GARY TYLER
WITH ELLEN BRAVO

ONE SIGNAL
PUBLISHERS

ATRIA

New York   Amsterdam/Antwerp   London
Toronto   Sydney/Melbourne   New Delhi

ATRIA

An Imprint of Simon & Schuster, LLC
1230 Avenue of the Americas
New York, NY 10020

For more than 100 years, Simon & Schuster has championed authors and the stories they create. By respecting the copyright of an author's intellectual property, you enable Simon & Schuster and the author to continue publishing exceptional books for years to come. We thank you for supporting the author's copyright by purchasing an authorized edition of this book.

No amount of this book may be reproduced or stored in any format, nor may it be uploaded to any website, database, language-learning model, or other repository, retrieval, or artificial intelligence system without express permission. All rights reserved. Inquiries may be directed to Simon & Schuster, 1230 Avenue of the Americas, New York, NY 10020 or permissions@simonandschuster.com.

Copyright © 2025 by Gary Tyler

All rights reserved, including the right to reproduce this book or portions thereof in any form whatsoever. For information, address Atria Books Subsidiary Rights Department, 1230 Avenue of the Americas, New York, NY 10020.

First One Signal Publishers/Atria Books hardcover edition October 2025

ONE SIGNAL PUBLISHERS / ATRIA BOOKS and colophon are trademarks of Simon & Schuster, LLC

Simon & Schuster strongly believes in freedom of expression and stands against censorship in all its forms. For more information, visit BooksBelong.com.

For information about special discounts for bulk purchases, please contact Simon & Schuster Special Sales at 1-866-506-1949 or business@simonandschuster.com.

The Simon & Schuster Speakers Bureau can bring authors to your live event. For more information or to book an event, contact the Simon & Schuster Speakers Bureau at 1-866-248-3049 or visit our website at www.simonspeakers.com.

Interior design by Davina Mock-Maniscalco

Manufactured in the United States of America

1 3 5 7 9 10 8 6 4 2

Library of Congress Cataloging-in-Publication Data has been applied for.

ISBN 978-1-6680-9732-8
ISBN 978-1-6680-9734-2 (ebook)

For my mother, who will always be remembered as the heroine of my story for using every means possible to ensure that what I endured was not in vain. People say heroes are those with exceptional powers. My mother was simply a woman who loved her child and wanted the best for him. She drew on that love and commitment to make sure the world knew the injustice done to me and the defiance and hope she helped to instill in me.

CONTENTS

PROLOGUE: Man on Fire	xi
CHAPTER 1: The Day the World Changed	1
CHAPTER 2: Awaiting Justice	19
CHAPTER 3: Presumed Guilty	35
CHAPTER 4: Welcome to Angola	48
CHAPTER 5: The Guardians	56
CHAPTER 6: Not Giving Up on Life	72
CHAPTER 7: Still Fighting to Survive	83
CHAPTER 8: Learning to Tone It Down	100
CHAPTER 9: Fighting for the Right to Education	111
CHAPTER 10: Making Change from the Inside	120
CHAPTER 11: What Kept Me Going	133
CHAPTER 12: Pardon Me	149
CHAPTER 13: Qualified to Do Anything with Nothing	161
CHAPTER 14: Promises Kept	175
CHAPTER 15: Cast the First Stone	189
CHAPTER 16: The Long Arc	204
CHAPTER 17: Free at Last	215
CHAPTER 18: Stitching a Life Together	223
EPILOGUE: Reflections	243
ACKNOWLEDGMENTS	247
RESOURCE LIST	251
NOTES	253

STITCHING FREEDOM

PROLOGUE

MAN ON FIRE

I had been on death row less than seventy-two hours when I was startled out of my sleep by a horrifying scream. It sounded like it was right there on tier C. I got off the bunk and went to the bars of my cell. All of a sudden I saw a glow above me. I realized I was watching an inmate on tier B engulfed in flames. Someone had doused him in gasoline and set him on fire.

I was seventeen years old, barely five feet tall, and less than a hundred pounds. Watching that glow was a shocking reminder that I was helpless. Here's an individual that's burning up. He's not a fresh fish like me, he's been here, and look what happened. How am I going to keep that from happening to me?

Angola—the State Penitentiary—was already living up to its reputation as one of the bloodiest, most dangerous prisons in the country.

Growing up in St. Rose, Louisiana, you hear a lot of horrible things about prison life, Angola in particular. People in your community who've gone to prison get out and tell you how things are. You remember it all, especially as a kid. It's like having a haunted house in the middle of the neighborhood. You don't want to go in that house. You don't even want to pass it at night, you're that afraid of it. That's how it was hearing about Angola, and now I was in it. How would I survive? I knew the men were dangerous, but I didn't know who was more dangerous than the next. Who could I trust?

Nobody. I was in cell 8, one of twelve on that tier. We were a mix of death row and CCR—close cell restricted, or solitary confinement. I had walked in there with nothing but the clothes on my back. Every day I had twenty-three hours by myself in that six-by-nine-foot cell, and one hour to get a shower and walk the tier. I felt bare, like I didn't have anything. There was a metal bed and a little metal stool, both bolted to the wall, a toilet and a sink, bars where anyone walking by could see you. Even when I was occupying the cell, it felt empty.

When I first got to Angola, one by one guys from the tier came to stand in front of my cell to introduce themselves when they had their hour out. The first thing in my mind was, They're trying to lure you in to hurt you. I was this little kid among strangers. You could see them coming. Some were all scarred up—they call them their battle scars. They were built like gladiators, like they were meant to fight on the battlefield. That's what Angola was for many of them, a battlefield. They were telling me if there's anything I needed, they'd be willing to help me. They were giving me things to read: "Here, see this newspaper, read what they're saying about you." Many had heard about what happened to me.

I felt like I was in a den of wolves. I suspected everyone. But seeing that man on fire forced me to grow up fast. I had to learn about my environment, get to know the people I was around. I realized I couldn't think like a child in there.

THIS IS THE STORY of how I wound up on death row and stayed in that prison for nearly forty-two years. I went into Angola as an adolescent and emerged as a man. I achieved things others would never have thought a person could accomplish in prison. I found guys who were like angels that came to protect me. They became family, mentors, people who enlightened me, taught me how to understand what had happened to me, how to survive, how to depend on my instincts and not judge a book by its cover. In time, I became a big brother, an uncle, a mentor to many guys. Some guards who used to dog me came to call me *Mister* Tyler.

In these pages, you'll learn how I was falsely accused, how I fought for my life in one of the worst prisons in the nation. You'll find out how the system failed to render justice, even though the evidence that I was innocent was so apparent. And you'll see how, despite it all, I was able to survive and thrive, to avoid bitterness, to learn to forgive, how I came to embrace life and make change in other people's lives.

CHAPTER 1

THE DAY THE WORLD CHANGED

October 7, 1974, was the day the world changed for me. I remember each detail like it happened yesterday, every face, every conversation, every run-in with authorities.

We'd heard rumors there would be a fight at school that day between white and Black students. That was nothing out of the ordinary. I was a Black kid being bused under a court order to a white school in the middle of a white community in the rural South where people despised us and let us know it. Racial tension was high. Fights were a ritual.

The fight had actually started the previous Friday, at a football game between Destrehan High School and one of our rivals, St. Charles Borromeo. I might have been part of the fists flying except for a white social worker named Nancy Lemoine, who had invited me and my cousins, Ike and Frank, to go to the game with her and her two children; her son went to Destrehan. This woman had come to our school to try to bridge the racial gap. She had a wonderful smile and a spirit that was off the chain. When you saw her, you could detect a good soul. Over time she had gotten to know me and several other Black students. Ms. Lemoine saw something in me—she knew I spoke the truth. When she set up a grievance committee for Black kids to talk about inequities in school practices, she selected me to be one of the representatives.

That Friday night, October 4, Ms. Lemoine drove her wood-paneled station wagon to where we lived, a newly built housing development in St. Rose called Preston Hollow, and took us to the game. It was sweltering as usual. In the fourth quarter, as we were rooting for our team, a commotion started on our far right. We could see it was a fight between Black and white kids. I can't say how it started because it was thirty to forty yards away from where we were sitting. A lot of people started rushing over there. Ms. Lemoine gathered all of us kids right away and got us to the station wagon, making sure none of us would get hurt or be part of the fighting. Then she dropped me and my cousins back in Preston Hollow.

Over the weekend, there was talk that things were going to pick back up on Monday. But Monday started like any other day. Despite the racial tensions, I was an adolescent and I was looking forward to going to school. I wanted the education, but I was also thinking about looking good for the girls. I put on a thin silk body shirt under a fitted knit shirt, sky blue and white with a collar. It was cool outside, so I wore a jacket and my little brown jersey gloves. Kids thought they were hip with those on.

Arriving at school was like the quiet before the storm. You didn't so much notice the tension because the kids getting off the buses were greeting each other, smiling and laughing. Destrehan High was a big, three-story building right off River Road, the major thoroughfare that runs through St. Charles Parish. It had a parking lot in back where the buses would swing around and drop off the Black students. Like always, we congregated outside the gym on the east side of the school. White kids gathered on the other side, in the field by the football stadium or by the industrial arts complex.

I was off the bus ten minutes or less when I heard the deep voice of Principal Wheeler on the loudspeaker saying, "Gary Tyler and John Lee, report to the principal's office immediately." I thought, This isn't good. I knew they were going to harass me. The white principal didn't like that

I was vocal about how the teachers and administrators favored the white youth over the Black. The assistant principal, John Smith, who was Black, didn't seem to like it either.

Earlier that semester, Ms. Lemoine had invited both men to a meeting of our grievance committee. We met in an overflow room in the auditorium. It was one of those moments where I had a lot to say and was ready, but I was still nervous since I didn't know how things were going to go. There were nine of us, five Black students and four white, with our chairs in a circle and two chairs waiting for the administrators. John Smith showed up first, and Wheeler came five to ten minutes later. Ms. Lemoine had everyone introduce themselves and tried to set the parameters, making clear this was a meeting to air grievances that the Black students had. Several Black kids put out how unfair things were, how the administration favored white students over Blacks. The white kids in the room backed us up. As usual, I waited to see what others would say and got my adrenaline up so I could be more direct and forceful when I spoke.

John Smith was six feet two, in his late thirties or early forties. I reiterated to him specific examples the others had mentioned. "You go around pretending to be the Black students' friend and have our backs," I told him, "but you're not there for us, you do not speak up for us." He began squirming and got all flustered, to the point where it looked like he was going to explode. This was a guy who wanted to be called Shaft. When the movie with Richard Roundtree came out, he used to go around the school sporting a leather jacket and a hairstyle like Shaft had, slick and smooth. I saw right through it. I refused to call him by that name, like some of the kids did. I called him John Smith.

"You say you want to help us, but you're really selling us out," I said. "You're a pretender, an Uncle Tom. You don't care about the Black students. You go hard on them if you see them ditching class, then smile in the face of white students doing the same thing."

Principal Wheeler was a little older, his hair starting to gray. When I told him what I'd witnessed him doing and what other kids had shared with me, he changed several skin tones. "You're detached from your duties and what you're supposed to be there for, to treat the students with respect and honor, to encourage them, prepare them for the future," I said. "You're prejudiced. You're a racist. You don't treat Black kids the way you treat white kids. You're quick to suspend a Black kid without even listening to what they have to say and you talk down to them." When Wheeler tried to refute it, I put out more examples. Other kids said, "Yeah, he's right, you do do that."

Wheeler kept saying, "I don't recall that, I try to be fair with everybody. I don't see color. Everybody who knows me knows that I'm fair."

"If that's the case," I said, "why do we have so many complaints against you?"

John Smith tried to defend him. "I've been knowing this man a while," he said. "I've worked with him, I think he's a fair man."

"Of course, you'd say something like that," I told him, "because you work underneath him."

Ms. Lemoine did her best to keep things under control. "Gary, you can be more polite," she said. I was a kid—I had no filter. I didn't know twiddly dot. I just knew that what I saw was unfair. I was like a vessel taking in what many Black kids were saying about discriminatory treatment. Back then I sometimes had a stutter. But when I got in front of a group it went away, like with the country singer Mel Tillis.

So I had reason to be wary when I heard my name on the loudspeaker that Monday morning. As I headed to the principal's office, Ms. Lemoine came over. "What do they want?" she asked. I threw my hands up and told her I didn't know. "If it's anything pertaining to the fight Friday night," she said, "I want Mr. Wheeler to know you were with me. I was the one who brought you, and I was with you the whole time."

John Smith saw us talking and hurried over. "Gary Tyler," he said, "you know you're being called to the principal's office. You need to go now." Like I was supposed to run. I let him know that's where I was headed.

My intuition was right. I saw John Lee coming out of the office, arguing with Principal Wheeler. John Lee was a friend of mine. He was at least five inches shorter than Mr. Wheeler, a stocky kid with dark skin and an Afro. I heard him tell the principal, "You're wrong, you're lying. I don't know what you're putting me out of school for." Wheeler made it clear: "You need to leave the school grounds now, before I call the police."

As John Lee shook his head and walked off, the principal saw me and called me in his office. He shut the door. "Gary Tyler," he said, "I'm suspending you for three days. I got reports from your teacher that you were causing problems in the classroom and that you never show up."

I looked right at him and said, "How can I cause problems in the classroom if I'm never there?"

He knew I'd caught him in a lie. When I hit him with that, his face turned red and he said, "I'm suspending you for three days. You need to leave the school or I'm going to call the police."

I asked for a pass to show my parents, and also, if I got stopped by the police, they'd want to know why I was out of school. Principal Wheeler told the secretary to give it to me, so I took that slip of paper, dropped my books off at my locker, and left. I'm thinking, Okay, I got this suspension slip, I got the day off now. I got three days on my own.

Little did I know I had only a few hours.

WHEN I LEFT THE building, kids were still outside. No one had rung the school bell yet. I saw John Lee with some other Black youth on the Mississippi River levee right across the street, so I went over there. But the water was receding and it was going to get full of mud. I told them, "I'm not going to get all muddy. I got suspended, I'm going home."

John Lee came with me and we walked over to River Road. Like the other Black kids, we lived too far to walk home so we had to hitchhike. It didn't take long to get a ride back to our community. Preston Hollow had federal-subsidized housing for first-time Black homeowners. It was modest homes, and it was all Black people. At the front of the subdivision was a big lot overgrown with weeds. People would sit there under the trees, on overturned buckets and some broken-down chairs. We saw a good friend named Calvin Taylor on one of those chairs drinking a beer. John Lee and I sat down to tell him what had just happened with the principal.

That's when an unmarked car pulled up, with an officer in plain clothes. I later found out his name was Joe Giglio. In the vehicle were two youths he had picked up for truancy, looking out at us from the back seat. I didn't know them, but I later learned one was named Boobie, the other they called Lurch. They went to New Sarpy Middle School. When a white man had two young Black kids in the back of his car, we knew he was a cop.

Giglio looked just like Tom Selleck, tall and slim with a mustache; he appeared to be in his late twenties. He came out of the car with a gun on his side, walked up to Calvin Taylor, and said, "What are you doing out of school?"

"I don't go to school," Calvin told him. "I have a job, I'm eighteen years old."

Joe Giglio pointed at me then. "What about you? What are you doing out of school?"

I told him, "I'm suspended and I'm not going back. I'm looking for a job."

He wanted me to come closer. I said no and started walking off. I knew he'd arrest me for truancy even if he saw the suspension note. We exchanged a few words. Four years earlier, in 1970, when I turned twelve, my parents had sent me to stay with my oldest sister, Ella, in Los Angeles, where I wound up spending two years. They knew there was racism there, too, but they wanted me to get away and experience something different. In L.A., I learned the words "pig," "honky," "fuzz." Just like at home, the police there were people with guns who abused their authority and had no respect for Black people. I used a couple of those words now. My parents always told me to be mindful how I interacted with people, not just elderly people but white people. "Try to make it home safe," they'd tell me. "Don't talk back to white folks. Don't look at white folks. Just make it home." But after my experience in California, I had changed a lot.

When Giglio drove up, I guess he was thinking, I got me a bunch of truants to arrest. He said "Come here" again and reached for his gun. I pointed my middle finger at him and walked away. I was just a sassy kid who took risks. The guy shook his head and went back to his car.

John and Calvin called me a fool and we laughed it off. I had no idea I'd see Giglio again before the end of the day.

John Lee left then, so I started walking home. I saw my cousin Jerry doing some painting at his mother-in-law's house and stopped to say hello. He wanted me to help, but I didn't want to get paint all over my clothes. Back at my house, I ran into Ulrich Smith. He was a couple years older than me, no longer in school, a friendly guy with an athletic build and a good spirit. My parents were allowing him to stay with us. His girlfriend had just had a baby, and he was happy because he'd gotten a job working at the Bunge grain elevator in St. Rose. "They hired me!" he told me. "Man, I need to get some clothes from my mother's house. Come with me." His mother lived in New Sarpy. I really wanted to get some rest, but reluctantly I gave in. This was my friend. So we walked to River Road and hitchhiked all the way to New Sarpy, where Ulrich got two paper bags of clothes from his mother's house. On the way back, a P.E. teacher Ulrich knew from the New Sarpy Middle School picked us up. He said he was going to the Red & White store, not far from Destrehan High School, and he left us in the store parking lot.

As we crossed River Road to hitchhike the rest of the way home, another unmarked car pulled up beside us, this time with Deputy Sheriff V. J. St. Pierre and a second officer, a stocky guy named Mike Babin. I knew St. Pierre; I'd had some run-ins with him before. He came to our community to give Black kids a hard time. He was a Vietnam vet who had been wounded in the war—he lost his right leg and a portion of his left hand—and got a Purple Heart. St. Pierre was also a racist.

For someone with a prosthetic leg, St. Pierre was quite agile. He popped out of the car and asked where we were going. Ulrich told him we were on our way to Preston Hollow. St. Pierre got up close and immediately started patting us down, hands not just up and down my legs but between my legs as well. He wasn't that tall, maybe five foot eight, but still a lot taller than me. "You're under arrest," he said, his voice full of hate. "Get in the car." This time there was no walking away. I knew not to fool with the guy because people said Vietnam had messed him up. We got in the back seat. St. Pierre got in front, leaned over the seat, and started going through Ulrich's bags, then he reached over and frisked us again. "We got a call saying some Black youth were causing trouble at Destrehan High School and left there heading west, away from the school," St. Pierre said. "You're the only youth I've seen."

We were headed east. We had to pass by the school to get back home.

He looked at me and said, "Gary Tyler, what are you doing out of school?"

I told him I had that suspension slip and I showed it to him. He snatched it out of my hand with a look of disgust, like we were the people he was looking for and I was just lying. We were two Black males, the ultimate suspects. The other officer put the car in gear and drove us back to the school, where he flagged down John Smith.

"Are these the youth you called about," St. Pierre asked, "the ones who were causing problems?"

John Smith looked at us and said, "No, Gary Tyler was suspended this morning. He shouldn't be on school grounds."

St. Pierre was not happy. "Get out of my fucking car," he told us.

"You're not going to bring us to St. Rose?" I asked.

"Get the fuck out of my car," he said, and took off.

You could see full buses leaving the school even though it was only one thirty. Ulrich and I debated whether to hitchhike or catch one of those buses. We knew from what St. Pierre said that there had been a disturbance at the school. Ulrich wanted to make sure his brother was okay, and I wanted to make sure my brother and two cousins were okay, so we decided to take the bus.

That turned out to be a big mistake.

St. Pierre had left us out in front of the school. As we turned at the far end of the building, we saw some teachers carrying a Black student named Karen LeBoyle toward the back of the building. It looked like she was out cold. Someone had thrown a rock or a bottle and cut her head. She was bleeding real bad.

Ulrich and I looked at each other and walked a little faster toward the gym. As we got closer, we could hear a commotion. All the Black students were huddled there. Police officers had separated kids by race and were ushering the Black students onto the buses. I saw my brother and cousins, and Ulrich saw his brother. "Man, they're going crazy out here," my brother Terry said. "They're sending us home." He said school officials and the local police department had canceled classes because they couldn't control the situation at school. It was complete pandemonium, students being injured, fistfights, things being thrown at the Black students while the buses were being loaded. The police packed us on bus 91, which was not the one we normally took. It was full way beyond capacity.

They just loaded us on, three to four kids in a seat and others standing, people from all different neighborhoods. You could see out the window but not down the aisle because you had kids standing all the way back.

The buses moved out slowly. Just thirty yards away we could see a big crowd of angry white people attacking the buses as they drove onto the parkway. They were throwing things at us—bricks, rocks, bottles, everything they could get their hands on, beating on the bus with bats. There were houses of white families right on the border of the school grounds. Whenever there was a fight on school grounds, people would come out of those houses with whatever they could use as a weapon. What kind of person picks up bats and shovels? You see that in medieval days when people were on the hunt for witches.

The police loading our bus told us to keep the windows shut. Instead of diverting the buses, we all had to go through that large crowd. If you were trying to protect kids, why send them through a mob and do nothing to stop the violence? It reminded me of scenes I'd seen of attacks on civil rights marchers in the sixties. Even with the windows closed, we could hear shouting and screaming. We couldn't decipher exactly what they were saying, but we could hear racial epithets, could see and hear objects bouncing off the bus, bricks and rocks, all kinds of stuff. The bus was actually rocking.

People inside the bus were hollering, too. I was sitting in the middle of a seat between Larry Dabney and Michael Campbell. The next thing you know, we heard a pop sound. It was probably louder outside the bus because we had the windows shut. All hell broke loose. Kids on the bus started screaming, "They're shooting at us! They're going to kill us!" They panicked and started pushing to the front of the vehicle. Larry jumped up from his aisle seat. Michael crossed into the seat in front of us because he was by the window, and I ducked down, thinking that would take me out of harm's way. People in the aisle were rushing together, making a big pile of kids in the middle of the bus. Others were scrambling over the seats, trying to get to the front. I heard girls hollering and crying. It alarmed the driver, Ernest Cojoe, an auxiliary policeman of St. Charles Parish who was also Black. He was a small guy, but you could look at him and tell he'd been in the military—he was clean-shaven, hair cut low military style, didn't allow any shenanigans on his bus. He stopped the vehicle, opened the door, and stepped onto the road. That's when officers ran up and told him to get back on the bus. We could hear them shouting at him to park on the side street, Destrehan Drive, next to a vacant lot bordered by a ditch.

A group of local police and state police officers surrounded the bus. They ordered everybody to get back in their seats and stay there. We didn't know what to expect because the police were talking to us as though *we* had done something wrong. Two white officers came to the back of the bus, stood in the aisle far apart and started yelling: "Leave everything where it is and get off the goddamn bus." They took us off one by one, patting each one down. The way they were treating us added to the fear of the students, especially the girls. No one knew what to expect because the white crowd had gotten larger and more menacing. The officers were taking off all the boys first and searching each one. As I approached the front of the bus, girls were pulling on my arms, terror-stricken. I tried to be brave, but though I didn't want to show it I was scared like everyone else.

When I finally got off the bus, Deputy Mike Babin searched me thoroughly. He had me take off my hat and glasses, and empty everything from my pocket. I complied, and after he was done he ordered me to jump across the ditch onto the vacant lot, where the rest of the Black students were standing. As I got my balance, I moved around the group. I saw some kids posing for a picture being taken by a state police officer and I struck a cocky pose with the group.

After the photo, I turned and saw that my cousin Ike was not too far behind me. I watched them pull him aside. "What's going on?" I asked. Deputy Babin told me they were arresting Ike because he had a chain with a twenty-two bullet in his pocket. "There's nothing illegal about that," I said. "They can't arrest you for that. Officer, you didn't say anything about the bullet I have around my neck." It was the same as my cousin's. The officer gestured for me to come back across the ditch. I was getting ready to do that when state police officers drew their guns on me.

I tried to explain that an officer had told me to go back across the ditch. Deputy Babin was very attentive but didn't say a word. Other youth were behind me. A cop was pointing his gun directly at me. I said, "You're pointing a gun at me, what if the gun goes off? I'm going to sue you because you aren't going to be able to say it was an accident when you have a gun pointed at me. You have all these witnesses, they see what you're doing. I'm just trying to get across the ditch because the man told me to do it. They're arresting my cousin."

Then out of nowhere came one lone officer, Nelson Coleman. He had to be at least six feet four, a big, corn-raised country Black dude in his fifties. I'd never seen this guy in my life. He walked up to me and said, "Son, what's your problem?"

"I'm not your son, I have a father," I told him.

He looked at me like I was out of my mind. "Son," he said again, "you're under arrest for disturbing the peace and interfering in a police officer's job." Then he grabbed me by the seat of my pants and lifted me up. I felt like a rag doll. I was like a little kid on his tippy-toes being dragged by his parents.

Coleman had a long gun, either a shotgun or a rifle. He handed that to the state police officer and took that officer's pistol and started walking with me through the mob. Here was a Black police officer marching me through that same white crowd that apparently had someone shooting at our bus. The crowd started circling in on us. Officer Coleman panicked. That gun he had lay right on my shoulder near my head. I started to panic, too. "Move the gun," I kept saying. "Move the gun." I don't think he heard a word I said. Other police officers came in and dispersed the crowd and we made it to the school grounds.

Coleman's car was at the school parking area, where the buses were still coming through. He put me in it and told the deputy, "Watch my vehicle." Just then Karen Moore, a Black student, came out of the school hallway. When she saw me in a police car, she said, "Gary, you didn't have nothing to do with the shooting of that white boy." This was the first I heard that a white boy had got shot. I told her I didn't know anything about it.

Joe, a white kid who was my tennis partner, walked up to the car. He asked the officer what I was arrested for. "Disturbing the peace," the officer said. Both Karen and Joe heard him.

I SAT IN THAT police car until they cleared everyone who was still on the school grounds. I could see they put the Black kids who had been on bus 91 back on that vehicle, headed to the New Sarpy police substation a couple miles away. The deputy got in the car and drove me there as well, without making conversation. He parked in front of the station, two feet behind that bus. I watched them bring the kids off, including Ulrich, but I was still in the patrol car. I also saw officers go back and forth onto the bus, but I couldn't see what they were doing.

At one point, the deputy put another kid, Michael Jenkins, in the vehicle with me. When I asked Michael what happened, he told me, "Man, the Black officer arrested me because he heard someone call him an Uncle Tom and he picked me out. Said I was disturbing the peace."

It got sweltering hot in the car. That morning when I left for school, it had been cool enough for a light jacket. I'd brought it home when I stopped there earlier and met Ulrich. But I still had my little gloves in my pocket and the knit shirt over my silk body shirt.

Now I was soaking with sweat, so I took off my outer shirt. I saw a lady from Preston Hollow whose daughter was at the substation. I called her name and asked her to call my mother, who by that time would be home from work. The lady went right across the street to a trailer house with a white family, who let her use the phone. About ten minutes later my mother drove up to the station. The lady showed my mother where I was, still in the police car.

When my mother walked to the car window, I could see she was worried. She asked me what was going on. I told her they arrested me for disturbing the peace. That's when Officer Coleman came over. "He's the one who arrested me," I told her.

Coleman said, "You're his mother?" She said yes, this small woman tilting her head back to look up at him.

"You need to teach your boy some manners." My mother seemed to be relieved that the charge was minor, but she was still concerned.

By then I was soaking wet. I had a hat with glasses, my gloves, this wet-assed shirt. I asked if I could give my shirt and the other stuff to my mother. Nelson Coleman said yeah. As she took my things, he told her, "It won't be long. We're just processing everybody now." They were questioning kids and letting them out one by one to their parents.

After a while, someone came for Michael, and then they finally got me out of the car and brought me into the substation. Ulrich was still there. They set us together in an office right off the lobby. I asked Ulrich what they'd arrested him for. "I called the man Uncle Tom," he said. "They arrested me for disturbing the peace." Turns out Coleman had arrested him at the same time as Michael Jenkins. We knew they weren't going to say they were arresting you for calling someone an Uncle Tom.

"I got the same charge," I told him. We thought it was no big deal. They would release us. We definitely weren't interfering with the officers doing their job.

A white officer came into the room and started processing Ulrich, then turned to me and asked my name, date of birth, how old I was. "My name is Gary Tyler," I said. "I'm sixteen years old."

It was like I turned on a switch. "You motherfucker," he yelled. "Why didn't you tell me you were a juvenile?"

"You just asked me!" I said.

He tore the paperwork in half and ran out.

Ulrich and I were both rattled by that. Then St. Pierre, the sheriff who'd picked us up on River Road, came in and saw the both of us. "Why didn't you all go home when I fucking told you to?" he said. I pointed out we'd been heading home when he picked us up. I was too flippant for them, a young kid who always had a response ready.

"I'm going to find out what happened from the others on that bus," St. Pierre said.

I could see fear on Ulrich's face. I knew he had just gotten a job and wanted to take care of his baby. I was kind of intimidated, too. We'd just heard about somebody getting shot.

The next thing you know, other officers came in, including Coleman, the Black officer. St. Pierre stood over me and said again, "Why didn't you go home the way I told you?"

"I was going home," I told him.

"You was on the bus," he said. "What happened?"

"What?"

"What happened?"

"Nothing that I know of."

"You're lying, you were on the bus, you know what happened."

"No," I said. That's when he hit me with his fist. I never saw it coming. He started hitting me again and ordered the others to move Ulrich Smith out of the office. "This motherfucker has a hard head," he said. "Give me something to beat this Black motherfucker." The whole time he was calling me the N-word.

Nelson Coleman, the Black officer, told him, "The only thing I have is this flapjack." A flapjack is a lead ball laced in leather. It's designed to punish. Coleman handed over the flapjack and St. Pierre went to beating on me. He started hitting me hard on the tops of my legs, my arms, my shoulders, then my face and my head. The other officers started punching on me, stomping on me, five or six of them, all except Coleman—he just stayed in the room and watched.

I kept saying, "Man, I don't know what you're talking about."

St. Pierre said, "A man is a mini-goat." I didn't know what the hell he meant, unless he was telling me I sounded like a mini-goat.

There was so much blood. St. Pierre was grabbing my hand, pushing it in the blood and trying to push it in my mouth. "Eat your blood," he yelled. "Eat it, eat it." Even though he was splattered with blood himself, he didn't stop.

They beat the hell out of me. I was hollering, screaming in pain. Giglio, the officer who had words with me in Preston Hollow, came in to give them a warning. "Listen," he said. "They still have mothers out here. They can hear what's going on. You all are going to have to take and move this somewhere else. They can hear this child screaming and hollering."

They stopped the beating then. St. Pierre said, "We're going to move him to the back room." They grabbed me, lifted me up, and started marching me to the back of the station. But the only way there was through the lobby. I saw a bunch of Black mothers sitting there. When the officers marched me out, I locked eyes on my mother and saw the horror on her face. I was a bloody mess.

"Mister, please, can I talk to him?" my mother said. "Please, mister." They ignored her.

No mother in the world should be put in a position like that, especially in the lobby of a police station, hearing a beating, a child's voice, hearing officers cursing, using vile language. All the mothers had been hearing this, thinking, Lord please don't let it be my child. And the moment that door opened and they were bringing someone out, whose child was it—my mother's child.

I could see the faces of the other women, the sigh of relief it wasn't their child, but also horror: Is my child next, or have they beat my child already like that?

The cops brought me to the back room and started beating on me again. St. Pierre said, "I don't want to hear nothing till I find out who murdered my cousin." That's when I realized the kid who'd been shot had died and that he was related to St. Pierre. "Pull your goddamn pants down," St. Pierre told me. "I want to see what a black ass looks like." He tried to knee me with his peg leg in the back of my leg. He hit me with the flapjack. Other cops kicked me in my privates. One kicked me in the front and one kicked me in the back. My balls were swollen. My lips were big, my eyes were swollen all round, my head was bleeding.

Then they sent Officer Coleman in to talk to me. "Gary, listen," he said. "Just tell us what happened." I guess they thought I would talk to him because he was Black.

"I don't know what happened," I told him.

"If you did it, say you did it," he said. "The only thing they'll do is send you to a juvenile institution. You'll be there a couple years and get out."

"For something I didn't do?" I said. "I didn't do anything."

He said, "You must know something."

"I don't."

"I'm trying to help you," he told me. "Just give us some names."

I said, "I don't know anything."

"Who's capable of that?"

"I don't know."

He kept trying to get information from me. Other police came in and gave me paperwork to sign. I refused. They said, "Sign to say you don't know anything." Even as a kid, you watch so many cop stories and they tell you, don't sign anything. It's not like I was an airhead. I did know that much.

They started beating me again. They proceeded to beat me and beat me and beat me.

At some point they all left and I was in the room by myself. All these thoughts went through my head. Were they trying to frame me for something I didn't do? Beating me for something I didn't know? Why were they targeting me?

A few minutes later, they came rushing back into that little room. It startled me. An officer walked to the table beside me, and that's when I noticed there was a green bus seat right behind me. I was hurting, I was confused, I hadn't noticed anything about what was in the room. If that seat had been a snake, it probably would have bit me. When the police officer walked by my side to get to that seat, I saw him pick a gun off it and hold it in his hands.

I didn't know what to think. It was like they wanted to catch me doing something. They'd left me alone without putting handcuffs on me. Maybe they expected me to get hold of the gun and get my fingerprints on it, or take the gun and try to escape. I know if I had done that, they would have felt justified shooting me on the spot.

The officer who picked up the gun took it out of the room. Those police knew what they had left in there when they'd left me alone. I didn't put it all together for a long time.

By now I was a complete mess. My pants were ripped. They forced me to stand up and then told me to sit down, and tried to pull the chair out from under me.

They really dealt with me that night. I was hurting, in pain, I was crying. It got to the point where I was numb. I cursed them out and everything. That didn't faze them one bit. The beating went on for a long time.

At one point someone said, "How old are you?"

"Sixteen," I said. "I just made it on July 10."

"Okay, you need to call your mother," the officer said. Apparently she had left, since no one would talk to her and I had two young brothers and a sister at home. Most likely she also wanted to call my father and let him know what was happening. My mother and father had been around during the Emmett Till lynching. They knew about kids getting murdered.

"Tell her to bring in your birth certificate," the police told me. "What did your mother take when she saw you?" I told them my top shirt, hat, and gloves. They gave me the phone and said I should tell her to bring everything back. I did, and soon she was there with my father. The two of them had my things and the birth certificate. This time they let my mother and father in the room. My mother's face was covered in tears. Even my father's eyes were watery. He was a big man, six foot four, 270 pounds, a guy who'd started working in the fields when he was nine and now handled three jobs, but that night he looked broken. I could see the horror and fear as my parents took in what these officers were capable of.

RECENTLY, I WATCHED THE movie *Till*. I saw how Emmett Till's mother examined his body with her hands. It reminded me of when my mother came into that room and how she ran her fingers from my head to my face to my shoulder. There was blood everywhere. When she hugged me, it hurt. The cops left us alone for a while, and she just felt me, touched my arms, my leg. I told her how they beat me and she wept. My father sat there shaking his head, like he couldn't believe what he was seeing. My mother was powerless. My father was powerless. They couldn't do nothing at all.

Mothers are the wonders of the world because of how they love their children. Any child, the first love of their life is their mother and father, especially their mother. They always expect their mother to protect them, no matter what. My mother would have been willing to put her life on the line for me. That day, she was petrified and she couldn't do anything. She pleaded and begged to talk to someone. They ignored her like she didn't exist.

I can still see the look on her face.

Those officers didn't care who saw how bloodied I was. They didn't care that I was a child. They knew they had power over the life of a Black child who they wanted to confess to something, and they were going to get it out of him if they had to beat him to death. St. Pierre was behind it, the same man who had patted me down on River Road, who had brought me back to the school, who had led that group of officers that laid in and took part in the brutality. "I'm going to find out who killed my cousin," he kept saying.

There was no benefit of the doubt, none of that. That's how the police operated: a bunch of heartless, brutal thugs.

After my mother left, they put me in a holding cell in the substation. They didn't give me nothing. Again they told me to eat my blood. I wasn't a human being to them. The people who tried to kill me, who beat the hell out of me, how could I expect they were going to show me some humanity?

Earlier, when I was in the police car, I was thinking I was going to be released into the custody of my family. I was just being arrested for disturbing the peace. That's minor. To me it wasn't that bad.

While they were beating me, I didn't know if I was going to live or die, all the hatred coming out of their mouths, calling me the N-word.

I was confused. I couldn't make connections. How did it get to this, from me protesting the way they were arresting my cousin over a piece of jewelry that wasn't illegal, to something this big?

I was so exhausted, I went to sleep on the metal bed in that cell.

I didn't go home that night.

I didn't go home for forty-one and a half years.

CHAPTER 2

AWAITING JUSTICE

Young and naive as I was, I still believed they would release me. During every day I spent in the parish jail, I thought someone would come and say, you can go home. Even after they beat my butt and denied me medical attention, even when they only allowed my mother and father to visit me and kept me from everybody else, I was still thinking they'd find out the facts and release me. They'd learn that St. Pierre had patted me down before driving me and Ulrich back to the school, and that he knew neither one of us had a gun. They'd examine the photos of me standing with the other kids waiting to get on bus 91 and see there was no way I could have hidden a gun under those tight-fitting clothes. Larry and Michael would say we were squeezed in the same seat and, of course, I had no gun. Everyone on the bus knew the shot came at us, not from us. The jury would listen to Ernest Cojoe, the bus driver who was a war veteran and knew for certain that no gun was fired from inside his vehicle.

But the justice I waited for wasn't happening.

The morning after my beating, a bunch of officers came in and took me from the holding cell at the substation. I was still wearing the same bloody clothes. No one had given me a toothbrush or any chance to wash up. When I was curled up behind bars the night before, I heard deputies saying, "That's him in there," like they were looking at an animal in a zoo.

The deputies who escorted me that morning didn't handcuff or shackle me. I guess because I was small and there were so many of them, they weren't afraid of me. They positioned themselves in front and behind me as they walked me out the side door. I saw all kinds of reporters and flashing lights. The officers closed in around me so people wouldn't see how bloodied I was. Some of them even went after the photographers and started grabbing cameras. They were in a frenzy as they rushed me forward and put me into the back seat of a car. All I knew in that moment was that I was in pain and I was scared. After what had happened the night before, I had no idea what they'd do next.

Some older white guy in a suit was behind the wheel. I didn't know who he was. It was just the two of us and he could see how badly battered I was. He drove to the Luling–Destrehan ferry crossing and I realized he was bringing me to the St. Charles Parish jail in Hahnville. When we parked, he leaned over and asked if I was all right. I told him, "No." He asked if I needed a doctor and I said, "Yes." But I never did see a doctor. I still have the scars on top of my head and around my eye from those lacerations. I still live with the psychological trauma.

After arriving at Hahnville, I was taken to a cell on the third floor. Unlike the cell at the holding station, this one had a solid door. Someone had to open a hatch in order to see you. The cell also had two windows, one in the front and one on the side that allowed me to see outside. Right across the street was Hahnville High School. It was a large old brick building just like Destrehan High. I could see buses coming in, kids getting off, walking around the school grounds, going to school activities. The sight hit me hard. I was just like any other kid, going to school, wanting to get an education, having fun, then all of a sudden my life took this horrible turn. Seeing those kids made me think how much I missed being able to interact with classmates, people I would possibly never see again.

I quickly made friends with two other prisoners on the floor, Melvin

Brown and Bertrand Richardson, both Black men. Melvin was in the cell next to me, a Vietnam veteran in his thirties. Though I didn't know him, my family had known his for a long time. Bertrand, a muscular guy close to the same age, was to his right and had been in prison before. When officers put me inside my cell, the two called my name. Melvin and Bertrand had news for me: They'd learned from the television that I had been charged with first-degree murder of a thirteen-year-old white boy, Timothy Weber.

I was terrified. The words felt surreal. Still, from what the guys were telling me, I was a juvenile and the most they could do, even if they convicted me of killing Timothy Weber, was to send me to the juvenile facility in Scotlandville, Louisiana, until I was twenty-one. That's the same thing Officer Coleman told me when he was trying to convince me to sign a statement. I believed them all.

My immediate concerns were being stuck in the same bloody clothes, needing to see a doctor, wondering when I'd be able to visit with my family. My cell had a toilet and a bathtub, but the tub had no running water. In order to shower, I had to be transported to an empty cell at the end of the hall. That didn't happen until two days later. The doctor never came.

On Thursday, my third day at Hahnville, I finally got to see my parents. The deputies brought me out of the cell down to a holding room where the two of them were waiting. They were relieved to see me, but I could tell they were worried. My mother rose to meet me as I walked in, to hug me and make sure I was all right. My father was working hard to hold himself together in a situation he had no control over. They'd also brought along a middle-aged white man. This guy had told the officials he had some position with a legal aid organization. When we were alone with my parents, he let me know he was really a reporter with *The Times-Picayune* and he wanted to hear my side of the story. Back then and still today, many Black people in rural communities like St. Charles see white people as a symbol of power. That's how I felt when I met this guy, that my family knew somebody with power and influence who could help. My father had made this connection for me. One of his jobs was managing an apartment complex in Jefferson Parish around Metairie. My father was known as a good worker. He knew a lot of influential white people there.

In the middle of the interview, the police rushed in and pulled the guy from the room. I was shocked. Apparently, someone had figured out who he really was. I still don't know whether he ever wrote that story. Police officials probably took away any notes he had.

My parents had brought me some clothes. They could see I was still swollen from the beating. I knew they were hurt and concerned like any parents would be. The jail was hardly a friendly atmosphere. When the deputies had brought me down, they kept me separated from the other prisoners who were visiting family in the yard and took me to the little conference room. It was evident they weren't going to let me see anyone but my parents. Five of my ten siblings were still living at home and three were adults who lived nearby. We were a close family who loved each other a lot. But for the first month, until my injuries healed, only my parents were allowed in. Mostly it was my mother who came. I knew my father wanted to be there, but he had to work hard to support the family, getting up at five in the morning and not getting home until eleven or twelve at night. Now they had to afford an attorney, too. I'm sure it was quite daunting for both of them.

My family did everything humanly possible to get me representation. Because they were from the South, they knew how cruel and how deadly white people could be. No matter how lightly I may have taken whatever lay ahead, they never took it lightly. They were afraid these people were going to take my life. I knew they'd do anything they could for me. "Son, do the best you can to hold on," they said. They assured me they were going to find an attorney.

I HAD MY FIRST preliminary hearing a week or two later with Judge Brennan, an older white man who looked larger than life. "Do you have an attorney?" he asked me. "If not, we will have one appointed." I told him my parents were getting someone.

And they did. My parents found a lawyer named Jack Williams. Back then, people like my family who were poor thought all attorneys were criminal attorneys, so they didn't know to ask about his experience. I learned later that someone had referred a more experienced defense lawyer to them, but the guy wanted $2,000 up-front. My mother said that was like $2 billion to her. The attorney was about six feet two, a slim white guy in his forties with receding hair and spectacles. I didn't meet him until my second court appearance a month after my arrest, in November 1974.

At the time, I was really worried about what the newspapers were saying about me. I didn't have a television yet, but I did get to read the papers. My case was all over the news, and they were painting me as a villain. The papers reported I was supposed to have signed a statement against myself. Those people damn near murdered me because I refused to sign papers, and here they were claiming I put my signature on something? I met Jack Williams about thirty minutes before we went into the courtroom and mentioned that article to him. "That's a complete lie," I told him. "I didn't confess to nothing. I didn't sign nothing."

In the courtroom, Williams made clear he was my attorney and asked for copies of all the evidence that had been submitted. Specifically, he wanted any documents related to the so-called confession or any other statement I had made. The St. Charles district attorney, Norman Pitre, told the judge, "We don't have any statement that Gary Tyler confessed or said he shot a gun." My attorney complained that the papers were reporting this. Pitre said, "We don't know anything about that." I knew the police and the DA were behind those stories. Leaking that to the newspaper was their way of poisoning the well, stacking the deck against me.

I wasn't the only one in the news those days—David Duke was all over it as well. Who didn't know David Duke? Black people tell their children about the Klan when they're very young. The attack on our bus happened at the same time Louise Hicks was leading a campaign against integration in Boston schools. I found out later that David Duke had gone to Boston with his minions to stir up the racial pot. When this thing happened in St. Charles Parish, David Duke got wind of it and came back down the following day. He wanted to be seen laying a wreath on Timothy Weber's grave. He wanted to send KKK security patrols into the area, he said, to "protect whites." He kept feeding the public racist statements about taking the community back from "these Black savages and murderers."

Despite all this activity and bad press, Williams told me I'd get off. I'm thinking, this is the guy who's going to represent me, help me convince the jury that I'm innocent. The man was saying, "Don't worry, you're going home. You don't have to fret about anything." From what he knew about the case, he said, he thought they were going to drop it.

That day in court, he entered a plea of not guilty and asked for bail. The judge made it clear they don't give bail on first-degree murder charges.

THE MONTHS DRAGGED ON. It never dawned on me that they would hold me for so long. At our second meeting, Williams told me, "From what I'm gathering, they don't have anything solid. That's why they're prolonging it." I believed him.

I was still thinking the worst that would happen is them sentencing me to the juvenile detention center in Scotlandville, called the Louisiana Training Institute, or L.T.I., which was about a hundred miles from my home in St. Rose. That wasn't too terrifying. I knew that place. I had spent some time there.

Twice I had scrapes with the law but managed to avoid getting sent to L.T.I. In 1972, I was with my brother Steve and four other guys when we broke into a neighbor's house on Turtle Creek. One guy found some old Spanish pesos and went to a shop to try to buy stuff with them. He got caught. He gave the police the names of everyone involved and they charged all of us with burglary. The others were sent to the juvenile facility, but I was put on probation because it was the first time I'd ever gotten into any trouble.

A few months later, a friend and I were passing through a laundromat. My friend put some money in a candy machine, but nothing happened. We both started shaking the machine. The owner of the place came out and called the police, who arrested us for attempted robbery. Luckily, there was a woman in the laundromat who had witnessed everything. She came to court and said exactly what happened, that we were just trying to get what my friend paid for. Both of those times I appeared before Judge Ruche Marino. This time he dismissed the charge and confirmed that I hadn't violated my probation.

In September of 1973, my luck vanished. I had stayed home from school that day because I wasn't feeling too well. My sister Bobbie Nell asked me to go to the store for her, so I got dressed and headed out to the sweet shop to get what she needed. Everything was normal and quiet there, just a few people hanging out. But on my way back, I ran into V. J. St. Pierre. Everyone knew the guy; he was one of the police officers who liked to come through the community and harass Black youth, especially teenagers like us. He was the same one who had arrested me for the Turtle Creek burglary. He got out of the car to stop me, made me get into his vehicle, and asked me where I was coming from. "The store," I said, holding up the stuff in bags in my hands. St. Pierre started driving down Mockingbird. "Ask my sister," I told him.

He stopped in front of my house and blew the horn. Bobbie Nell came out and saw me in the back seat. "Did you send your brother Gary to the store?" St. Pierre asked.

"Yes," she said.

But the guy just drove off with me. He told me I was under arrest and transported me to the Hahnville Parish jail. Someone had claimed they saw me in a house on the corner that had been burglarized.

A week later, a guy named Kenny Shield, who'd been caught after escaping from juvenile detention, came to Hahnville. When he found out what I was in for, he told me, "Look, I was the one who did that break-in. They mistook you for me." We were similar in build and complexion, though he was a little heavier. We both had small Afros. I watched Kenny Shield write Judge Marino saying he was the one who broke into that house. But it didn't matter. In October of 1973, I was sentenced to L.T.I. I got out the following April.

At first, we didn't have guards out there—we had house fathers and house mothers. Young kids were escaping from the place all the time. In December 1973 or January of 1974, they brought in some Angola prison guards with horses to patrol the perimeter. Once the young offenders learned the escape route and how to do it, they still ran off the first chance they got. But I never did. It didn't cross my mind. I knew I wasn't going to be there forever. We did play some games with the Angola horsemen, though, when they were riding through the grounds. As soon as they were a few yards ahead of us, we'd yell "Run away!" and jump on the fence like we were all going to climb over.

Of course, I didn't want to be there. When Kenny Shield wrote the letter saying it was him, I was sure the judge was going to release me, but he didn't. He decided not to believe the letter. I didn't like it, but I wasn't afraid. My brother Steve was in the dorm across from mine, sent there for that Turtle Creek burglary. His friends became my friends. The food was pretty good. On the weekends when Big Momma and Miss Whitmore needed help in the kitchen, they'd tell the house fathers and mothers they needed someone and get me to work for them. During the day, I went to school. We also had recreation. I played football in Scotlandville, linebacker and defensive guard. I liked the house father, Mr. Smith, and his wife, Dorothy.

MY TIME AT THE parish jail in Hahnville was completely different. There were no classes, no recreation. Every weekday morning, they would feed us two boiled eggs and some grits. On Saturdays and Sundays, we had a pack of two little doughnuts. We were in cells, not dorms. I never did get medical attention. I had assumed the man who drove me there would arrange it when he dropped me off, but it never happened. I brought this to the attention of the jailer, Lockett, but I imagine when he inquired, they told him one thing and did nothing. When they locked me in the cell upstairs, no one was allowed to come in. Eventually, you heal.

That first week, something happened outside the jail and no one gave a thought that I was there inside watching it. There was construction on both the jail and the courthouse. Every worksite had a manager's trailer. I was on the third floor, in a cell by myself, in the corner of the building. The trailer was right down from me. That Thursday or Friday night, a terrible fire broke out. It was so intense, it completely burned down the trailer. Turns out the contractor had been drinking. He fell asleep and burned himself up. I was right there by the window, watching as fire engines arrived and firefighters came out with his charred body. Having to watch them dig through the rubble and locate his body and put it in a bag was horrendous. I'd never seen anything like that.

Soon after the fire, things got much worse. Deputies who worked at night started passing through the parking lot and shining their vehicle floodlights into my cell on the third floor, calling out my name and threatening my life. Bertrand and Melvin told me to keep away from the window and keep the lights off at night. "They can see your silhouette from the window," Bertrand said. "You're an easy target. Stay away. These white folks are dangerous. These white folks will kill you."

I started sleeping on the floor. That didn't stop me from hearing them curse, call me the N-word, say they're going to kill me. These were their ways to intimidate me.

One Thursday, an officer named Kenneth walked into the jail and came looking for me. He knew I was on the third floor but not which cell. First, he went to the bullpen where they had the white prisoners. They didn't integrate jails back then; they had a separate bullpen for Black inmates on the second floor. I could hear Kenneth asking those white bullpen guys where I was.

"Somewhere on the other side of the floor," they told him.

I was in cell 1, Melvin in cell 2, Bertrand in cell 3. The door to cell 4 was open so the deputy could see nobody was in there. Kenneth started with my cell. I was laying in the bed and the hatch on the metal door opened. I realized someone was peering in. The lights were off and I could tell he couldn't see where I was. He knew the door was locked because he pulled on it. Then he walked to Melvin's cell and asked, "Where's Gary Tyler at?"

"Why?" Melvin said.

"What you looking for him for?" Bertrand said. "Why don't you leave him alone?"

Melvin backed him up. "Yeah, leave that boy alone," he said.

It wasn't hard for Kenneth to figure out which was my cell. He went back and sprayed mace in through the hatch. That mace hit me right in the face. I hollered and Kenneth ran downstairs. My friends shouted for me to wash my eyes out with water. They started screaming and hollering and banging on their doors to get the attention of the jailer. Lockett was actually off duty but lived in a house right next door. He was an older man, tall with a solid build and gray hair, who'd been a jailer there for a long time; his wife cooked for the prisoners. Lockett came up to see what all the noise was about. Bertrand and Melvin told him the deputy had come up to harass me and shot mace in my face.

I also told my mother when she came to visit. She talked to Lockett, too. The next day I was told he went to Judge Marino to complain. Lockett was in charge at the parish jail, but he only worked during the daytime. He had no control over deputies who came at night. Later he told me what he said. "If something happens to Gary, it would be on me," he reminded the judge. "I won't take responsibility." The judge put orders out that deputies couldn't go in there messing with me anymore.

I wasn't the only one in danger at the parish jail. Earlier that year, a group of six Black people had been arrested for robbing a place in Killona, Louisiana, across the river next to Hahnville. I met them when V. J. St. Pierre had locked me up for the burglary Kenny Shield did, before I was sentenced to the juvenile facility in Scotlandville. Two of that group were young women, Chris and Althea.

In December of 1974, several police officers came to the parish jail at night. We could hear Althea and Chris screaming on the first floor. By then, Bertrand and Melvin had been transferred to Angola. A guy named Michael Weber was in the cell next to me. We were trying to figure out what was going on. We watched them bring Chris up to the empty cell on our floor about five feet away from me. You could see she was crying and had been beaten up.

Turns out Chris had managed to escape. She had made it out of the jail and had started running down River Road. The deputies gave chase. They caught her and brought her back to the parish jail, put her upstairs near us. Chris was hollering and screaming and crying. Later, I was standing by the door of my cell and I could smell smoke, could see it coming from her cell. I went to yelling out the window for Lockett and the maintenance guy, Plummer, to come up there because her cell was on fire. They rushed up the stairs. I learned from the trustee, Michael Dupre, that Chris had taken her clothing and put it in the middle of the floor and set it on fire, then laid right in the middle of the flames. They dragged her out in time. At some point, Chris and Althea were released from the parish jail, along with Althea's brother Rockhead who had also been arrested for the robbery.

It was well known in the community that white police officers went into jail cells and raped Black women, and that seemed to be what had happened here. This was a few months after the incident with Joan Little, where she was raped by the night jailer in North Carolina. It was happening all around the country in small towns. Althea was only in her mid-twenties, one of six kids. From what I gathered, the parish had a history of this type of assault. Years later when we were in Angola, Rockhead confirmed that both Althea and Chris had been sexually assaulted.

EXPERIENCING THESE ATTACKS ON me and other prisoners was horrific. I was a young kid trapped in there for something I didn't do, accused of murder, being witness to all this corruption in the parish jail and the community. It was hard to process it all, especially having deputies shouting through a bullhorn that they're going to kill you. I didn't know how it was going to turn out.

What kept me going was the tremendous support I had from my family and from the Black church in St. Charles Parish. But that's as far as support went. During that time, you had demonstrations around the country for workers' rights, union rights, women's rights, other stuff, but it never got to that little country town in St. Charles Parish, Louisiana. It was just me, my family, and my church, small town people.

We were also up against David Duke, who got a lot of people riled up in the neighborhood. There was talk to the point where Black people in our community armed themselves. About a third of the people who lived in Preston Hollow were from New Orleans. They were cut from a different cloth from people raised in the plantation culture of the rest of St. Charles. Black people in Preston Hollow were not afraid of the KKK. They knew about night marauders and all that. They were saying, "You ain't coming through here. If you do come out here, we're going to meet you with force."

That was no comfort for me, though. Captive as I was, I was at the mercy of David Duke and his followers. I wasn't able to do anything to defend my name. The harassment against me was coming from a parish that would later cast a large percentage of votes for David Duke when he ran not only for Congress but for governor of Louisiana. He played on fears and prejudices of white people, telling them Black people are uppity, it's time to put them back in their place, they're trying to take over our community, run over our school system.

The old Confederate powers were able to define and set in motion how they were going to go about prosecuting me. They kept me in the parish jail for over a year. They set my trial date for November of 1975, so they could try me when I was seventeen. That made it easier for them to classify me as an adult and give me the death penalty. Back then, if they found an adult defendant guilty of a capital offense, the person automatically got the death penalty. The judge and jury had no discretion. All the power structure had to do was put together a jury to their liking who would find me guilty of first-degree murder. Automatically, I'd get sentenced to die.

For most of my time in Hahnville, I didn't know any of this. The few times I did see my attorney, he told me, "They aren't going to find you guilty." I was sixteen years old and I was desperate. Cops were talking about killing me, so anyone saying stuff like "We're going to beat this, you're going home" was saying what I wanted, and needed, to hear. I didn't know Jack Williams was a divorce attorney. I didn't know he was talking smack, that he was going to be the one to sell me down the river. At those moments, he had my undivided attention. You're told that white people know what's going on and they're going to make things happen, they know how to talk to each other.

I came to find out this attorney was doing nothing; he was only trying to get as much out of my family as he could, knowing they were poor, working people. Every week he wanted to know where his money was at. My family had to host suppers, fundraisers, get the churches involved to pay for legal expenses. But at the trial we found out he hadn't spent that money on anything that would help me.

Given what happened in the parish jail and how little Williams was doing to prepare me, you'd be surprised at how adamantly I still believed that the truth would prevail. I thought the criminal justice system operated in a different sphere, not that it was used as a tool for racists. I believed that if you were innocent and had witnesses, you'd be found not guilty. I had the bus driver, my seatmates, and the other sixty kids on the bus. I was going on all that to prove my innocence.

Because if I hadn't believed all this, it would have been a whole new chapter in my life. I would have escaped from that parish jail.

I actually did sneak out of the place three different times, but just overnight. Getting out wasn't that hard. As a jail trustee, Michael Dupre was entrusted with the keys. He was the one bringing food and letting me out to take showers since I didn't have one in my cell. You're in a place long enough, you observe, you make friends. Mike was a couple years older than me, a white kid from St. Charles who kept getting in trouble. The jailers looked out for him. When he went to Hahnville, they made him a trustee.

I wanted out.

I started by talking to Mike. At first, he used to open my door and let me wander from the third to the second floor. I'd visit Rockhead and the other guys in the bullpen there who'd been involved in that armed robbery in Killona. Then I saw there was a door upstairs on top of the building. I thought about how I could get up there and climb down.

"Look, man, I want to leave out here on Friday," I told Mike one day. "I just need to get out for a bit. I'll be back. Do you have the key to the door upstairs?"

"No problem," he said. "I got you. If you come back, bring me some weed." He left my door unlocked—they used to lock it with a big key and a padlock. I took a wrapper twist-tie from one of the loaves of bread my family brought me when they visited and jammed it into the padlock so it wouldn't work.

Friday night I got out of my cell and went upstairs to the roof; the door was unlocked. There was a wall up there with a fence. I climbed that wall, got over the fence, and landed on the roof of the catwalk that connected the jail to the courthouse. The rest was easy. The catwalk led to the second floor of the courthouse building. From my cell, I had observed what was out there. I found a way to ease down the gutter pipe, stand on the roof of another building, and climb down to the ground. Behind the jail was a Black community. No one knew me there and I walked right through, down the road that hit River Road. I had to hitchhike to get to the Luling–Destrehan ferry to cross the river to St. Rose.

I watched a car slow down for me and whose car was it? None other than Officer Nelson Coleman. I thought I was busted for sure, but I played it cool. I opened the door and got in the passenger seat. Even though I immediately recognized his car, he didn't recognize who I was. I sat there next to him. Officer Coleman kept his eyes on the road and asked me where I was going, and I told him the ferry. "Be careful," he said when he dropped me off. I watched him the whole time I crossed River Road to see if he was going to turn around, but he just kept going. I got on the ferry, which was free, and when it arrived, I got off and hitchhiked to St. Rose. A guy named Red who was out in front of the Kart and Karry store saw me and kept on calling my name. "Chill out," I told him. "I'm on furlough." I continued walking and found my cousin Jerry, who worked on the ferry but was off that night. We went to my brother Mac's house; he was having a little party. Early the next morning, Jerry brought me back to the jail with some MD20/20 wine and some weed.

The second time I left was on a Saturday and did the same thing, hitchhiked with no problem, took the ferry, and caught a ride to Preston Hollow. My cousin Jerry brought me back that time as well.

The third time, I'd made it to Preston Hollow when I spotted my mother and my Auntie Lady in the car with my baby brother Richard. The two of them were drinking some beer, parked in front of my aunt's house on Mockingbird. My mother had gotten wind that I'd been out a couple times and brought it to my attention when she came to visit. I didn't confirm or deny it. They were both blown away when I walked up to the car.

"What are you doing out?" they asked me. We sat there for a while and then rode around. "You're going to get into a lot of trouble," my mother said. "We're bringing you back." This time we didn't take the ferry. We took the long way over the Huey P. Long Bridge in New Orleans. To ease their mind, when we got to the jail, I told them how I got out and how I'd climb back up. They parked in the lot of Hahnville High School across the way to watch me. I promised I'd flick the light on in my cell to let them know I'd made it without a hitch. They waited for my signal and then I saw them drive away. Years later, after the movie *Thelma & Louise* came out, my mother told me she and Auntie Lady had started calling themselves

Thelma and Louise. They realized they could have gotten in a lot of trouble back then. But at the time this happened, my mother didn't care. My father never found out.

After the trial, my mother regretted driving me back to the parish jail. "If I'd known this was going to happen to you," she told me, "I never would have brought you back."

The first time I left, it wasn't a certainty that I was going to return. But I returned each time because I believed the truth coming out would allow me to go home for good. In the Black community, despite the harm and detriment society has done to us, many Black people tend to believe what the Bible says, "the truth will set you free." I also believed in God and thought God would make sure the right thing would happen.

If I'd understood the gravity of the situation at the time, there would have been no question about it. One of those times I wouldn't have gone back. Later, when my mother told me about her regret, we talked about what I might have done. I would have tried to get to California and let the politics play out. Jerry Brown was the governor back then and he was against the death penalty. I don't think he would have approved of extraditing me back to Louisiana.

But in my heart, I know I never would have made it to California. As soon as the guards found out I'd gotten away, they would have sent people out looking for me and tracked me down. The power structure in place wouldn't have stood for the escape of a Black kid charged with shooting a white kid. The truth is, whoever might've found me would have probably killed me out there instead of bringing me back.

MY BLIND SPOT CHANGED shortly before the trial started. Michael Dupre hurried into my cell and told me, "Gary, I just heard them downstairs talking about they're going to give you the death penalty. They're going to put you in the electric chair. They're going to kill you." I completely panicked. I hollered out the window at a maintenance guy, told him I wanted to make a phone call. He brought me down and I called my momma.

"Who'd you hear that from?" she asked.

"The guy Mike who's a trustee here. He heard them talking."

My mother freaked out. She called Williams. "They're not going to give him the electric chair," he insisted. "He's too young."

But I knew right then that I'd been wrong all along. They were determined to kill me.

CHAPTER 3

PRESUMED GUILTY

Time crawled for me while I was in the parish jail. The months piled up. I didn't expect to spend my seventeenth birthday there that July, eating a lemon cake my father made and watching my family leave for home. There were days I thought would never end. And then, finally, the trial date was set for November 5, 1975.

You might think the trial itself flew by, but it did not.

The first morning deputies came to the cell and took me to the courthouse to meet with Attorney Williams. Throughout the trial, I was never shackled or handcuffed. I was allowed to wear my own clothes—jeans and a T-shirt, same as I wore every day in jail. By then my face was familiar from all the publicity, so the police knew there was no way I could escape. During breaks that first day, I went out in the big hallway with everyone else. The guard assigned to me, a guy in his mid-twenties who I knew from the parish jail, stood on the other side of the hall. He let me hang out in the stairway with Larry Dabney and Michael Campbell, the schoolmates who'd been in the same seat as me on bus 91. Like me, they didn't have facial hair yet. We all wore our hair in a bush; Larry's and mine were a little bigger than Michael's. "They got you bad, man," they both told me. "We were there with you."

These were the guys who knew the truth and would testify for me. I was feeling somewhat hopeful but also antsy. I hadn't seen my lawyer more than four times before the big day. Several times while I was waiting for trial he had lied to my parents, telling them he was going to see me and then he wouldn't show up. He never talked strategy with me. He didn't prep me for what to say or how to present myself on the witness stand. I had no idea what to expect or how to behave. The only thing he did ask me—during jury selection, with arguments set to begin soon—was who I wanted for witnesses.

"I feel you should subpoena everybody on the bus," I told him. I was thinking he already had their names and was going to speak with all of them. But Jack Williams told me that wasn't possible.

"Why not?" I asked. "I told you, it will help our case to talk with every student who was on bus 91."

"It's too late," Williams said. "We have to get some witnesses. Give me names." The guy looked professional with his black business suit and yellow legal pads, but he reminded me of the Nutty Professor, all over the place.

So, I gave him names: Larry Dabney and Michael Campbell, who shared the seat with me on the bus. My cousin, Ike Randall—he was the one whose arrest I was objecting to when Officer Coleman dragged me off and charged me with disturbing the peace. Ulrich Smith, who was hitchhiking with me when V. J. St. Pierre stopped us and brought us back to the school together. Ulrich could tell the jurors that St. Pierre had patted us down and didn't find any weapon.

The only ones Williams agreed to were my cousin and Michael Campbell. "Those others," he informed me, "they can't testify for you. They're state witnesses." He read the names off the state's list, which also included Natalie Blanks and Loretta London, two other schoolmates who'd been on the same bus. I never expected that. But okay, I thought, whoever brings them up to testify, they'll be under oath. They'll have to tell what they saw that day. And that would prove I didn't have anything to do with Timothy Weber's death.

These were people I knew. When they'd come to the courthouse the previous October for the grand jury investigation, I had called down to them from my cell window. They each hollered back up to me, asking me how I was doing, saying they couldn't wait to see me that day. They didn't know the grand jury wasn't going to call me, and neither did I. Natalie Blanks, Loretta London, Larry Dabney, Michael Campbell—they had all stopped to stand in the construction area to talk with me, until the police told them it was an unauthorized area and ran them off. Natalie and Loretta had both visited me at Hahnville. Larry Dabney and Michael Campbell had just been showing me moral support in the stairwell. They dapped me and shook my hand. I believed their testimony would help.

The trial kicked off with jury selection. I didn't know how the process worked, but my heart sank as I saw the candidates. I may have been a kid, but I wasn't a dummy. I was looking at a lot of old white people. There weren't more than a few Black people in the room; the other side struck all but one of them. The questions were direct, short, and precise. The prosecution was mainly asking about people's integrity and fairness: Could they hear the facts of the case and render a decision of first-degree murder, knowing it would automatically lead to a death sentence? Many Black people don't believe in the death penalty. Any hesitation, that person would be gone.

The one Black woman they might have chosen really floored me. When the other side asked whether she thought I was involved, this woman's answer was "Yes." Why? She thought I wouldn't be there otherwise. I couldn't believe what I was hearing, to have a Black person say something like that, knowing you're talking about a teenager being tried for his life, and you're supposed to give a fair and impartial decision.

I learned that day about striking people from the jury pool. That woman was also struck, this time by my attorney.

I told Williams, "Why don't you try to get some young people on the jury who'll see things my way?" By "my way," I meant, "the truth." But there weren't any young people called up. We would have to convince a jury that was all white, all older.

At one of our four meetings, I had asked Williams about trying to get a change of venue for the trial. Guys in jail taught me that term and told me

I couldn't get a fair trial in St. Charles Parish. Bertrand Richardson, whose cell was next to mine until he got shipped to Angola, had been to prison before and learned some things there about the law. Williams had pushed back. "People in this parish know your family," he said. In fact, Black residents were only a quarter of the parish population at the time, and none of them wound up on the jury. But Williams never filed a request to move the trial somewhere else.

TRIAL ARGUMENTS STARTED ON Monday, November 10, and deputies tightened things up. No more hanging out in the stairwell. They told me I couldn't talk to anyone besides my lawyer. At every pause in the proceedings, deputies would take me back to the jail waiting room or to my cell. The only person in a cell near mine at the time was an older guy named Robert Jasmine. We didn't speak about much of anything. I wasn't even allowed to talk with my mother on the phone.

As we settled in for opening arguments, I sat at the defense table with Williams and a couple young assistants, a woman and a man, both white. I looked over at the prosecution table and saw a slew of people. That made me feel even more alone. We're outnumbered, I thought, and outnumbered means outgunned. They had the district attorney for St. Charles Parish, Norman Pitre; the assistant DA, Harry Morel, who I recognized as the guy who had driven me from the substation to Hahnville and asked whether I needed a doctor; and L. J. Hymel from the state attorney general's office with a whole bunch of his associates. The room was a typical courthouse scene like in *To Kill a Mockingbird*, a big space but without any balcony upstairs. I noticed when I turned around that they had people standing in the back. The judge sat high up. We were in an old brick building like the jail; the two buildings had gone up at the same time. But unlike the jail, this place was air-conditioned. I was sweating anyway.

As is always the case, the state went first. Norman Pitre made the prosecution's opening statement about how they were going to prove me guilty. I could see he was orchestrating the state's case, calling every move, but I was too nervous to follow the particulars. When Jack Williams made his initial remarks, he just asked the jury to be open-minded and listen to the facts of the case. There was nothing compelling or dramatic in what he said. My heart sank a little more.

Then Assistant Attorney General L. J. Hymel rose from the table to start the questioning for their side. The guy made me really uncomfortable. He reminded me of a Klansman without his robe. I felt like I could see the anger and hate erupting within him. He could have been one of the racist characters in some movie. You look at these films, you see the hate in their faces and their voices, how they are always agitated and resentful. Every time my attorney said something, and especially when I testified, L. J. Hymel responded with disgust. It was like he was cursing me out, yelling, "Get this Black motherfucker out of here."

One white deputy after another went up to the witness stand. Some said when they heard a shot, they saw smoke by the back of the bus. Others did not. Only one officer said he saw a gun sticking out the window, and that guy had been standing the farthest away from the bus. They all said they searched the bus in the lot around the corner, and they all agreed they didn't find a gun. Deputy Mike Babin had to admit that a "normally" experienced officer would have noticed any slit and bulge in the seat the first time they searched the vehicle. He also mentioned that the gun had been stolen from the Kenner Indoor Firing Range in Jefferson Parish.

John Smith, the assistant principal, trying to look more like a professional educator, wore a suit instead of a leather jacket. He said some BS about why they suspended me. He did think the shot came from the bus. But he had to testify that there was no puff of smoke by the back of the bus and that no one held a gun out the window. "If something had been sticking out of the window and held for any length of time," he said, "I would have seen it. I had a clear vision of the bus."

One person whose testimony I thought might help me even though he was a prosecution witness was the bus driver, Ernest Cojoe. "It couldn't have been fired off of my bus because if it was, I would have heard it," he said with confidence; he would have recognized the sound. "I mean, a .45, when you shoot a .45 it carries a lot of noise and somebody's eardrum would have been hurt." He was also on the bus the whole time the police searched it. He was the one showing them how to unlock the seats. Cojoe described how a deputy held the particular seat where I'd been and turned it around and around and then put the seat back, "and said he didn't find [a gun.]" They searched bus 91 on the side street and then again for two hours at the substation. In all that time, Cojoe testified, there was no slit or hump in that seat.

I felt a sense of vindication seeing how adamant Ernest Cojoe was about that, just like he was adamant that the shot couldn't have come off his bus or he would have known it. Everyone on that vehicle heard a pop sound from outside. He thought someone was shooting at the bus and he stopped to make sure no kid on the bus was shot. I watched him walk away from the witness stand a proud man, firm in his description of what he had witnessed.

The police and the AG were trying to make the crime fit me by singling out the seat I had been sitting in. Ernest Cojoe showed how that argument was bullshit. Here was a man who spent twenty years in the military, an upstanding citizen and also an auxiliary police officer, highly respected in the community and a firearms specialist in the military. I felt relieved—he was the driver and the owner of that bus and he was there when all this happened. Like the rest of us on bus 91, he had assumed we were under fire.

But would that be enough? He was also Black.

I knew Deputy Nelson Coleman was not my friend, but when he got up to speak, I was still expecting him to state exactly what happened, how he arrested me for disturbing the peace when I was bad-mouthing the state police and other officers. But Coleman made it seem as though he'd been watching me all along and arrested me because he thought I looked suspicious and was trying to leave the scene. I was thinking, When the hell did that happen? The police had everything blocked off. We were in a vacant lot and they had a perimeter all around as they took us one by one off the bus. They had photos of that. I had been trying to jump over the ditch because the police were beckoning me to do so. Coleman claimed he walked up and called me by name.

"No, he did not!" I turned to Williams and jabbed him in the side. "He's lying! That day was the first time we laid eyes on each other!"

Eventually Coleman had to admit that, with all the police around, there was nowhere to go and that he had arrested me for disturbing the peace. When Williams asked whose peace I had disturbed, Coleman said, "Mine."

He also acknowledged that he was close to the bus at the time of the shooting and hadn't seen hands with a gun sticking out the window. If there had been anything like that, he said, "I'm quite sure I would have seen it."

Before I could let that soak in, I was hit with a triple whammy when my friends from the bus took the stand. First, Loretta London claimed she saw me with a gun on the bus and that I handed it to her. I thought, Who is this person? She looked the same—bronze skin, small build—but what was this coming out of her mouth? The Loretta I knew was smart and concerned about other people, but the girl on the stand was all nervous and couldn't look in my direction. Larry Dabney got up next and said he heard a shot and saw me with a gun right after, saw me hand it to some people, including Loretta, and a few minutes later saw me hide the gun in a hole in the seat. Was this the guy who just the other day had dapped me in the hallway? The next morning, I watched Natalie Blanks raise her right hand and say that she and I were sitting in that seat together, by ourselves, that she saw a gun in my hand and watched as I "shot it out the window" and "put it in the seat." She kept her head tilted down and avoided any glance at me, shifting nervously in the witness chair as if she were on Ritalin or something.

Each time I jumped up. "That's a lie!" I told my attorney. "Why is she saying that? What is he talking about?" I demanded Jack Williams object. It hurt so much till I wanted to cry. Natalie Blanks did not sit in a seat with me at all. I had been sitting between Larry Dabney and Michael Campbell.

I felt like I'd been punched in the gut. These were Black kids I went to school with, some I grew up with—me and Natalie Blanks went back to first grade together—people who knew I was innocent, getting up and lying under oath about what happened. How were these people testifying *against* me? I couldn't breathe, and I couldn't stop fussing at Jack Williams.

Instead of attacking their credibility, my lawyer just kept telling me to calm down, he was going to deal with it. Sometimes he laid a hand on my shoulder or on my thigh. He could tell how tense I was; I think he was trying to keep me from making a complete spectacle of myself. The judge admonished me. I knew I was reacting emotionally, but I was caught completely off guard. These kids were lying, and my life was on the line.

Then I had to listen to Herman Parrish, the head of the crime lab who was supposed to have examined my jersey gloves for gunpowder residue. At the start of the trial, my attorney made a motion to strike those gloves as evidence because the information had never been disclosed to him. Judge Marino ruled on my behalf. Williams was happy about that. But the AG immediately appealed to the Louisiana state court; within twenty-four hours they overruled Judge Marino's decision. So Hymel was able to introduce those cotton jersey gloves I'd had in my pocket—the state claimed I used the gloves to hold the gun out the window. Herman Parrish swore he'd tested them and detected some gunpowder residue.

My parents had given Williams $500 specifically to hire his own expert. I knew how many suppers they had to cook and sell to come up with that money. I looked around for our expert, asked Williams where he was. My lawyer never replied, because he hadn't gotten anybody. I sat there and shook my head in disbelief.

After the state presented its witnesses, it was the defense's turn. Patricia Files and my cousin Ike Randall, both students on bus 91, spoke on my behalf, but I could tell the prosecution was going to dismiss them as a friend and a cousin. Hymel said Patricia Files would do what she could to get me off. "Right," she told him. "Because I know he's innocent."

Then Michael Campbell got on the stand. Like Loretta and Larry and Natalie, he looked nervous and intimidated, like he didn't want to be there. By this time, I assumed he was going to do the same as the other students. But he didn't. Michael made it clear that I was sitting between him and Larry Dabney and that I never had or fired a gun. He said when V. J. St. Pierre questioned him at three in the morning, "They asked me, did Gary have a gun, and I said 'I ain't seen none.'" And that's not all. Michael Campbell said the police "were trying to make me say other things, too, like they were half-trying to put words in my mouth.

It's not true that I looked out the window and saw a gun go by." The seat was not torn when he got off the bus. He heard one pop sound, saw no smoke. And he saw two or three white people outside the bus with guns.

Finally, somebody was speaking the truth! I nodded my head and thought, Thank you, Michael, for telling what really happened. I prayed the jurors would hear him. I wanted Jack Williams to get up and demand an investigation into how the police conducted their questioning of my schoolmates. Even I could see the AG was basically leading the testimony, guiding what each of them would say. But my attorney didn't do any of that. The jury would have to weigh Michael's words against the conflicting testimony from Natalie and Loretta and Larry.

Ulrich Smith also testified for our side, but he was no help. He claimed he didn't see me on October 7 until he was coming back from New Sarpy and we tried to hitch a ride together. He did say V. J. St. Pierre stopped us on the road by the Red & White store and took us back to the school, but he left out how this officer arrested us, frisked me, and found nothing. When my lawyer asked if Ulrich would have noticed if I had a gun when we were on the road or in the police car, his answer was: "I didn't look at him that close." Again I was yelling at Williams: "He's not telling the truth up there!" I couldn't believe it. I was devastated. There were no questions about Ulrich's own arrest for calling Officer Coleman an Uncle Tom, nothing about him seeing St. Pierre beating me.

I was hearing people who I thought were my friends and had my back and were going to speak the truth about what happened. It was crushing. I was beginning to fear I didn't have a chance in hell.

THE TRIAL TRANSCRIPT SHOWED how desperate I had become by the time I got on the stand. I had to convince the jury that I was innocent, but I didn't know what to do. I was a kid who was in the grip of death. When they say a drowning man will grasp at anything to keep from drowning, that's how it was. I tried to stick to the truth. The AG said, "Tell us what happened that day." I interpreted that as, tell them everything I heard and saw. Yet when I described what St. Pierre said or Nelson Coleman or anyone else, the AG kept objecting that I was relying on hearsay. I was admonished a dozen times about hearsay. I didn't know what the hell hearsay was. I just repeated everything said to me that day. When the AG objected and the judge chastised me, I'd go right back to the same approach, to show I was telling the truth. I felt it all needed to be included in the record. Then the judge would say, "Strike that from the record."

I can laugh about it now. I was a juvenile who didn't know anything about the law, jumping up and yelling, waving my hands and acting out. I was being tried as an adult and they expected me to act like an adult.

It was so crazy to have people I knew up there testifying about things that never happened. I started to lose it, to the point where I went to saying some of the things witnesses against me were saying, thinking maybe that would get the jury to believe me. If I talked about having a gun, I thought, a pistol different from the gun they said was the murder weapon, they might believe me when I said I didn't fire that gun and neither did anyone else. It wasn't rational. "Something was passed to me," I said. I acted like there was a gun passed around and I was part of that. I mimicked other witnesses out of desperation, hearing them lying and them knowing it was a lie.

I did tell them about the beating and how they treated my mother. When Hymel cross-examined me, I said Ulrich had seen me getting beaten.

"He didn't say anything about that when he testified, did he?" Hymel said.

I told him, "You didn't ask him."

My emotions were definitely in it. I was full of anger and anguish. If I could have stormed out of the trial, I would have done it. "They're lying," I wanted to say. "This whole thing's a sham. I'm going home."

I believe my mother's testimony would have helped. She would have spoken the truth, hoping to reach those on the jury despite the other things they were hearing. She would have told them about the tight clothes I was wearing that day and how I never could have hidden a gun in them. She'd have said how it felt to be in the lobby along with the other mothers waiting for their children, how she heard my cries as I was brutally beaten, and how the police refused to talk to her when they were bringing me through to the back, where she heard them keep on with the beating. The jury would have listened to her describe what my body looked like, what my injuries felt like as she held me later that night.

But they never did call my mother to testify.

On November 14, 1975, after closing statements, Judge Ruche Marino gave his instructions to the jury. First-degree murder "requires a specific intent to kill or to inflict great bodily harm upon more than one person," he told them. The state had introduced a second person, Roland LaBranche, a white student who'd been standing near Timmy Weber and said he'd also been injured that day, but he himself described the injury as a "nick" on the arm. I didn't see how you could call that "great bodily harm."

But the judge didn't stop with the definition of intent. He told the jurors that, even though a person is presumed to be innocent, in this case they could presume "that the defendant intended the natural and probable causes of his act." I wasn't sure what all those words meant, but it sounded like he was telling them they could presume I was guilty. I thought that's what the jury was supposed to deliberate about.

While Judge Marino gave those instructions, Jack Williams just sat there. He didn't say, "I object." He didn't say anything at all.

The case was now with the jury. I was back in the parish jail waiting with my attorney in a holding room, the same room where my mother and father visited me the first week I was in Hahnville. After only a couple of hours, the police officers who stayed with us received a message that the verdict was in. Immediately the atmosphere in the room shifted. Everyone was tense, stoic. When I saw how fast the jurors had reached agreement, I had a sick feeling. In my head I heard the judge's voice admonishing me, the AG yelling objections. And yet, I felt a glimmer of hope because somebody on the jury might have believed me.

We entered a courtroom that was already full. The jury hadn't come in yet; the judge wasn't behind the bench. Jack Williams was telling me, "We gave it our best shot. We got our message across." That gave me no comfort. When I looked back at the faces of Black people in the room, they looked full of dread.

The judge and jurors came in a few minutes later. The bailiff got up and announced, "Hear ye, hear ye, the court is now in session. The Honorable Judge Ruche Marino presiding." We all rose. I heard the judge ask the jury whether they had reached a decision and the foreman answer, "Yes."

I was watching the jurors' faces. I didn't feel warmth from anyone.

Some gave me a stern look, others avoided my eyes. No one showed any compassion. No juror was weeping. The way the men were sitting, they gave off the impression that they'd done their job, they'd done what was right for the community. Their faces reminded me of photographs I've seen with white men standing underneath a Black person hanging on a tree like it's a trophy. A soulless look. In their eyes, I probably wasn't a human being.

I had to stand and listen to the judge read this jury's unanimous decision. It wasn't long: guilty of murder in the first degree. Once he announced that, I became detached from everything. The sentencing would come later, but I knew it was automatic. The state got what it wanted. It had determined my fate.

BEHIND ME, THERE WAS a commotion. From some people, I heard cries of relief; from others, a gasp of surprise and disappointment. I thought at least I'd see my family in the courtroom and feel their support. Only then did I realize they'd kept my entire family out of the proceedings. I had just assumed they were somewhere in that packed room. The only family member I spotted that day was my sister Bobbie Nell. They must not have realized she was my sister. After the verdict was read, they wouldn't let her or anyone else come near me.

As the deputies walked me back along the catwalk that connected the courthouse to the jail, no one spoke. I remembered the first time I'd been on that covered walkway, when Lockett accompanied me to my initial court hearing. At one point he noticed me looking at a trapdoor above our head. "That was the hanging gallows," he told me. They used to execute people by putting a noose around their neck and dropping the person from the third floor down through that trapdoor. The practice stopped when Angola got an electric chair and executions were transferred there.

I knew about the hanging gallows from inside the jail. The room where the executioner stood and placed the noose around the prisoner's neck was across the hall from my cell. But the trapdoor was what made it real for me. We'd pass below it every time they transported me between the jailhouse and the courthouse.

As we made our way beneath it that Friday, I couldn't help wondering how many bodies had dropped in that very spot, how many people they had lynched in this parish jail. I could feel the souls of those men. I was walking in their footsteps.

CHAPTER 4

WELCOME TO ANGOLA

When the deputies brought me back to jail after the verdict, they moved me to a different cell at the farther end of the building, away from the parking lot and the street. Before, people could look up from the street and see me in my cell at night. Bertrand and Melvin always told me to keep my lights off or someone would shoot me through that window. I think Lockett worried there might be repercussions from the white community. In the South, vigilante groups grabbed people out of jails and took action instead of waiting on the court. St. Charles had its own dark past.

Alone in that cell, I was consumed with regrets: Why did I go to school the morning of October 7? When the principal suspended me and I hitchhiked to Preston Hollow, why didn't I follow my first mind and stay home instead of going with Ulrich Smith to New Sarpy? Why did I come back to the parish jail when I had three chances to leave? I beat myself up for squandering the opportunity. I also thought a lot about why those students lied on me. They were teenagers like me, still out there having fun, going to school, parties, football games. They had their whole lives ahead of them. It felt like the ultimate betrayal. To me, they were as much at fault as the police and the prosecution.

Still, I knew whatever happened was in the past. I had to deal with what was ahead of me.

I didn't see my mother that night. When my family was allowed to visit, they had to come upstairs and stand in front of the hatch in my cell door with the food my mother had cooked for me. The guards wouldn't let us visit out in the yard like everyone else. It broke my heart to see my mother trying to be strong and positive. "I'm disappointed in that lawyer," she said, "but we have a good chance of winning on appeal. Don't give up." I know mothers try to be strong for their children and put a spin on things. But I could hear in her voice that she was winded. My mother knew the system, knew stories from when she was growing up in places like Ruston and Tallulah, Louisiana. On more than one occasion she had told us about the killing of Emmett Till in the 1950s in a similar small town in Mississippi. She'd also gotten to know Althea's family; she had heard how the jailers had raped and beaten Althea and Chris. Now my mother's son had been accused of murdering a white kid. How could a Black mother like mine trust the system?

My sentencing came about a week later before a packed courtroom. This time my family was there. Judge Marino asked me if I had anything to say before sentencing was imposed. I had to choke back my anger at how wronged I felt. "I am not a speaker," I replied. "But I figure on the day of the trial, we had everything in order and the deputies, well, they didn't do me right. And I want everyone to know, whatever happened, I don't want anyone to have prejudice against my family or anyone else. And revenge . . . this isn't on my mind. I would like everyone to have a decent life."

Then I listened as the judge announced the sentence: "You are to have a current of electricity of sufficient intensity to cause your death, pass through your body and be applied and continued until you are dead." I felt hollow and numb all over, full of dread and despair. At the age of seventeen, my life was at the mercy of an unjust system. I didn't see any way to change what the prosecutors and judge had orchestrated.

The guards took me straight back to the cell. The only person I was allowed to see that day outside of prison staff was my attorney. Security got really tight. I can still see the shock on Lockett's face when he came to my cell, how he kept shaking his head in disbelief. He felt my family's pain. Other than to say, "I'm sorry," he was speechless.

Things were uneventful the first few weeks after the sentence came down. Then early one morning before dawn, several deputies startled me by rushing into the cell unannounced and yelling at me to get dressed. It was Monday, December 15, 1975. My heart pounded as I jumped out of the bunk. Were they coming to kill me? No one had informed me of any upcoming dates except one: May 1, 1976, the day set for my execution.

Those deputies charged in like a bunch of thugs. They wouldn't let me bring anything with me. I heard them giving the same orders to Robert Jasmine in a nearby cell. I could tell he was really scared. So was I.

When they took me downstairs, I saw Officer Coleman. "What's going on?" I asked him, thinking he at least would tell me. "Where are they taking me?" He didn't answer. I asked if I could call my mother, and he flatly refused.

The other guards left me alone with him downstairs and went back up. I didn't have handcuffs or shackles on and I was there with just Officer Coleman, who paid me no mind as he sat across from me. It occurred to me to run out the building because the door was open, but I didn't know who was out there waiting for me. There had once been a slave rebellion at the plantation over in Destrehan. When the militia had come from New Orleans, they maimed and decapitated those involved and put their heads on pikes on the Mississippi River. It was as if they were warning every slave: "This is what will happen to you if you revolt." I didn't know all the details of that story until later in life, but I did know that was the way law enforcement treated me and other Black individuals. I knew they were not to be trusted, including Nelson Coleman, regardless of his skin color.

I could hear keys and a door opening upstairs, and then a shaky voice asking, "Where are we going, mister?" I got out of my chair and looked up the stairs. I will never forget the fear I saw in Robert's face. He was gripping the railing as if someone downstairs was waiting to do him harm. Robert seemed relieved to see me and I was glad to see him as well. Once they finished the paperwork, they took us both out to Officer Coleman's patrol car.

Coleman and another deputy drove us to the Luling–Destrehan ferry. My cousin Jerry was working as a deckhand that day. When he looked in the car window, I could tell he saw someone was in the back seat. He came closer and recognized it was me. I gave a little wave. Jerry looked at the police. "Where you going?" he asked them.

"Angola," they told him.

My heart was heavy because of all I'd heard about that prison, full of inmates committing murder and sexual slavery, with violent attacks on prisoners from guards and inmates alike. But I tried hiding whatever fears I had. Jerry asked to speak with me, but they refused. Bullheaded as I was, I hollered out for him to call my momma and let her know. The officers were not pleased. Sure enough, an hour or so after we got to the prison, guess who was at the front gate? My mother. The guards told me she was there, but they wouldn't allow me to see her because I was still being processed.

All the time I'd been at the parish jail, all during the trial, they never cuffed or shackled me. But when we were a quarter mile from Angola, Officer Coleman pulled the car over and said, "This is where we put the handcuffs on you. We don't want them to think we don't cuff our prisoners." I got it. I may have been small, but I was going to be a death row inmate at the toughest prison in the country. How would it look if I arrived without being restrained?

Coleman and the other deputy checked their weapons and we walked through the front gate. Once we were inside, they took the cuffs off me and walked back out. "Good luck," Coleman said.

I was going to need it.

ROBERT AND I WERE immediately separated and I was escorted to processing for death row. I felt a real sense of loss, even though the two of us weren't close. I realized I was on my own in this place I dreaded. The reception officer, Sergeant Carl Kimball, led me down the hall to the ID department, run by an old prison guard named Floyd Gauf. He entertained himself by saying cruel and demeaning things to every prisoner who came through. While I was being processed by an inmate who worked for him, I overheard Gauf talking to a young white guy who had also just arrived about how he had to cut his hair. "You're going to have an old man waiting for you down the walk if you don't cut it," Gauf kept saying. I didn't know what "down the walk" meant, but soon learned that's how they referred to the Main Prison. The guy was really mad and upset, but Gauf kept it up, taunting and laughing until the inmate left. When I got to Gauf, he tried making his little jokes, but, much to his annoyance, I wouldn't give him the satisfaction of saying anything back. After taking my photo with the death-row number C-127, he arranged for me to be brought to C tier on the ground floor.

I had to summon all my strength to face whatever was on the other side of the big steel door in front of me. I'd heard so many horrible stories about this place. I hung on to the words my mother told me when all this started. "Son, you have to be strong for the both of us," she told me. "No matter what happens to you, you have to be strong."

A guard used one key to open the steel door and another to open a panel box where he hit a switch. I heard a cell door rack back. "Cell eight," he told me. I was to walk there on my own. I immediately became very alert to my surroundings. Ahead of me was what looked like a very long hallway, though Lower C is actually the shortest of the tiers for guys on death row or put in solitary, which is known at Angola as CCR. The tier has twelve cells instead of fifteen, all on the left side, with the cell numbers painted on a panel above the bars. Looking down the hall, I saw these little flashing objects hanging out of the cells. I was intrigued and tried to figure out what they were. Turned out prisoners used gum to fasten pieces of mirror to either toothbrushes or pencils so they could look down the hall and see who was coming. Every time they heard the keys, they would stick their mirrors out to see what correction officer might be coming to prank them. Basically, these men had learned the art of survival.

As I walked past, I looked at these guys watching me from behind bars, shaking their heads, trying to figure out who I was. No one was talking. I could tell some of them recognized me because of the news reporting. I glanced around; their cells appeared to be really deep, like a long vacuum or like looking down a hole. But when I got to cell 8, I realized it was only about six feet wide, nine feet long.

The door immediately clanged shut behind me. Everything vibrated. I quickly learned that when a door closes or someone hollers in a structure made of stone and concrete, you can hear it throughout the building. The place smelled like urine and mothballs. All I could think was, How the hell am I going to get out of here?

The cell itself was totally different from the parish prison. It was smaller, painted a military green. Instead of a solid door it had bars, also painted green; I would be visible to anyone walking by. The furniture was limited to a metal bunk, table, and stool, all bolted to the wall. A toilet and sink were mounted on the other wall. The space had no windows and no cells across from it. There were big windows, though, on the other side of the tier. You could see the hillscape and green trees, but what most caught my eye were the guard towers lined up along a security fence. No more watching school buses. The only movement I would see was the changing of the tower guards three times a day.

I sank down on the bunk and counted two blankets, a sheet, a pillow, and a mattress. The mattress was so damn hard, it was like sleeping right on the metal bunk. There was no give, no softness whatsoever. The same was true of the pillow. The blankets were green military blankets, old and scratchy. I soon learned the mattress, pillow, and sheets were made out of cotton they grew there in Angola, a former slave plantation with eighteen thousand acres. That's roughly the size of Manhattan.

Because they'd rushed us out of the parish jail, all I had were the clothes I had put on that morning. Most of the things that mattered to me, the few possessions I'd been able to accumulate, I had to leave behind: my little TV and radio, my Bible, the rest of my clothes, photos taken at Hahnville with family members. I really missed those photos. They had become my comfort zone, a source of love that partially filled the void of loneliness. But I soon found out that in the cells on death row, you weren't allowed to put anything on the walls. At most you were permitted one picture on the little table in your cell.

Fifteen or twenty minutes after that door slammed shut behind me, they slid food trays under the cell doors. I remember it being red beans and rice. I didn't eat a thing. My appetite had disappeared as I tried to adjust to my new surroundings.

I was a young kid with no idea whom he could trust. I realized I couldn't go in like a Pollyanna when I didn't know the difference between Who and Who. The only thing I knew for certain was that I was on death row. And that I had a prescribed date for my death.

While I was processing what might come next, I saw an arm stick out of the bars down the tier with a mirror and heard someone calling, "Hey, man." One by one, as individuals got their hour outside the cell, they stood in front of mine and introduced themselves. They expressed interest in me, but I was wary—I didn't know who was for real. I realized the tier held not only death row inmates, but also inmates in CCR. In fact, only one other guy, Claude Hopkins, was officially on death row with me at that time. A lot of the guys had been in these cells for eight to ten years already. Some, like Jesse Washington and Joe Gleason, were former death row inmates still waiting to be re-sentenced after the *Witherspoon* decision in 1968, which had raised questions about the constitutionality of the death penalty and put executions on hold until 1976.

Just in time for me.

That first day in Angola, I got introduced to more than just the guys on my tier. I found out about a guy called L'il Fire Black, who was confined in a holding cell separated from CCR. They housed him there because he had enemies everywhere, people he'd harassed. But apparently he was also after Billy McCoy, who was a cell away from mine. When L'il Fire came out for his hour on the tier, I heard splats and Billy cursing. "I told you I was going to get you," L'il Fire said. The next thing I knew, there was a horrid, rancid smell. L'il Fire was actually slinging human waste on Billy McCoy.

It seemed to go on for a very long time. I wondered how anyone could have so much waste to throw. Apparently, he'd been saving it up in these little milk cartons. The free people—that's what we called the guards, a legacy of slavery times—had to have known all this and must have been in cahoots with L'il Fire. I realized later that they actually encouraged that kind of behavior, to keep prisoners divided.

Finally the guards put handcuffs on L'il Fire and transferred him back to his original cell. The whole tier smelled foul. Inmate orderlies—prisoners with certain work responsibilities like delivering food and cleaning the tier—brought out mops and soap and water. But that's one thing about human waste, once it sets, it ferments, and the smell gets worse and worse. The smell can take weeks, months to go away.

It was December and it had been hot or at least warm during the day. At night, that's when it got cold. The first night I fell in and out of sleep. I was in a place I'd never been to before and where I didn't know anyone. People were shouting, screaming, racking the bars. The smell was horrible. It was like being in a madhouse. I made up my mind: I knew I had to man up or be manhandled. I moved from fright mode to fight mode.

CHAPTER 5

THE GUARDIANS

By the next day, all the guys on my tier had come out and introduced themselves to me. Several told me they were familiar with my case. I still didn't know who to trust. But by day four, after watching the guy who had been set on fire on the tier above me, I realized I had to figure out who was for real. An experience like that stiffens your spine.

Learning to trust is a process. I'd heard so much about this world—the violence, the mayhem, the rape, the brutality—and now I was in the middle of it. I couldn't start trusting someone just because he walked up with a smile on his face. Like anywhere, Angola had the good, the bad, and the ugly. I realized I needed to read each person, observe what he said and what he did.

It was easy to tell the bad. For example, early on, Gilbert Montegut stole my watch and plotted with security to cause me bodily harm. I considered Jessie Washington as the ugly, though it wasn't his fault. He stayed loaded with medication because that's what the prison system does—dope people up as a way to control them and keep them docile.

The first guys I really got to know were Ronald Lewis, who everyone called Bockaloc, and Colonel Nyati Bolt. They were the most politically aware people on tier C. A couple things that won me over were the radical behavior they exhibited toward the guards and the camaraderie they had with each other. Soon after I got to Angola, they organized a hunger strike to protest the inhumane way the guards were feeding us, shoving the tray under the cell door, treating us like dogs. I saw how Bockaloc and Colonel Bolt were still respected by guys who had different political perspectives, because they were about doing the right thing. If anything bad happened to any prisoner, they would make a fuss about it.

As we came to know each other, they told me about their lives before Angola. Colonel Bolt, a slim, light-skinned guy in his mid-thirties, was an escapee from Chino who had also been at San Quentin, where he knew the revolutionary George Jackson. California had a program of using inmates as firefighters; Bolt had been on one of those crews. He escaped and went to Shreveport, where he was originally from, robbed a place there, and landed in Angola. Bockaloc was very tall and could easily have been mistaken for a basketball player. He was a civil rights activist and had been involved in the Black nationalist movement. Earlier he'd been sent to a federal prison for a bank robbery, but wound up in Angola because he also owed state time.

The day I arrived, I had received two "kites"—a note delivered by an orderly—from Herman Wallace and from Albert Woodfox, who were in solitary on different tiers. I didn't know yet, but soon learned, that they were both members of the Black Panther Party who'd been framed for the murder of a guard named Brent Miller in 1972. Basically, they wanted to say they knew about my case, were sorry to hear I was in Angola, and if I needed any help, to just let them know. They knew the guys on my tier and were really good friends with Colonel Bolt and Bockaloc. "Trust them," they told me. "You're not alone."

Bockaloc was the one who took the lead with me. Our conversation went something like this:

"What kind of support do you have?" he asked.

I listed it off. "My mother, my father, my sisters, my brothers, my grandparents."

"No, what organizations?"
"What do you mean?"
"Any group supporting you?"
"Yes, my church."
"Any political organizations?"

I couldn't even answer the question because I didn't know what that meant. "I don't know," I said. "Uh-uh."

"Do you want people to know your story?"
"Yeah."

"Because if you don't get support, these white folks are gonna kill you, boy. You're the youngest person on death row in America, and they're serious about killing you. You're accused of gunning down a thirteen-year-old white boy."

Hearing that put more fear in me than anything. Guys in prison, who know better than anyone, were saying, "These people are going to take you out." Bockaloc told me, "You need help, a lot of help. What we need you to do is write out your story and make a plea for support."

I knew I had to appeal to whoever I could get on my side. But I didn't know where to begin. I was educationally challenged and mortified about it. I simply could not compose a grammatically sound sentence. My syntax and composition were deplorable.

Up till then, my education had been hollow. I was just a high school student attending integrated schools where Black students got ignored by teachers and harassed by white students and administrators. When I was going to an all-Black school before integration, the teachers put their time in with us. During lessons and instruction, they didn't just speak to the class as a whole but they came to each and every student in the classroom, a hands-on type of schooling. The teacher made herself known. "If you don't understand," she'd say, "I will come to you or you come to my desk and I'll explain more." Then, in 1968, when I started sixth grade, the courts ordered the schools to be integrated, which meant we were moved to what had been all-white schools. Everything was totally different. We were made to sit in the back while the white students were in the front, with a row that was usually empty as a buffer between us. When the teacher finished instructing the white students, she took a beeline turn and went back to the front.

That's the kind of thing that really hurts a child's education. It did for me; my reading and writing skills plummeted. I didn't have the attention of teachers like I'd become used to. Besides the lack of instruction, there was so much conflict, I couldn't concentrate.

I put up a facade to hide the fact that I'd become only a semi-functional reader. But when I got sent to L.T.I., in Scotlandville, in 1973, there were teachers who took an interest in my education and encouraged me to study hard. They were always on my case and didn't tolerate any excuses. I'll never forget the dedication Mrs. Sandiford, Mrs. Williams, Mrs. White-Green, and Mrs. Petticoat put into my learning. I began writing letters to my mother and brother Jimmie, who stayed in contact with me. I felt really good about my accomplishments and strived to know more. I read magazines (*Ebony, Jet, National Geographic, Time, Newsweek,* and *Reader's Digest*) and newspapers (*The Morning Advocate, The States-Item, The Times-Picayune,* and *The Louisiana Weekly*). Whatever material was available in the institution, I read. It gave me a new attitude and better self-esteem. But when I went back to Destrehan High, with its "integrated" classrooms segregated by rows and by instruction methods, I became conditioned like the other Black students. We all knew we had to sit in the back, just as the white kids knew they were up front and center. I needed a lot more help with reading and especially with writing. That wasn't happening.

I was afraid my lack of education would seriously hamper any progress surrounding my case, but I was lost and too ashamed to discuss it with anyone. Fortunately, Bockaloc and Colonel Bolt looked at what I'd written and said, "We're going to help you with that. And here you go, read these books." They first gave me books and magazines of theirs to read that were interesting and relatively simple, to improve my reading and writing skills. As I read, I'd ask them, "What does this word mean?" They gave me a dictionary and said, "Look it up. This is how you use the keys to break a word down." At the same time, they kept working with me to compose my letter.

I learned the two of them had been involved in political activities when they were on the streets. They knew a lot of organizations like SNCC, the NAACP, the NAACP Defense Fund, the US Organization, and the Black Muslims. They were quite well informed and they had connections. Here I was, this little kid, being housed on the same tier as they were.

One thing these guys made clear was how the mainstream media worked. They kept telling me, "There are two sides to the story, but only one side when it comes to newspapers like *The Morning Advocate*, *The Times-Picayune* and *States-Item*." Those were the main newspapers in Louisiana, out of Baton Rouge and New Orleans. They just fed off of each other's articles. Bockaloc and Colonel Bolt had connections with other newspapers, like *The Louisiana Weekly*, a Black publication out of New Orleans; the *Bilalian News* of the Muslims; the *Militant*; *The Guardian*; the *Fightback!* newspaper—publications that were sympathetic to cases of injustice. They had me reading all these. They had subscriptions.

That's when I learned about Joan Little. I knew about George Jackson's brother, Jonathan, who'd been killed when he tried to free his brother in a courtroom. I already knew a little about Angela Davis, arrested for allegedly trying to help him. When I was out in California in the early seventies, I had collected signatures on a petition for her. But I didn't know politics. That was a strange animal to me. Until I met these guys at Angola, I didn't understand why things happened, how various injustices were connected, who benefited, and who all paid the price.

I worked on many versions of my letter, which was the first thing I'd ever written about what happened to me. Each time I'd show it to Bockaloc and Colonel Bolt. They'd go through it, tell me to strike this out, add this, be more clear about that, and I'd go back at it. "People need to hear it in your voice," they told me.

I began the letter by describing my arrest. "When I was arrested and charged with this murder that I did not commit, everyone involved in the stoning of the school bus should have been arrested as accessories to the crime," I wrote. "That includes the authorities, since they did nothing to stop the attacks." It felt really good to say that. I linked my conviction to past and present attacks on Black children and said the plain truth: "It is a known fact that no Black can get a fair trial from an all-white jury, especially in the South." I appealed for support and legal help: "Let us not let a Black youth die in the electric chair or spend the rest of his life behind bars because of some sick people's hatred and racism. Because if we do let them victimize me, we are telling these people to do with our brothers, sisters, sons and daughters anything they want to do."

After finishing the letter, I felt a sense of pride and dignity. I felt redeemed. Finally in mid-January 1976, we all felt it was ready to send out. I called it "A Letter from Death Row." The guys on the tier gave me envelopes and stamps. They had written the addresses of magazines and newspapers they knew, for me to mail out my letter widely.

Soon after I sent out "A Letter from Death Row," I started getting a flood of responses. My story caught fire. Churches, schools, universities, Black radio stations and organizations around the country took up my cause. Walter Collins, a veteran of the Louisiana Student Nonviolent Coordinating Committee (SNCC), helped set up a New Orleans–based Gary Tyler Defense Committee. He worked with the Southern Conference Educational Fund (SCEF) to make the movement national. That July, two thousand people marched in New Orleans demanding my freedom.

AT FIRST, WHEN THE guys on the tiers at Angola gave me books to read and offered to help me write "A Letter from Death Row," I found myself struggling and embarrassed. Not to say that a kid should know what terms like "imperialism," "capitalism," "communism" meant, but a proper education would have given me the tools to break the words down and figure out how to comprehend them. The stereotype of men in prison was that they were lowlifes and cretins who didn't know how to read or write. I'd been misled to believe that every prisoner was the dumb "Bubba." But at Angola I was around some very educated men. Bockaloc and several others had served in the military. They were active in the Civil Rights Movement and became members of the Black Panther Party and other groups. They were smart, and the books they were reading were complex. Bockaloc even gave me a book on Socrates and Plato that I tried to read but had to set aside.

Words like "colonialism," "dialectical materialism"—for me, those were mind-blowing. I didn't even know how to pronounce them. My new friends recognized my literacy level right away. What really impressed me was how supportive they were, how considerate and understanding. They took their time, like men taking their time with their own son. They were never arrogant. The guys were already appalled that I was in their prison so young. They knew it was a setup meant to destroy me completely. In order for me to make it, they understood they had to help me educationally, philosophically, psychologically. Each of them stood up and gave their best to me. Under their guidance, I learned a lot.

The only person who ridiculed my attempts was Gilbert Montegut, the guy who'd stolen my watch that first week by fishing it off the table in my cell while I was sleeping. People heard him say I was being "pampered." Word also got out that security had him bothering me. The other prisoners on the tier confronted Montegut. They made it clear he had to back off me or suffer great bodily harm. Reluctantly he changed his behavior.

There were three televisions on the tier mounted on cans—we called them butt cans, because they were painted red for guys to put cigarettes in—and one day we were watching a TV show about ex-cons in California who had successfully completed some experimental program. Among the people they featured was my brother Jimmie, who had spent a year and a half in prison for grand theft auto. Montegut immediately recognized him and called out to another inmate, Rory Mason, who we called L'il Man, "Look at Bilbo on TV!" Only a few people knew that nickname. Both were friends with my brother from their time together in Scotlandville. When I came out to shower, I told Montegut that Bilbo was my brother. That day totally changed his attitude toward me, and he also started to spend time helping with my education. He even confessed at one point that the guards Jerry Wells and David Veeds had solicited him to kill me by stabbing me in my cell while I was asleep. They were going to cover for him and make it look like self-defense.

READING THE RESERVOIR OF materials the guys gave me—from Malcolm X and Martin Luther King to George Jackson, Karl Marx, and Ho-Chi Minh—helped me to make connections between poverty, racism, the role of police in my community, the reason for such high rates of incarceration. For the first time, I started making sense of my own life experiences.

I was really young when I first saw news about the Civil Rights Movement on TV, saw Black people under attack by Klansmen and police in places like Birmingham and Selma. That wasn't something I could comprehend at the time. When my family moved into St. Charles and I used to pass by the plantation there, I just thought it was someone's big old house. What I did grasp was how protective my parents were of us. They warned us not to be caught walking through a white community. Right on Hansom Place in Kenner, Louisiana, where we stayed when I was young, there were Black people living on one side of the street and whites on the other; we weren't allowed to cross to the other side. Nearby was a place we called "the dog street" because if we went on it, white people would sic their dogs on us. At least we felt safe at Washington Elementary, an all-Black school on Clay Street where the teachers cared about us.

It was bad enough that Black kids were singled out in the community where we lived, but it got even worse after school integration. Kenner Elementary was right in the center of the white neighborhood. If I missed the bus, I had to walk through there to get home, with constant harassment along the way. At school I felt like I wasn't wanted and had to listen to kids calling me the N-word. In 1969, I was being harassed so much, I didn't want to go to school. That was when my mother sent me to stay with her sister in Preston Hollow.

While I was at my auntie's, I switched to Pecan Grove Elementary, also a recently integrated school. I thought it was going to be less awful, but it really wasn't that different from the one I left. One afternoon they had interclass athletic competitions. Growing up, my cousins and I had always challenged each other about who was the fastest. I knew the 50-yard dash was something I was good at and could possibly win. Four students volunteered for this meet; I was the only Black kid. We all went to the starting line and before the teacher could say, "Go," the others took off running. I took off behind them and wound up ten to fifteen yards ahead of them at the finish line—a clear-cut win. But the white student who came in second was declared "the winner." The other white kids cheered and laughed and patted him on the back. I protested vehemently but was ignored by everyone except the Black students, who were shocked by what had happened. After that day, I refused to participate in any school activities.

The following year, the house my parents had paid for in the third section of Preston Hollow was completed and we all moved there. My mother wanted my sister Ella, who lived in Los Angeles with her two daughters, to see the new place, so they got a ticket for her to come out that June of 1970. I was Ella's favorite sibling and she was mine. "Come back to L.A. with me," she said. I was really excited—I'd never been anywhere. My parents agreed. A week later, we caught the train to L.A.

I hadn't been in L.A. for more than a week when I got into a fight with the bully of the community, a dude they called Red. He was light-skinned, skinny, and tall, and he was trying to get my niece and her friend to fight each other at a house across from my sister's. When my other niece ran over to get me, I went with her right away. And when Red came at me, I got the best of him. Soon afterward, back in my sister's yard, I saw three young guys walk in. I was thinking they were coming to jump me so I grabbed a shovel.

"We heard about a new kid beating up Red," they said. "We want to be your friends."

My sister lived in south L.A., out in Watts. Every summer they had the Watts Summer Festival in Will Rogers Park. I saw the Jackson Five and Sammy Davis Jr., *Cotton Comes to Harlem* with Redd Foxx, and Black Panther Party rallies. I was twelve years old. Then I heard about the shootout that happened at the county courthouse with Jonathan Jackson, and the arrest of Angela Davis. As time went on, my new friends and I started passing flyers around, getting people to sign petitions to free Angela Davis. In California, Black people were different from those in the South. They weren't submissive or subservient. They were audacious and outspoken—especially the Black Panther Party. Those were Black people feeling proud and standing on their own feet, insisting on self-determination. I saw how it made a lot of people feel about themselves, seeing the Panthers dressed in black berets and black leather jackets, standing at attention. That was something I wanted to be.

I was going to Russell Elementary in South Central L.A. We had a little parade at school and a group of us decided we were going to dress up like the Black Panthers. My brother-in-law Melvin had a black beret he let me wear. I knew there was some type of symbolism that mattered, and that the Panthers were revered and respected in the community. One day when

I was wearing that beret, some police officers stopped and accosted me and a few guys I was with.

"Give me that beret," one said.

When I moved, everyone else scattered as well. We jumped fences and ran through alleys. For us, it was familiar territory. The cops never caught up.

My second year in L.A., I attended Charles Drew Junior High School. They had Black History programs in school that taught us about the Civil Rights Movement.

STILL, BACK THEN, I hadn't put it all together. As the months in Angola went on, I was gaining a profound appreciation of what Black people had gone through during the Civil Rights Movement. I learned more about the Black Panthers and other groups, Black men and women who decided they'd had enough of over-policing and police brutality. I saw how they were fighting against an unjust system. Things that had been ambiguous started becoming clear.

As a kid, I thought the people calling me the N-word and giving me the middle finger were dangerous and crazy people I needed to stay away from. From my mentors and protectors, I began to understand there was more to it. These white folks, themselves working people, had been taught that Black folks were nobodies, inferior and harmful. I learned about the intentional ways those lies got spread. The guys educating me connected this to capitalism, that there was a class of people in charge who benefited from racism. People running the system do what they can to divide people up by race or gender or class—"Look who's taking your job or moving out of the ghetto and into your neighborhood!"—so we'll focus on blaming each other and not look at who's responsible for the economic deprivation and hardship of people. And who benefits? The rich. They control the media, what stories get told. The children of the rich are going to top schools while the children of working people struggle because funding keeps getting cut from public schools and put into private schools. Those in charge then use educational deficiencies as "proof" that Black people are intellectually inferior to whites and only get ahead because of programs like affirmative action.

I also learned how the power structure uses force to intimidate people and maintain the status quo. One book that deeply affected me told the story of the Scottsboro Boys from the 1930s. It was hard not to put myself in their position and identify with them. They were young like me, falsely accused of raping two white women. There was no way they were able to defend themselves because the deck was stacked against them. Afterward, reading how prison guards raped Joan Little in her cell, I reflected on what happened to Althea and Chris in the parish jail. I realized these incidents weren't isolated. Whatever was taking place was systemic.

For a while, I got into Black nationalism. I was moved by reading about Malcolm X's experience after he went to Mecca and realized there were Muslims of all races, from the whitest white to darkest dark. He remembered a white woman approaching him one day asking what she could do to help, and Malcolm told her there was nothing she could do. He later changed his views and wished he could have been more open to her.

From people like Malcolm, George Jackson, and Martin Luther King, I began to understand something else, the need for discipline, leadership, and integrity. Disciplined people are able to control themselves and conduct themselves respectfully. They know how to listen. They're not apprehensive about everyone. They take into account how other people see things.

After all that had happened to me, I realized I was primarily operating off my emotions, not thinking about the consequences of my actions. I didn't analyze, I just reacted. The May 1 execution date was postponed while new lawyers were appealing my case, but the death sentence hung over me. I was past being bereaved—I was a raging tiger cub. That meant I made myself an easy target for security. Thanks to the political conversations and reading I was doing, I realized that if I was serious about getting out of there, I had to find another way. The guys I was around on the tier, they led by example. I'd look at them and say, "I want to be like that guy." But in order for that to happen, I had to put some work in.

SOME OF THE GUYS who became most important to me were housed on different tiers from mine. They did an extraordinary thing several months in.

The guards used to come to the tier and pat our cells down on a regular basis. Jerry Wells and David Veeds were two white correction officers assigned to death row and CCR. They encouraged a lot of mischief among the prisoners. I became one of the people they would shake down. On May 27, 1976, they came into my cell, ordered me to go up to the bars, handcuffed me, and made me step out. They were going through my stuff, tossing letters that I had received from family, friends, and supporters and what other little property I'd accumulated. They went into the sink and then came out and said, "We found a shank here." What that meant was they'd had a shank made—a metal spoon sharpened into a weapon—and planted it in my sink. They wrote me up for contraband and property destruction, and said I was getting sent to a place called the dungeon.

I asked to make a phone call and called my new appeals attorney, Jack Peebles. He came to Angola to represent me at the Disciplinary Board Court. The guy in charge was named Bill Kerr, assistant warden of treatment. "This is not a courthouse," he told us, meaning we didn't have the right to plead our case. They found me guilty and gave me ten days in the dungeon on Rule #1, possession of a weapon, and ten days on Rule #19, destruction of state property.

I had no idea what the "dungeon" meant until they put me in there. I just thought they were moving me to another cell isolated from everybody. Instead, they put me in a cell with four other prisoners on death row. They were packing a lot of us in that space, which was about the same six-by-nine size as our regular cells. There were no beds or seats in the dungeon—we were all on the floor. The food came on one tray, some combination of beans, rice, and turnips. We sat on that concrete floor, digging our plastic spoons into the tray while a rat or two scurried along the wall looking for crumbs. I realized this was part of the process I would have to go through and I resolved that I would survive it. I would not let them get the best of me. Somehow I learned to compartmentalize the degradation and dehumanization and keep it separate from who I was as a young Black man with a clear objective—to get out of prison.

On day three or four, Albert Woodfox checked into the dungeon and was put in a nearby cell. Once he left a few days later, along came Jerry Johnson, a Black nationalist who was a comrade of Woodfox and Herman

Wallace. And after that I saw Wallace himself, who had been framed for that guard's death along with Woodfox in 1972. It was like they were on rotation. This was the first time I came in close proximity with them. They had been sending me kites, but only now did I get to see them and hear their voices. They were letting me know who they were and finding out if I needed anything. Even though they were in an adjoining cell, we were finally able to talk up close.

Albert, Jerry, and Herman took turns in the dungeon like shift work to bear witness and send messages to those around us. They knew how corrupt and crooked the guards were. By their presence they were communicating to the other prisoners in the dungeon with me, "If you do anything to Gary, any opportunity arises, I'll do you some grave harm." They were known as "dungeon warriors" who had no fear of security; they weren't going to let anything happen to me as long as they were there to prevent it.

Later I found out that Colonel Bolt and Bockaloc had sent them a message about the shank. If Woodfox and the others wanted to show solidarity for someone who was in the dungeon, they would tell a guard, "Send me to the dungeon. I got a lot on my mind right now. Put me there before I do something crazy." The guards would let them do that. People called it "downtime."

I had already learned about Woodfox—his nickname was Fox—from the guys on the tier. Fox wasn't the type of person who boasted about who he was, but he had a reputation in prison, the way he and the other Panthers set an example with their own conduct and worked to organize their tiers. They taught inmates to pool their resources and educate themselves, to stand up to the guards together, to lay off being violent with each other. He was doing that on D tier upstairs. Herman Wallace was doing the same on A tier.

The first time I saw Fox was when they brought him to the dungeon. I was watching a guy with a big old bush on his head. He had a skin disease where he appeared very light-skinned, almost white. His voice was stern and powerful. He wasn't a big man, but he had stature. We stood at the bars of our cells and talked.

"We have your back," Fox assured me. "Many people are watching what happens to you. Despite where you're at, you can make the best out of a bad situation." It was like a clarion call, letting me know people were paying attention and rallying to my defense. I noticed that when Albert talked, people listened. He didn't play, and he spoke truth. He also spoke words I wanted to hear. How could you not respect someone, whatever they might have done before prison, when they worked to help other inmates? Fox and Hooks—that's what everyone called Herman Wallace—were on a whole other level, telling guys the history of our people, that they needed to be proud of themselves. People really need that when they're down and out in prison.

ON MY TENTH DAY in the dungeon, a Friday, I was in one of the cells with three other people. The guards brought a Black guy, Scully—his real name was Clarence Williams—to the cell on the other side. Scully was arguing with the guards, because when they opened the door to his cell, all he saw inside were two white men, the Lambert brothers, James and Larry. Scully wanted to get placed with another Black guy, Clarone Bates, who was in a cell by himself. Clarone was a really big guy. They didn't put cuffs on him, they put chains. I knew the guards feared him and didn't want to take a chance opening the cell door, afraid they'd never get him back in. Scully's pleas fell on deaf ears. Reluctantly, he went in with the Lambert brothers.

At about 7:00 p.m., the guards came to pass out blankets. We went to sleep and were awakened by hollering and sounds of beating from the next cell. I looked through a small hole in the wall where they had unscrewed the bunks. I could see Scully lying on the floor not moving, his head in a strange configuration. Something was wrong. "It's Scully," I told the guys in my cell. "I believe they killed him. I don't see him breathing." I was horrified.

We heard a lot of racking and then guys in the next cell calling for Major Phelps, the free man in charge that night. (Prison guards have military ranks like police officers do.) He opened the door and pulled out the two Lambert brothers and also a third guy, John Valdez, who apparently had been put in the cell secretly after Scully was already in. Major Phelps went to cursing them out. We heard Clarone Bates hollering as well. That's when we got confirmation: They had strangled Scully to death.

The next morning I got out of the dungeon. After ten days, they had to give you twenty-four hours back on the tier, including an hour out to shower and walk. During that time I did a telephone interview with a Black radio station out of New Orleans; I talked about my case and also what had just happened to Scully. Someone asked me why the free people let me do that interview. My answer: "Why'd somebody make a movie about the Keystone Cops?" It's not like we were dealing with the smartest people in the world. They weren't thinking, Gary Tyler has been in the dungeon, he can talk about this incident.

The following day the guards brought me back to the dungeon for the rest of my twenty-day sentence. A little later Albert Woodfox and the others checked themselves back in. I was really relieved to see them. Otherwise, who knows who the guards might have put in my cell to go after me.

On my first day at Angola, I knew it would be bad, but I didn't expect it to be as bad as it was. I didn't expect to see a guy set on fire. But most surprising, I didn't expect to find guys there who would become my protectors and my family. It took men at Angola who read the paper, watched the news, who knew me before I even came to that prison, to educate and mentor me. They gave me a lot of inspiring things to ponder. In more ways than one, they saved my life.

THERE WERE ALSO A few guards—Gregory Sanders, David Knapp, Norman Blue, and Peter Riley—who secretly kept watch and periodically checked on me. They empathized with me because I was so young and fending for myself in a hostile environment. They were young, too, and hadn't become hardened guards; three of them were Black, still a small minority among corrections officers. The inmates would say there was a good shift and a bad shift. A bad shift was one with Wells and Veeds. When these other four guys were on, we'd consider it a good shift. They didn't harass us. We didn't have a hard time using the phone. They'd help if we needed something.

Still, my situation was terrifying. I remember seeing an interview with Rubin "Hurricane" Carter on Tom Snyder's *The Tomorrow Show*. Watching Hurricane Carter talk about how he'd been raped of his freedom, I asked myself, How am I going to be able to deal with what's ahead? I'd been convicted; I was on death row. Was my cry going to be heard or fall on deaf ears? I felt lethargic and off-kilter. I was struggling to find myself, to regain my balance.

But the seeds of a new way of thinking were being planted. I was listening to people like Colonel Bolt, Bockaloc, Woodfox, older guys steeped in knowledge who spoke with certainty, with authority.

While I was in the dungeon, the mail I was getting grew so much, they had to bring it in sacks to my cell. Within a few weeks of sending out my story, those newspapers began writing about my case and readers were seeing it. I'd started to get letters and Western Union telegrams from all over the country. The numbers of people rallying to my cause kept growing and growing, and so did my mail.

Four months after I first sent my letter, the growth in supporters was bringing me a ray of light at last.

CHAPTER 6

NOT GIVING UP ON LIFE

I had my protectors inside Angola teaching me how to win public support and how to stay safe. But within months of my letter I also had a new set of protectors outside, lawyers who were trying to get my conviction overturned, or at least keep the state from executing me.

Ever since my conviction, my family was desperate. Their son was on death row and people were talking about an execution just a few months away. Even though we lived a hundred or so miles from Angola, my mother was driving almost every day to visit me—she did that until the rules changed in late 1977 limiting visits to twice a month. She was afraid the day she didn't come to visit, they'd find some other way to kill me. "I'm all right," I'd tell her. "I'm managing."

"They go this far, sentencing an innocent kid to execution, they could do anything," my mother would say.

Several weeks after I went to Angola and before I was sent to the dungeon, my mother told me she'd been approached by new attorneys who were interested in taking on my case free of charge. Jack Peebles, the lawyer who later represented me before the Disciplinary Board Court, and Lolis Elie Sr. both came out of New Orleans. Jack Peebles was a white attorney who'd been heavily involved in the Civil Rights Movement in the South. Lolis Elie, who was Black, worked on local civil rights cases.

"They heard how horribly the case was handled," my mother said during one of our visits. Peebles thought my first attorney should have gotten a change in venue. "No way in the world should the case have been tried in St. Charles Parish, where the incident took place," he told her. The new attorneys hated how Williams had dropped the ball on so many things, especially failing to object to the judge's prejudicial instructions to the jury.

These two men were there for me. Unlike Williams, the two of them visited often and were very attentive despite the fact that my family wasn't giving them any money. They stayed in constant contact with my mother. They were trying to save my life.

I told Peebles how folks lied and how the kids on the bus all knew it was a farce. They knew that Natalie Blanks, bless her soul because she's no longer with us, had psychological problems. I'd known her a long time. At one time at Destrehan, she'd been my girlfriend. We had gone to first grade through third or fourth grade together in Washington Elementary School in Jefferson Parish.

So Peebles sought her out, and first Natalie and then Loretta London recanted. That's a legal term I wasn't even familiar with at the time, but I quickly learned it meant they took back their testimonies. They also made clear why they'd given false statements about me in the first place: The police had forced them to.

In an affidavit in early March of 1976, Natalie Blanks described how she said she wasn't sitting with me and didn't know anything about me having a gun, but she was told that she'd be charged as an accessory to murder unless she said exactly what they told her to. She was sent to see the district attorney, who had referred to her young baby and told her, "Do you want to be in jail? . . . Don't you want to be here to raise your baby?" In her own affidavit, Natalie's mother said she informed the prosecutor L. J. Hymel before my trial that Natalie wasn't trustworthy, that she was under psychiatric care. Hymel just dismissed it. The prosecution had made Natalie the center of their case—she was the only one who testified that she'd seen me fire a gun.

Natalie's mother also brought in her cousin, Sylvia Taylor, herself an attorney, who swore in an affidavit that she'd notified Hymel and Norman Pitre and Judge Marino about Natalie's credibility problems, including that she'd once falsely claimed to have been kidnapped. None of that mattered to the prosecution or to the judge. And none of it got communicated to Attorney Williams or the jurors.

In her deposition that same month, Loretta, who had gotten married and now went by Loretta Thomas, said the police had threatened her, too. When she told them she never saw me with a gun on the bus, they insisted she say yes, she had seen me, and that I'd given the gun to her afterward. Loretta said one of the policemen started "hollering" that he was going to give her ninety-nine years because she was "an accessory after the fact." Like Natalie, Loretta told the attorneys she'd been afraid. She'd felt helpless. She hadn't known what to do.

I have to say, I had mixed feelings when I heard about this. These were kids I had considered friends who had lied on me in court. I still felt deeply betrayed and wronged by people I thought I knew. I was consumed with what they had done to me, knowing my life was on the line. Thinking about what had happened in the courthouse affected my ability to deal with my difficult circumstances in prison. It was like having to fight two battles at the same time. To be honest, I still held them at fault.

At the same time, it was a huge relief that they came forward and acknowledged the police had pressured them to lie. It was a vindication, because I'd been saying all along that Natalie wasn't sitting in the seat with me, that I never held a gun out the window or shot it. I was thinking now I would automatically be released from prison. I'd go to court, have a hearing, and the judge would dismiss the conviction and free me. I was such a kid still. You're talking about someone who had always been told that the truth will eventually prevail. My parents would say, "Never lie to me. The truth will always come out." Somehow, in spite of everything that had gone down, I still believed that.

ON MARCH 10, 1976, Jack Peebles filed with the state supreme court asking for a new trial based on this new evidence. Eight days later, the state court sent the case back to the original trial court in St. Charles Parish. I got transported from Angola to the parish jail until the hearing, which was set for April in the same courthouse. But this time would be different, I thought. This time witnesses would be telling the truth.

The day I arrived at Hahnville, Lockett came to see me in my cell. He stood by the door and shook his head. "Why did you come back, Gary?" he asked me.

I thought he meant, why were we fighting the case. "I want to get my conviction overturned," I said.

"No, why did you come back here that night?" Lockett had a look of disbelief on his face. "I was standing by the kitchen window and I saw you climbing out. I recognized it was you. When I came back the next morning to hand out the food, you were in the cell."

During the time I was in Hahnville, Lockett had taken a liking to me. I was one of the inmates he always checked on, and often we would talk. Maybe I reminded him of a grandson. He was a very kind old guy. He never was rude, never spoke down to me, always had a friendly smile. Because he lived right next door, he checked on me on a daily basis. It used to give me a sense of security, especially when he stood up for me when that police officer came looking for me and sprayed mace in my cell.

But at the time, I hadn't known the man had any idea that I had left the parish jail. I thought the only individuals who did know were Michael Dupre and the inmates I was friends with on the second floor. Turns out Lockett knew, too, and never said a word. He was a deputy sworn to uphold the law. He could have taken action, could have caught me or informed other officers. No telling how that would have turned out. Instead, he remained quiet about it. And when I came back for this hearing and he opened the latch to my cell, the expression on his face was kind of surprised, like "You?"

I was shocked to find this out. It wasn't that any of the prisoners had told him. He saw me with his own eyes. He recognized me. I guess to him, it was a relief that this young kid at least was getting out, either to give them a run for their money or get lost where they could never find him. Lockett wasn't going to be the one who would get me in trouble. He'd been there so long, he'd probably seen a lot of bad things happen, and he didn't want anything to happen to me on his watch.

I grinned and gave him an appreciative look, like "Yeah, you got me." He was a good man. The inmates in the parish jail, whenever they had a problem, that's who they called on.

The new hearing went on for a week in front of the same judge, Ruche Marino. My lawyers had tried to get him recused because he had witnessed Sylvia Taylor asking for and getting immunity for Natalie Blanks. Giving someone immunity could imply they were in on a crime and that could prejudice the jury. Ruche Marino denied he'd ever heard any immunity discussion or that any had been granted. It was his word against Sylvia Taylor's. No surprise, the judge overseeing the recusal motion believed his fellow judge, so we were stuck with Marino.

L. J. Hymel, Norman Pitre, and Harry Morel represented the state. I wasn't worried about them. Natalie and Loretta were coming back and saying what really happened. When my two schoolmates got on the stand and testified, and then their parents and Sylvia Taylor did, too, I sat back in my seat thinking everything was going good. My attorneys were doing a great job. Natalie and Loretta were correcting their lies. On each day of the hearing, I thought, This is the day I'm getting released.

Then, on April 23, the judge rendered his decision. I couldn't believe it. In his opinion, Natalie Blanks had told the truth at my trial the previous November and was lying now. I didn't understand everything he said, but I got the essence of it: It didn't matter what evidence our side introduced. There would be no new trial.

ONCE AGAIN, I WAS crushed and hurt and angry. Part of me felt defeated. But this time, I knew there were people out there protesting on my behalf. Some of them had been present in the courthouse, and when they brought me outside—Deputy Schmill had me by one arm, Mike Babin was holding the other—I saw the crowd, people from Tulane, Southern University at New Orleans, and others. As I listened to them chant "Free Gary Tyler," I felt this exhilaration. "These are my supporters," I thought. "I got to be strong, I got to let them know this is not over, I'm going to weather this storm." I couldn't raise my arms because the deputies had their hands on me—you can see that in a photo. But I gave the crowd a defiant pose. They were saying, "Free Gary Tyler. Free my brother." I wanted them to know "I'm not giving up. I've come too far. I'm not going to keep doing things as a child." I would start acting like a man.

Even in defeat, we were making progress. More people—myself included—were understanding that what I'd experienced wasn't just happenstance. It was one more example of how the legal system treated young Black men, Black people in general. My reading and conversations had shown me that the system was rooted in this kind of injustice.

Peebles told me he was appealing the decision back to the Louisiana State Supreme Court. I didn't understand the process, but I understood he wasn't giving up either. And he was preparing for another avenue as well with the U.S. Supreme Court.

Just before I was taken to Hahnville for this hearing, I'd heard rumors of a case before the U.S. Supreme Court, a lawsuit by a man named Stanislaus Roberts challenging the constitutionality of the Louisiana law that demanded an automatic death penalty for anyone convicted of certain crimes. Roberts's attorney argued that giving the jury no discretion in sentencing was a violation of the Eighth Amendment prohibiting cruel and unusual punishment. Roberts was also on death row in Angola, on a different tier from me. I hadn't met him yet, though I would years later in the Visiting Shed, a large room inside A Building that looked like a big cafeteria, for prisoners and people who came to see them.

People were saying that the court had heard his case, and it looked like the ruling was going to be favorable and overturn his death sentence. I didn't understand the legalese, but being on death row and having the guys talk about it, I understood it was an opening, a possibility that something good was going to come. The state continued the stay of execution date for me and others until the Supreme Court made its decision.

When Peebles and I talked about this, he raised the possibility that, if Roberts won, my case might be remanded from adult court to juvenile court. He felt I had a great chance of beating the charge there. Once again, I was like someone underwater grabbing at anything at all I hoped would keep me afloat. One more time I was thinking, naively, that if the case was overturned, I'd automatically get to go home.

As much as I hung on to the Roberts case, I wasn't that familiar with the details because I was caught up in my own. But when the decision came down that summer, everybody on death row heard about it—they all had their attorneys, too, who were following the case.

On July 2, 1976, the U.S. Supreme Court ruled that the automatic death sentence for certain crimes was unconstitutional. The ruling affected adults and juveniles not just in Louisiana, but also in Texas, North Carolina, Georgia, and Florida. Those states all had similar legislation and all of them had to change.

You could see the relief, you could feel it, you could hear the deep sigh coming from all the guys on Angola's death row. We no longer had execution dates hanging over our heads.

I should have known it was too good to be true. Some weeks later, the attorney general, William Guste, a Democrat, filed a motion that despite this U.S. Supreme Court ruling, my death penalty should remain and my execution be carried out. Why? Because, AG Guste argued, under a 1974 constitutional change, the state supreme court might have the power to review a sentence to see if it was excessive. "The death penalty would never be mandatory if always reviewable," he told the newspapers.

Hearing that, I thought, Wow, why are they so determined to kill me when I'm innocent, I didn't do a damn thing?

A few days after the ruling came out, I was transferred to a local jail. There was no reason for the state prison of Louisiana to have custody over me. Because this was not a new trial but a resentencing, the district court still had jurisdiction. St. Charles Parish had the old parish jail in Hahnville but the authorities felt it wasn't secure enough because my case had become highly political. Vigilantes might try to cause me harm. So they transferred me to a place called Convent in St. James Parish. That's where I spent my eighteenth birthday.

THE JAILHOUSE IN CONVENT was nothing like Angola. It was fairly new, it was clean, and it didn't have more than six of us in the whole facility. The other prisoners had heard a lot about me. I was a popular guy.

At Convent, my cell had two bunks and a shower. We didn't have recreational activities, but they did allow our families to bring us food. We were also allowed to have money. The six of us used to get our little money together and have the radio dispatcher, a twenty-year-old Black woman, call police out on patrol to buy some chicken and bring it back for us. The officers didn't mind.

My family, friends, and supporters used to visit me a lot. Convent was closer and more accessible than Angola. People from the community came. So did newspeople from leftist magazines and newspapers. I needed them to get the word out because the mainstream media remained indifferent to my situation. They were stuck on the information coming from the courts. Bottom line, that reporting was biased.

On October 20, I was expecting to see some family members since they were there all the time, so I got worried when no one showed up. I had a strange feeling that something was wrong. It turned out a Norwegian tanker had hit the *George Prince* ferry, one of the Luling–Destrehan lines, and killed seventy-eight people, including my cousin Jerry. Eventually I heard from the jailer that there had been a bad accident. I got a late visit that day from family members who told me my cousin was trapped in a cabin on the boat. They were looking for his body along with the others.

It was a horrific day, a blow to my whole family and to me. Jerry and I were very close. Although he was several years older, he was someone I looked up to and had really bonded with. He used to work on a garbage truck driven by a friend's daddy. When I was fourteen, Jerry and his friend asked me if I wanted to make a little money. On Friday nights, four of us would go empty the garbage cans from Preston Hollow to St. Rose and then all the way to Destrehan, New Sarpy, and Norco. When morning break came at about 6:00, we'd finish and shower. They'd give me some money and we'd go shopping for clothes and shoes. Jerry took care of me twice when I took a night out from Hahnville. Whenever I called on him, he was always there. I was really going to miss him. In our family, cousins were like brothers. I felt a kind of suffocation. I knew I would never see him again and I couldn't do anything about it. I couldn't even attend his funeral.

I also remember the day two prisoners from Angola, Tommy Mason and Jerry Cooks, stayed over with us at Convent. They had a speaking engagement at a local church the next day, part of a program Angola had where prisoners traveled to talk to young people, and they spent the night in the local jail. Tommy and Jerry knew about me. Cooks was from New Orleans and was an inmate counsel—what they call a jailhouse lawyer. Tommy Mason was from Shreveport and worked on *The Angolite*, the prison newspaper, with Wilbert Rideau. They shared their life stories with young people, encouraging them to make better choices and not be influenced by peer pressure. I really enjoyed talking to them that night at Convent. They said they were glad to see me because they'd heard so much about me. "Don't give up," they told me.

I was determined not to, even when the state supreme court turned down our request for a new trial in February of 1977. I focused on the re-sentencing hearing coming up.

ON MARCH 8, 1977, deputies flew me in a helicopter to Hahnville for that hearing. I'd never been in a helicopter before. I was sitting by the door, handcuffed, as we got caught up in a rainstorm. The vehicle was shaking and the pilot had to lower his altitude to avoid the strong wind. For a moment he was talking about putting us down in a field. I just prayed we wouldn't crash. Here I was fighting not to die in the electric chair, but dying in a helicopter crash wouldn't have been any better. Neither would being shot by some white supremacist. When we got there, the local sheriff pointed out that his department had snipers on the roof to protect me.

In spite of my experiences up to that point, from talking to the attorneys I felt there was a chance of getting the case remanded to juvenile court. The attorney general and the rest of the prosecution stuck with their defense that my death sentence should remain.

Judge Ruche Marino rejected the prosecution's argument, but he also rejected ours. This wasn't the first time the U.S. Supreme Court had required states to fix laws involving the death penalty. Following each of the other decisions, *Witherspoon v. Illinois* in 1968 and *Furman v. Georgia* in 1972, state courts had made clear that the convictions were fine, it was just the punishment that needed adjusting. End of argument. My conviction would stand. And the new punishment they wanted for me was harsh: Imprisonment at hard labor for life, with no chance of probation, parole, or suspension of sentence until I had served twenty years.

Judge Ruche Marino looked over his courtroom, attentive to everything that moved, a man in control. I stood there in a world of hurt, trying to process what this meant. The decision was definitely a blow because, foolishly, I hadn't anticipated it. I still thought, The law is the law and the truth will prevail. Indoctrination is hard to wipe out. I knew there was a political system at play, but I hadn't yet fully understood how the system worked.

That was when I began to ask myself, What am I missing? I was ignorant about so many things. Thanks to my mentors, when I went back to Angola I began to understand much more. "The legal system is racist," Colonel Bolt told me. "It doesn't work for us." The people in charge had the cake baked for me and wanted to make sure I had no way to get out. But Bolt also said, "You should never give up. Struggle is constant—we can't afford to stop. Remember that victory is inevitable. You need to keep on fighting. People are depending on you to be strong."

THE DAY THE SENTENCE came down, they flew me straight back to Angola on that same helicopter. It's funny how, in light of this big loss hanging over me, there were two smaller things I was really upset about.

When the guards had targeted me in the early months on death row, they'd seen the kind of reading materials I had. They'd go through your stuff, one letter at a time, and throw it all over the place, just because they could. By the time they finished, your cell was a mess. They had done that to me many times. You're on death row, you've got a lot on your mind, and they'd come in to taunt you. "Sweep your cell out," they'd say, after you'd already done it. They'd insist the fork wasn't on the tray, even though they knew damn well it was. Anything to make your life miserable.

Once I'd been at Convent for a while, I got a referral to get my belongings sent there from Angola. You know what those people sent me? Three Bibles and a bunch of Christian newspapers. It was as if someone said, "We're going to make sure this heathen gets some religious material. That's what he needs." None of my books, magazines, or newspapers came back to me. I had bundled that stuff up and tagged it and knew it had all been in the property room. When I got back to Angola, I realized I had lost everything.

When the court order came for me to move to the local jail, I thought I'd never go back. Jerry Wells, one of the guards who had planted that shank in my cell, got into it with me. And I now regretted that, thinking that was the last I'd see of him, I'd had a few choice words for him.

Wells was a big guy, about six feet five, three hundred pounds. He was known as a "coon ass," as some Cajuns called themselves. Like most of the people who worked at the prison, he was from one of the families who'd been guards at Angola for a long time. Wells and many of the others lived in Marksville, a small town across the river from Angola. Those guards fought each other like cats and dogs, and they routinely harassed the Black prisoners. From the start Jerry Wells was after me, a Black kid accused of killing a white kid. His nickname for me was "Juvenile." He loved to provoke me, knowing he'd get a reaction every time.

"You'll be back," he told me.

"You're a motherfucking liar," I told him. "I will not be back, I'm going home."

The so-called justice system proved me wrong. I was going back to Angola.

After the resentencing, one of the officers escorting me there tried to console me. "Don't worry," he said, "there's a bright side. In the state of Louisiana when you get life, you only serve ten years and six months and you'll be out of prison." I wanted to believe him. I knew about people who had done that. But I'd heard my sentence. I had to go by what the judge said: Life at hard labor with no chance of probation, parole, or suspension of sentence until twenty years had passed.

Some of my supporters thought we'd won because I had avoided being executed. But my mother and many others knew that it wasn't justice. I was innocent. The focus now had to be on freeing me. Being sentenced to life at Angola was still a death sentence.

CHAPTER 7

STILL FIGHTING TO SURVIVE

It was a short helicopter ride to Angola. They put me back on death row until March 25, when I could be reclassified and moved to the AU, the Adjustment Unit. That's where newcomers went for several weeks before they were processed and classified to minimum, medium, or maximum security. Maximum was reserved for the prisoners Angola considered dangerous and at-risk.

AU inmates stayed in an open dormitory upstairs, and unless they had a medical condition, they went to work right away in the field picking cotton or doing other hard labor, for this place that still operated like a massive plantation.

I had a feeling the field was going to present problems for me. All of the guards there were white. My case was known, my name was known. A lot of those guards hated me before they even saw me. I'd heard they had made threats against me. Guards drove us inmates out to the field in what they called a hootenanny, a long rig with a semitruck pulling a trailer holding up to one hundred prisoners. They gave us flat shovels and had us digging trenches out in the blazing sun. Overlooking the field was someone known as the High Rider. That's the guard who sat on a horse with a high-powered rifle wearing a dark hat and dark shades so he could shoot anyone who tried to escape. The High Rider used to harass me a lot, so much so that Junius Lane, the guy who drove the hootenanny, stood up one day and said, "Man, what you harassing this kid for? This kid never done you anything wrong." I'll never forget that. Junius Lane was an old convict, a class A trustee, and he stood up for this young kid. I was eighteen and a half years old.

The first week, they had us hoeing the ditches. They'd order us either to "cut it low" or "cut it to the dirt." One morning in early April, it had rained hard and we had to dig a quarter-drain to clear the water out of the field. The field farmer was telling the guys in front of me and behind me to dig the trench two spades wide. Then he came to me and told me to dig four spades wide. I saw the scheme, to get me in trouble for messing up the job.

"What the fuck," I told him, "you want me to dig a goddamn canal out here? Fuck you!" I knew he was going to write me up for property destruction, so I thought why not, I threw the shovel out in the field. They called the patrol on me, handcuffed me, and put me in the dungeon. Then I had to go to Angola's D.B. Court, the Disciplinary Board. The board found me guilty of a work offense despite me explaining how the guard had tried to set me up—they all knew, but it didn't matter. They shut me in the dungeon for a few days, then suspended the sentence and sent me back out.

This time I was sent to the cotton field, where guards demanded a quota of a hundred pounds each. I didn't know anything about picking cotton. I said, "Man, slaves did this kind of work. I'm not doing this. Fuck you." They locked me up again for a work offense. I went back to the disciplinary board, where they found me guilty again. This time I had to spend ten days in the dungeon.

I was young and I was grieving. I saw other guys stand up to the guards, and that gave me the green light to be defiant, too. I felt I had a legitimate reason, being wrongfully convicted, and I wasn't going to conform to their rules. I got to a point where I didn't even care about the punishment. I could spend ten or twenty days in the dungeon. I got used to it. I'd made my point. I was letting them know that they might be able to control me physically, but they couldn't control me mentally.

***

WHILE I WAS IN the dungeon, a guy named Al Landry in a nearby cell started calling my name. He did it in a flirtatious way, a challenge, like he was coming out to get me. Then I heard the distinct voice of Billy McCoy—he was an educated guy and his pronunciation was very clear and memorable. I hadn't known he was in the dungeon, too. He said, "Al, I know you. You know you ain't nothing but a whore. If you find yourself messing with Gary, I'm going to deal with your ass." Al was calling my name like he was trying to impress the guys on the tier, and Billy McCoy called him out.

I originally was skeptical about Billy McCoy; I'd heard he'd been accused of raping another inmate. But I was starting to trust him. He stood up for me in the trenches when it mattered. I needed allies like that in prison if I was going to survive.

When the AU held the next classification board, they sentenced me to maximum security—CCR, or solitary confinement—because of what they called the "original reason for lockdown," that first work offense from the field. The regular board met every ninety days to assess inmates' conduct record to see if they were eligible to be released from maximum security. Over and over again, they used that "original reason for lockdown" as an excuse to keep me in solitary, what we called "the cells."

In their view, I had become "rebellious." They saw me as a threat. I'd learned early on that those who speak out and protest against the inhumane conditions in prison get confined to maximum security as punishment for standing up for themselves and others. It was no surprise that Fox and Hooks were the ones who'd been framed for killing Brent Miller in 1972, given how they organized among the inmates. Locking people up in solitary was the prison system's way of using power against us, who were already trapped. It was purposefully vengeful and vindictive, but the board had complete discretion. Still, I was determined they would not destroy me.

The building that housed people on death row and CCR was a separate structure with two stories. Downstairs were tiers A, B, and C; they had tiers A, B, C, and D upstairs as well. This time they sent me to C upstairs. People in maximum security didn't work in the field or anywhere else. We couldn't leave our cells except for that one hour a day.

One thing that helped me through that time was having more interaction with Albert Woodfox. Fox was on D tier upstairs. C and D were back to back. We used to holler at each other through the pipe chase, a narrow space between the tiers where the pipes were. We had to be careful, though. Sometimes a guard would sneak back there to see what we were talking about. On my hour out, I might see Fox in the lobby where the two pay phones were. It was an open area with tables lined up, where they fixed the food trays. Fox knew my desperation, knew how much I wanted out of prison. "I understand," he told me. "But freedom is not freedom until you free your mind."

I was in a place where I didn't know a lot of people and everybody was not my friend. I knew I had to be aware of my surroundings, to observe and listen, and to use common sense. I learned to trust my instincts. If I didn't feel right about something, I'd go with that feeling.

Fox and my other mentors gave me a lot of advice. About the free people, they said: "Learn which ones are cool and which ones are dirt, but don't trust any of them. They're not your friend. At the end of the day, they go home, you're still here. Always be aware of who you're dealing with. Don't let them provoke you, get in your head by playing little games where you can get yourself locked up."

About the other inmates, they told me, "Don't get into any bar fights. Just don't say anything if a guy gets irate or says something disrespectful. Don't respond right away because it could be a trap." Fox reminded me that those in charge of the prison at the time instigated divisions among prisoners to cement their own control. That's why they allowed sexual slavery, favored prisoners who dealt in contraband, and went after anyone who opposed such practices and tried to educate young prisoners. "If they keep us fighting among ourselves," Fox would say, "we won't resist them."

That's when I stopped being a kid. When you see the whole system come down on you, you have to grow up fast and learn quick. I couldn't act like I was in la-la land and everything was peaches and cream. People around me were getting killed, getting hurt really bad. Guards would tear-gas us in the cells. They might come on the tier and demand an inmate come out of his cell for some unfair reason, like an arbitrary rectal search. When the inmate refused, they'd shoot tear gas that permeated the whole tier. I learned to put my face in the toilet and flush to create a vacuum of air, wrapping a towel around my head to keep my face and eyes from burning. Once they ordered an inmate named Larry Calloway, who was on death row on A tier, to come out and he refused. The free people fired riot gas that burned off Calloway's clothes and the skin on most of his body.

Upper-C tier was known as the "outlaw tier" because there was so much turmoil and infighting. After several months there, I was transferred to Upper-A tier. I found out that security wanted to use more force on C tier and felt my presence would be an obstacle. By then there was a lot of publicity surrounding my case and protesters gathered at the front gate demanding my freedom. The prison was already under public pressure about the brutal beatings of inmates at Camp J, a disciplinary camp built in 1976 close to Lake Killarney, far from the Main Prison and CCR. It had been created as a control center for inmates who were labeled "incorrigible," primarily people who organized work stoppages and other protests. Camp J was known as a death camp because so many people died there, beaten really badly by security. There were numerous lawsuits about it.

The move to Upper-A actually served my best interests. I knew some of the guys who'd been moved there from downstairs, including Gary and Dennis Ledbetter, Akbar Lateef (Ronald Crawford), and Herman Wallace, who welcomed me and introduced me to Gerald Bryant, Henry Patterson, and Herman Nelson. These brothers were well disciplined and the most militant and active in Angola.

STILL, VIOLENCE LURKED EVERYWHERE. On every tier I was on, I saw inmates do a lot of harm to each other, throw human waste or hot water, bust open a battery and throw acid, heat up a can with wiring and throw that, whatever they could get their hands on. I witnessed men coming out of their handcuffs and stabbing someone. I lived among people who made zip guns in prison, bows and arrows. They made spears out of newspaper rolled up really thin, with toothpaste as a glue. Some inmates had relationships with the free people where the free man would open the cell door for them and let them kill another individual. My mentors taught me how to rig my door to keep someone from opening it when I was sleeping.

For me, prison was a learning field. It was a world I had no idea functioned this way, and I had no other choice but to pay close attention. I didn't want anyone setting me on fire or shooting me with a spear gun or bow and arrow. I was dealing with men without knowing why they were in prison, men with trauma and many with severe, untreated mental illness—anything could trigger them. People fought like tigers. Respect was the foremost concern. If you did the slightest thing someone saw as disrespect, they thought they were justified in killing you. The inmates looked like gladiators and prided themselves on confrontation. Just because someone was quiet didn't mean he wasn't dangerous. I watched, just like my mentors told me.

"You're not of this world," they'd say. "You're not built for it yet. You're new. Do as I say, not as I do." Many of them believed that I was innocent and they were willing to put their lives on the line for me. They knew I was young and impressionable and felt it was on them to keep me from going in the wrong direction. This was their world, they were saying—they were contributors, that's why they were in CCR. They didn't mind hurting someone if they had to in order to prove themselves. Those same challenges would come my way. They wanted to keep me from being dehumanized. Prison had a way of destroying good people.

Robert King, who we called Moja, was also a member of the Black Panther Party, with Woodfox and Wallace (Hooks), all widely respected for fighting to end rape and indiscriminate violence at Angola and organize inmates to work together. These guys had tremendous mutual respect for each other. The issue for me was, what path did I want to follow: those who educated themselves to understand the system and developed tools to combat the injustices and inhumane treatment, or those who'd been victimized by it and thought the only way to survive was to perpetuate that cycle?

I was clear I didn't want to perpetuate it. I wanted to be on the side of enlightening myself, getting the tools to understand my conditions, and working with other people to change those conditions. When the Panthers came together on a hunger strike, not everyone in CCR joined in.

But everyone benefited when the prison decided to cut slots in the bars to feed us humanely. That win changed some people's perspective about certain individuals and about people in general—and also about the possibility of change.

I had a good sense of right and wrong. It wasn't hard to choose which side I wanted to be on.

BUT THERE WAS A needle I had to keep threading: Don't let yourself be provoked, but know when to stand up for yourself. I wasn't a coward, and I knew what it meant to get in a fight and lose; I was determined to survive no matter what. When they sent me to prison, I made up my mind that if someone came to rape me or kill me, I would kill him. I'd been told, "You have to keep this on your mind: If someone gives you a knife, don't turn it down. That's a litmus test, that's when they'll judge you, decide you don't have the heart to defend yourself and they can do whatever they want because you won't fight back." I convinced myself that I wasn't going to fall into that trap.

I had started lifting weights in 1970 when I was staying with my sister in California. My brother-in-law was a bodybuilder and taught me. When I left California, I continued to lift. We didn't have access to any recreation when I was on death row, but in that six-by-nine cell, I did push-ups, tricep dips, sit-ups. I ran in place. I promised myself after getting the ass-whipping from V. J. St. Pierre and the other officers that I wasn't going to let myself be vulnerable to anyone like that again, not the free people, not the inmates.

Early on, when I was still on death row in 1976, during the twenty-four-hour break between my two ten-day sentences in the dungeon over that shank frame-up, a man called Leonard Buggage had come to our tier. He arrived out of Jefferson Parish with two capital punishment convictions. *Playboy* magazine publicized how ludicrous it was to give two death sentences when you can only die once. Buggage was five or six years older than me. He had started calling me "Casper," a derogatory racial term. No one makes a mockery of my color. "My name is Gary," I told him over and over again.

When I got out the dungeon for those twenty-four hours, I headed for the shower. I was used to guys asking to get some ice or turn the TV. Then I heard Buggage's voice: "Say, Casper." I was already on edge. Scully had just been killed and I was trying to figure out how to get the word out. At first I showed no reaction. I just walked to the window across from my cell, climbed up, unscrewed the long fluorescent lights, and started throwing them at Buggage's cell. The noise they made when they broke got a lot of guys' attention. Buggage was really surprised. Even though he'd been watching me, he didn't know I was going to aim at him.

That was the first time everybody saw me act up. Out of concern and respect, I had never gotten into an altercation. But this guy thought he could get away with continuing to disrespect me. "I told you not to call me by that name," I told him. After that, he never did it again. Later, we got cool with each other.

There were other times I had to stand up for myself. Once I was locked up in the dungeon with a guy named Vincent Simmons, known as Comanche. He kept telling me about all the people he'd beaten up. I thought he was trying to intimidate me. When we had political discussions on the tier and I'd ask a lot of questions, he used to say, "You need to shut up. You sound stupid." That really irked me. The guy was buff, and at that time, I was still a skinny little kid. I listened to him in that cell bragging about the things he'd done, and I told him, "I'm the type of person, if I have something to say, I tell the person directly." Comanche punched me in the chest, and I proceeded to beat his ass. He pulled a shank out on me, a toothbrush with a razor blade burned onto the edge. I didn't care. I ran up on him and took it from him. "I should cut your fucking neck," I said. But something told me, You are not a killer. If you do this, you're going to ruin yourself for life. I backed off.

BY 1983, BOTH HOOKS and I had been transferred from Upper-A to Upper-B tier. While there I got into it with a guy named Sammy Tropaz from New Orleans. He used to put on his shorts and wrap his wrists with ace bandages, do push-ups and walk around like he was some kind of Spartacus gladiator, like the actor Woody Strode. He and I started off being cool. But then everything changed.

Hooks got into it with a guy named Jewel Green, who folks called Seventh Ward. Just because Hooks or others from the Black Panthers were organizing on a tier didn't mean every inmate went along. There could be a knucklehead like Green who refused to cooperate and continued to cause problems on the tier. After a time, the inmates who were in solidarity with each other would force that guy off the tier. Jewel Green called Hooks out, not knowing Hooks was a peaceful warrior and would take action if needed. When the guards were taking them out for recreation, Hooks managed to come out of his handcuffs and attacked Jewel Green, not to kill him, but to let him know he was no longer welcome on B tier. Green went to the hospital and Hooks got locked up in the dungeon.

Someone tipped me off that an inmate named Roland Johnson, an instigator on the tier, was stirring up trouble for me. He told Sammy Tropaz that Hooks and I were planning to kill him. I don't think Tropaz believed it, but he was being manipulated. One day he came out of the cell next to me with a cup of human waste in his hands. I was sitting on my bunk bed watching TV. Sammy Tropaz reached into my cell and threw the waste on the wall. I knew Roland Johnson was watching with his mirror.

"I just wanted you to know that I'll throw this on you," Tropaz told me.

"Are you finished?" I asked. "I don't want to clean this up and find out you have more."

He said yes.

That was the first time someone had thrown human waste in my cell. As I cleaned it up, I knew if I let this guy get away with this, it would set a bad precedent and let others think they could do it, too. I had to protect my reputation. But I knew if I got Tropaz, I'd have to get the instigator as well.

I was clear I wouldn't throw any human waste. That would make me lose the moral high ground—only prisoners with no character would stoop to that. I had batteries, soap, mothballs, and baby oil in my cell. I decided to bust the batteries open to get the acid, mix it up with baby oil, and cook it to foment the battery acid. I also got newspaper, rolled it up real well, and soaked it down with baby oil to make torches. Tropaz's cell was next to mine. On my hour out on the tier, I started throwing battery acid and mothballs at him and lit the torches. I only meant to scare the guy. But as soon as I got those torches in the cell, they set his bars and the paint on the wall on fire. I had no idea it would burn that intensely. It was horrifying. When I turned around, I saw the mirror hanging out the door of Roland Johnson and shouted, "I'm coming for you next." He immediately called for the free men. I disposed of the rest of the stuff in my sink.

Johnson told the free men I had set Sammy Tropaz on fire. Smoke was coming out of that cell. I was praying I hadn't killed this guy. My heart was pounding as the blaze got bigger and bigger. I couldn't complete the mission and get the instigator as well, because Roland Johnson had called the free men. I looked at him and shook my head. "You're a rat," I said. The free men got there and handcuffed me through the bars. One thing I can say about Tropaz, when they asked him what happened, he told them he accidentally set his cell on fire using a "stinger"—aluminum wire attached to a can and connected to the lights—to heat up his coffee.

THE FREE MEN TOLD me to get my stuff and sent me to Camp J. This was my first time there. I knew all the stories about what went on there, but I had done what I had to do and I would deal with the consequences. Many people had gotten to know me by then. I wasn't someone other people in maximum security felt uncomfortable around. I was young and focused on getting out of prison. Because of the attention my case received, I was something of a celebrity in prison. Guys who met me for the first time would say, "Oh, you're Gary Tyler!" I was well known for standing up for what was right, because I was innocent. But when I needed to, I stood up for myself.

The guards transported me during the day but kept me in a holding pen till that night. When they took me to a cell in Camp J, we had to walk outside. I stopped and just stood there, handcuffed and shackled, looking up. It was the first time I'd been out at night for a long time.

"What are you looking at?" the guard asked me.

"The stars," I said.

The guy was surprised. This was something he took for granted. He took my cuffs off and led me to my cell.

Twenty-four hours later, they took me to the Disciplinary Board, tried me for that attack, found me guilty, and moved me back to the cells on Upper-A tier. Lucky for me, that's also where they'd moved Hooks. I really respected that guy.

Hooks had a personality that made everybody feel at ease. He was medium height, about 140 pounds, very fit, with dark skin and an African bush. He had a nice smile and he wasn't judgmental. Even the guards liked him, despite the fact that he was radical, because he was one of the most mild, rational individuals you could talk to. Hooks was always willing to help, and he was smart as a whip.

This man, who was seventeen years older than me, was like my sensei. I was around Hooks for many years. He was an organizer. He wasn't shy about what he believed in and liked to sew a Black Panther image on his clothing. I saw how methodical he was, always planning, always filing suits for himself and Woodfox, falsely accused of the Brent Miller killing, as well as for improved conditions for all the prisoners. He set the marching orders for everything. He was also the person who helped me maintain my humanity. I watched how he took his time, was patient, how he never boasted. And he was really there for me. When I had a hard time understanding something, he stayed with me. Hooks was the one who taught me how to read people, helped me develop emotional intelligence. I observed how he would listen, try to pick someone's brain, ask them, "Why did you do what you did? Don't you think you could have done it differently?"

Hooks made me realize my potential. He was patient with me at times when I was very difficult to deal with. And he always gave me good advice. "Don't do something that you'll regret for the rest of your life," he'd say. "Don't let the puppet master get inside your head and manipulate you. That's what the system wants to see. Don't go through life making enemies, especially of people who mean you well." Hooks also helped me moderate and understand my feelings when it came to women.

STARTING IN 1977, I was in communication with a young woman, Gilda Parks, from Orange, New Jersey. She had first written me a letter when I was in the parish jail in Convent awaiting resentencing. I got so much mail, I could never answer it all. But after I got sent back to Angola, something told me to go through my stuff and find that letter. Gilda had sent a picture of her and her six-year-old son. At the time, I was getting a lot of support from churches around the country. They'd said a prayer for me at her church and shared information about how to correspond with me. I decided to write her back. We kept up a great communication for several years.

Gilda was six years older than I was, a working mother who had just graduated from college. From the photos she sent me, I saw she was a beautiful woman, light-skinned with reddish-brown hair and freckles. I could tell from her letters that she was also a real nice person, sensitive and with a big heart. Gilda knew how hard it was for Black men in America and urged me to maintain my pride and fight for what's right. "Don't give up no matter what," she'd write, "no matter how hard things get. Believe that someday it will all be behind you and you will overcome your ordeal." I kept her updated about my case. She was always supportive. Over the course of several months of writing to each other, we fell in love.

In April of 1980, Gilda came to Angola and visited me for a three-day period. We were able to spend time together each day in a visiting booth, where I was behind a screen. She had a way of making me feel special and appreciated. She definitely had my heart. I could only feel her fingertips through the meshed screen, but as we talked, we caressed each other's fingers and looked each other in the eyes.

That last day she could visit on that trip was the most emotional time of my life in prison. Gloom filled my heart, and Gilda's face had gotten flushed. She began to cry because the end of our time together was drawing near. I tried comforting her, but my heart grew heavier and my eyes were full of tears. I couldn't stand seeing her like this. I realized how much we cared for each other and I surely hated to see her go. We kissed through the screen and expressed how much we loved one another. She gave me her high school ring, gold with a stone the color of sapphire. We promised to keep in contact. I called her later that night while she was staying at my parents' house before she left on a plane back to New Jersey.

But jailhouse relationships don't usually last long. After a while, ours didn't withstand the pressure either. She was kind about it, letting me know she didn't want to hurt me, but that there was someone else.

I became dysfunctional after that. I gave her ring and letters and photos to my lawyer, Mary Howell, and asked her to keep them. "If anything happens to me," I told her, "please mail these to Gilda." I could no longer concentrate on my studies. I lay in my cell sickening with hurt, and I wouldn't talk to anyone on the tier. The guys knew that something was wrong and tried to encourage me. I felt like my heart was impaired, as if it were sitting outside my chest. I became indifferent to a lot of things and found myself slipping deeper into depression.

Hooks saw I was having a hard time. "This is your first love," he told me. "In most cases, that's the one that breaks your heart. You have to learn from it. It makes you a better person. If you fall in love again, it won't be as devastating." He made me realize I had a responsibility to those who were fighting for me to stay strong.

CONVERSATIONS WITH GUYS LIKE Hooks helped me make it through each day, which could get really long and tedious. I spent a lot of my time in my cell reading and writing letters to my family and my supporters. Reading was one of the things that kept me in the world. I didn't read romance novels, like some prisoners did—I read newspapers and political books like Harry Haywood's *Black Bolshevik*, which taught me about the massacres in Black communities like Tulsa, Oklahoma, and Rosewood, Florida. I read Louis Tackwood, *The Glass House Tapes*, a confession exposing how the LAPD pressured Tackwood to be an agent provocateur spying on the Black Panthers. For the first time, I understood how corrupt and how sinister the federal government can be and how the FBI would destroy anyone they considered a threat to the system. That made me realize they had killed the activist Fred Hampton because he was young and radical and able to appeal to white people as well as Black, including people who had philosophical differences with him.

By then it didn't surprise me to learn that Angola had been created specifically for Black people by former slave owners during Reconstruction. After the Emancipation Proclamation, Black people were not really set free. The power structure came up with Black Codes, including laws against "vagrancy" that let them arrest people for not having a job or just going about their business. Then those in charge would force them into performing free labor for the same landowners and other wealthy whites who earlier had them enslaved, picking cotton or chopping sugarcane or cleaning roads. The courts' job was to serve the rich and keep the disgruntled in check.

I learned that the Thirteenth Amendment didn't end all servitude. It included one big exception: "as a punishment for crime whereof the party shall have been duly convicted." In 1895, 85 percent of the prisoners in Angola were Black. The number wasn't much different at 75 percent in 2011. Neither was most of the labor.

The more I read, the more I became consumed with the urge to learn the real history of America and the world—the history they don't teach in school.

I ALSO SPENT TIME working out. Because of a lawsuit filed by Big John Fulford, those of us in CCR were finally allowed to go out to the yard in 1978. At first, they'd only let three people out at a time. They had orders to keep us separate from each other, so they'd put us in different areas. There were three big yards and they divided that up. They'd give us a football, which we used to throw back and forth from yard to yard. We learned to throw with precision so it didn't go over the fence, which meant we'd have to wait till some guard brought it back in. There was also a basketball court at the end of each yard where we would shoot hoops by ourselves. The guards mostly didn't give us a hard time out there, except to cheat us out of our time. "Our time don't start until you take the handcuffs off us in the yard," we'd say. "Not when you put the handcuffs on us and bring us out the building." We were very adamant about that. Sometimes they let us out longer than forty-five minutes, probably because they got caught up doing other things, or maybe because they saw us having a good time. Whatever the reason, it felt so great to be outside and breathe that fresh, country air. Everything was green, and when the wind came through the trees, you could sometimes see deer.

After a while, they divided each yard in two and let six people go out at the same time. That meant everyone couldn't go out the same day;

you sometimes had to take your time in the hall. I'd run up and down the tier.

There were other things I did to keep myself mentally healthy as well. I listened to music—soul, R&B, jazz, but during that time I also started listening to Bach and other classical music. I played chess with Hooks, Alvin Moore, and a few other guys on the tier. I watched television, mainly the news. My parents would deposit some money in my account, and I used that to buy toiletries, ice cream or cookies, peanut butter and jelly with Ritz crackers and bread—basic canteen items.

I also took the time to keep my cell clean, for my satisfaction and to avoid being hassled by the free people. When they had GI day—general inspection—we had to pick stuff off the floor, our shoes and locker boxes. An orderly would shoot water and soap in the cells and we'd clean. Going after some infraction was a way for the guards to constantly harass you. You had to make up your bed, couldn't put anything in the bars. They'd use that to write you up and put you in the dungeon.

THOSE YEARS IN CCR felt like an eternity, with no end in sight. Then, in 1984, at a ninety-day board meeting, Major Teer and the assistant warden Peggy Grisham offered to let me out of CCR. I said, "You kept me here this long, you're not serious," and turned the board down. I knew they had political pressure on them about why they were keeping me locked up in maximum security. They really couldn't explain or justify that. But by now, I had grown accustomed to being in CCR; the other prisoners had become my family. Teer and Grisham told me they were going to have a special board on October 4 and I could change my mind.

When I went back and I told the others, they shook their heads. Guys like Hooks and Colonel Bolt said, "Gary, you've been in these cells for almost ten years. If I had a chance to get out, I'd jump at it." Fox heard about it and sent me a kite. "Man, you don't need to be in CCR," he wrote. "You've been in here too long."

They used to call me Nyeusi, Swahili for Black. Hooks told me, "Nyeusi, you need to leave, get a feel for how things are in the Main Prison population." It was like a light popped in my head. I realized that the people who ran Angola knew me. They wouldn't want me making trouble because there were too many people who supported me. And if things went bad, I could always come back to CCR.

When the special board took place on October 4, I accepted the move. By then, I'd been in maximum security for eight years, nine months, and four days. I was twenty-six years old.

THEY FIRST SENT ME to a working cell block in the Main Prison. I was still in a six-by-nine cell, but with two bunks and two prisoners instead of one. They put me on line 8 in the field to hoe; cut grass in the trenches and the canals; and pick cotton, corn, okra, tomatoes, watermelons, and cantaloupes. Line 7 was strong and hardened prisoners; 8 was what they considered soft and vulnerable prisoners, where they put anyone who was gay. I hadn't known that. I looked around me and said to myself, They're setting me up to fail. They're assuming I'll get into it with one of these guys or throw in the towel and say I want to go back to CCR.

I thought about getting the shovel and throwing it out in the field. This assignment was a form of dehumanization. But the prisoners I worked with convinced me to hang in there. I had blisters on my hands. They told me, "Pee in your hand to make it hard for the blisters." Those guys on line 8 worked their hearts out. They showed me how to do things, how to use the dish blank blade, which was like a cane blade or a machete but with a long handle. With their help, I became one of the best workers out there. I realized I couldn't fall into a trap and let those in charge say, "We gave him a chance but he squandered it."

Billy Tigler was the person in charge, known as the field farmer, on line 8. The guys in the line were talking about who I was. He remembered reading about me, and he took a liking to me. He was young and wore dark shades; he didn't smile and was quite hard on those who didn't do the work right. He also appreciated those who tried, and he knew how long I'd been in the cells. One morning when I came out, he said, "Tyler, you got the water bucket. You're going to sharpen the dish blank blades." Assigning me to sharpen those was his way of showing me favor. "I like your attitude,

Gary," he said. "I've been watching you. You come across more mature than a lot of guys. You carry yourself respectfully."

After a few months, a guy named James Singerton, instigated by a white inmate who didn't like my attitude, got into a fight with me. He hit me in the head with a cup and we got in a fight. I got locked up in the dungeon and they transferred me to a different line.

IN MAY 1985, I finally got classified out of the cell block and into Pine-1, a dormitory in the East Yard that held sixty people. Pine was where Albert Woodfox and Herman Wallace had been accused of killing Brent Miller. It was my first time in prison in an open space with so many other people. I was relieved to be out of the cells, but I also wanted to know how these prisoners with so many different personalities and habits, mainly bad habits, got along with each other. There were two urinals, five toilets, four showers that everybody had to share, one TV, and one telephone. Once again, I had to figure out where I fit in. It was wild, but I had more freedom than before, more opportunities to get involved in various activities. For the first time, I could walk to breakfast, lunch, and dinner, and I also had access to the canteen, where I could buy items like razor blades that weren't allowed in the cell blocks. I could go on callouts for organizational activities, sports, and weightlifting.

At Pine, I was assigned to work in the field on line 3. A guy named Mayeaux was the field farmer there. Eventually, he put me on as lead guy who took care of the water cooler, sharpened the tools, and measured the spots where we would work. You know why? Because Billy Tigler had told him, "See that guy Tyler? He's a good guy. He helped me run my line. Look out for him." Mayeaux took a liking to me, too.

I was proud to hear that praise. My mentors had helped me survive the cells. But in spite of all the mentoring, I still carried my emotions on my sleeves. At the age of twenty-seven, I was what they would call an angry Black man. Hooks used to tell me, "It ain't that serious. You need to control your emotions. Everybody is not your enemy."

I still had things to work out.

CHAPTER 8

LEARNING TO TONE IT DOWN

Don't let anyone tell you that people in prison are ignorant of what's happening in the free world. They keep up with the news probably more than people do outside of prison. And what I saw in the news was blatant racial disparities in the legal system. In my mid-twenties, the more I read and watched, the more I got caught up in my emotions.

Me and bitterness became real good friends.

One case that really disturbed me involved the racial slaying of a Black man in Denham Springs, Louisiana, in April 1982. Four white men, Todd Tarter, Johnnie Erwin, Randy Hooper, and Wayne Simmons, drove into a Black neighborhood and shot indiscriminately into a Black crowd. Tarter's gun killed Gerald Green, who was only nineteen years old. The four white men were all indicted on charges of manslaughter, aggravated battery, conspiracy to commit aggravated assault, and conspiracy to commit manslaughter. And what happened? Tarter was acquitted of the murder and his accomplices were set free.

Even more enraging was reading about a white kid named Ronnie

Acaldo. On Halloween in 1984, the seventeen-year-old got into a confrontation at East Ascension High School in Gonzales, Louisiana, with a Black youth named Joseph Buchanan. Acaldo went home and got a gun, took it back to the school the next day, and shot Buchanan in cold blood. This murder took place ten years and twenty-four days after what happened to me in Destrehan. In Acaldo's case, there was no question who did it. But look at the sentence he got. The 23rd Judicial District judge A. J. Kling Jr. decided Acaldo should finish high school, pay for Buchanan's funeral costs, and complete seven thousand hours of community service. Ronnie Acaldo would have no jail time whatsoever for manslaughter, just a seven-year suspended sentence and five years of probation. The judge thought Acaldo was too young to be sent to prison, saying his shooting of Buchanan was "an act of desperation from the undeveloped mind of a young man."

Here I was fighting to get out of prison for something I hadn't done while these blatant crimes were being committed and the police and courts were whitewashing them. My cries were falling on deaf ears. Black lives didn't matter at all. Those responsible for sending me to death row had no concerns about *me* being too young—there was nothing I could say or do to change their hearts and minds. They did a great job convincing people I was guilty and deserved to die, whether in the electric chair or by being forced to stay in prison for the rest of my life. They didn't see any humanity in me.

The cases I read about were typical of white justice in the South. Those in charge looked for any excuse not to send one of their own to prison. They'd let them go or give them reduced time, no matter how blatant their offense, while others, like me, were being framed and serving life sentences. Everything was flipped around. Injustice like this was overt and cruel, and seemed more so as I gained a much better understanding of why the system worked the way it did. These stories filled me with hate and resentment for those who had destroyed my life. After a while, my emotions began to have a psychosomatic effect on me. I developed symptoms of an ulcer, lost weight, and had trouble sleeping.

I didn't want to be this way. I'd known men who out of bitterness took their own lives, men who died of heart attacks and strokes. I wanted to live. But it felt like progress around my case was losing steam. I saw my life falling apart and I lacked the muster to pull myself together. I felt out of control, pissed off about everything. It was like being in a whirlwind of hopelessness.

THE TURNING POINT CAME when I began to reflect on what bitterness had done to an older prisoner named Louis Singleton. Louis had been in Angola since November 1961. I first met him in the dungeon in 1978. One day on the tier in CCR, he got into an extreme altercation with a prison guard over having a drinking cup sitting on the crossbar of his cell. The guard told Louis to remove it and he refused. Everything got quiet all of a sudden. The guard told him again and that's when Louis went off. For several consecutive days, he cursed out every prison guard who made his rounds on the tier. He blustered unintelligibly all night and day. I thought he would never stop. No one on the tier dared to intervene because they didn't want Louis turning on them.

After a few days, Louis finally settled down. I approached his cell cautiously to check on him. He turned out to be quite receptive to my overtures and we talked for a while. I learned he was originally from New Orleans and had been convicted in 1961 for killing an elderly Black woman who he was convinced had cursed him with voodoo. Louis was familiar with my case and spoke passionately about what had happened to me. After that day, I spent a lot of time talking to him. It turned out he had relatives living in St. Rose on Turtle Creek, so I told my family about him. They knew his people well and contacted them for me; I thought his family would want to know how he was doing. I felt sympathy for Louis and wanted to do something to help. Little did I know that he was estranged from his family, and he was not pleased at all when I disclosed my efforts to get them to visit him. He became angry and cold, going on and on about how his family had robbed him of his military pension.

Louis was a broken man on the verge of self-destruction. Thinking about him and his plight enlightened me. I understood I was starting to become like him, and I knew I had to change. I vowed to re-channel the negative energy I had into something positive.

Moving to Pine-1 in 1985 opened new opportunities. At first it felt strange to be in a dormitory with fifty-nine other prisoners. Still, it was like a burden was lifted off my shoulders and I welcomed the change. I was looking forward to pursuing personal goals I couldn't achieve in the cells. I wanted to further my academic skills by getting a GED and to focus on a trade. I knew it wasn't going to be easy, but I was determined to take on the challenges.

In order for me to make the move to the dormitory, board chairman Lieutenant Colonel Eddie Boeker and head classification officer Ray North wanted me to agree that I'd remain quiet about my case and stay clear of giving security any problems. Most inmates already knew about my situation—I didn't have to say a word. I agreed to their conditions and was released that same day.

Ray North saw I was a strong worker, so after five months at Pine working in the field, he assigned me to a job in the Main Prison kitchen. He also recommended I be made a class-B trustee, with more privileges and greater freedom to move around the prison. Deputy Warden Prentiss Butler overruled that recommendation and sent me back to the field until Ray North intervened and I was once again on kitchen duty.

A highlight of being in the dormitory was having physical contact with my family. All that time I had been in the cells, we couldn't hug or anything, there was always a mesh screen between us. The first time my mother visited me in the Main Prison, they still handcuffed and shackled me and brought me to the A Building Visiting Shed, where they took the shackles off and patted me down. The shed was a wide space like a cafeteria, with tables where families sat and organizations sold food at concession stands. Being able to embrace my mother and others in my family was a huge relief for them and for me. It was a great feeling to hold hands, embrace, sit at the table together up close with nothing to separate us. For most prisoners, visiting was a time to put on your best clothing and groom yourself. I also put on my best front. No matter what was going on, I told my family I was good.

I was pleased with the changes in my life, but I had another obstacle to deal with. During my time in the cells, I had grown dreadlocks and a full beard and had started wearing combat boots and a big African medallion carved out of mahogany. To me, dressing like this, with symbols representing self-determination for Black people and an end to oppression, gave me a sense of power, of authority. But in the Main Prison, it also stigmatized me. Some inmates were afraid to associate with me and dissuaded others from coming in contact with me. They'd heard I was a firebrand militant, a revolutionary, and they didn't know how to approach me. I couldn't care less how people perceived me. I was influenced by the Seven Principles of Ron Karenga, known as *Nguzo Saba*, celebrated during the holiday of Kwanzaa. These principles included *Kujichagulia*, the ability to name, develop, and speak for oneself, part of building a community and solving problems together.

Still, my concern was how the prison guards would take advantage of my appearance. I understood that what my look signaled was especially a threat to those prisoners who were determined to hold on to their illegal gambling privileges and sexual slave trade, preying on the young and weak while unscrupulous guards turned their heads. Those inmates knew I didn't condone their actions, and that made me a danger in their eyes. Manipulative and cruel free people would likely make me a target as well.

There were brothers I had known in CCR who were now in the general population, including Lawrence Jenkins (Kenya) and Dominique, as well as men I had met in the Main Prison, like Percy Tate (Baki) and Nelson Marks (Mwanafunzi). We formed a strong nucleus down the walk—that's how inmates referred to the Main Prison—where we got together every day to talk about political and social matters. We'd discuss problems within Angola and how important it was to create a base among prisoners. While we were a close-knit group that mainly stayed to ourselves, we understood the potential threats against us. And we knew it was inevitable that the group would be harassed or written up on some made-up rule violations by prison guards. Given the way we dressed in African colors—red, green, and black—and greeted each other, we stood out as a group of our own, guys involved in the struggle.

As I anticipated, I became a target. Certain guards would regularly call me from work, or wake me up in the middle of the night or early morning, wanting to shake me down. They'd go through my belongings with a fine-toothed comb looking for contraband. Some would even make a fuss about the type of reading material I had in my locker box. When they couldn't find anything incriminating to write me up for, they found other ways to harass me. They'd call me into the "boot," a small office on the walk, and make me empty my pockets, demanding to know where I'd come from and where I was going. They made it quite clear that I was not welcome down the walk and that they would be watching me. I was careful about what I did and where I went. I didn't want to jeopardize the others in our group. Although my friends were concerned and upset for me, they knew they couldn't risk having everyone else scrutinized and harassed as well.

It was a problem I had to deal with and I was up for the task. I had developed a meticulous lifestyle. Even so, I figured it would be just a matter of time before something happened.

ONE AFTERNOON IN AUGUST of 1985 I was in the dish scullery washing dishes with Kenya, Baki, and Mwanafunzi when I was informed by a guy we called Nap, Napoleon Moore, that I'd been accused of being the ringleader of prisoners who were arming themselves with knives to take over the walk. Nap told me this in confidence. "The prison officials say you want to stud up all the gal-boys," he said. "They're coming for you. Put protection on yourself."

Apparently some guys had gotten locked up for making shanks or weapons in the tag plant, where they manufacture license plates. The name Tyler came up—someone said Tyler had them making shanks to arm the gay prisoners so they could stop the rapes going on in the Main Prison. First the officials called in Melvin Tyler, who was working in the bakery section of the kitchen. Then they moved on to Floyd Tyler, the office clerk in the kitchen. They eliminated both after questioning them. There was one Tyler left, and they were saying it's got to be this Tyler here.

As soon as Nap left the kitchen, Lieutenant Gremillion came looking for me and told me I needed to go back to the dormitory. On the way, we passed the guard at the East Yard gate, Ducote, who pointed at me and said, "Not that guy there. The only thing that guy does is go to work and lift iron."

When we got to Pine, Sergeant Lartigue was the key man in the security booth. He was a decent guy who'd taken a liking to me. Sergeant Lartigue came in with us and turned to the other guards. "Gary? Gary Tyler?" he said. "He goes to work and comes back, doesn't hang out on the walk."

The guards didn't care. They tore up all my stuff. Mike Roberts was the lieutenant over the shakedown crew. "Why do you only have books by Black guys?" he asked me as he pawed through my stuff. "Why no white guys?"

I held up a book about Marxism-Leninism. "You're not familiar," I said. "These guys are white." That shut him up. He had pegged me as a Black radical so I must hate white people.

When they didn't find anything, they told me to put my belongings back and to get to work. An hour later, Sergeant Lartigue called me back to the unit and told me to pack all my property because he'd been ordered to lock me up. I immediately tracked down the yard supervisor, Lieutenant Colonel Eddie Boeker, who was at the gym. "What's going on?" I asked.

"Someone went over my head," he told me. "I don't believe you had anything to do with this." He let me know that an inmate by the nickname of Spider who worked in metal fabrication had gotten busted trying to smuggle knives down the walk. The story was that he was selling knives to prisoners and got caught while making his delivery. I didn't know this inmate at all, yet he had told the prison guards that he was bringing the contraband in for me. It was his way of trying to get out of trouble. He was aware of how unpopular I was at the time and felt he could scheme his way out of it.

Five guards came and locked me up in the dungeon. But the scheme didn't work because the same guy who tipped me off helped clear me of the charge. I didn't know until later that Nap was actually a confidential informant. He told me, "Gary, I watch you and see the things you do. Guys talk highly of you. I couldn't let them mess with you." He went to the lieutenant colonel's office and told him I didn't have anything to do with the knives.

Before I was released from the dungeon, or administrative lockdown, I had a surprise visit from Mike Roberts, the same shakedown lieutenant who had been giving me such a hard time and who had gone over the lieutenant colonel's head. "Our investigation uncovered that you weren't involved in the scheme," he told me. "I'm about to clear it up. But, Gary, you suffer from an image problem. You need to cut your hair."

    Later that day I was brought to see the lieutenant colonel himself and Ray North. After they removed the handcuffs and shackles, we had a candid conversation about my image. "Gary, we found out you weren't part of this," the lieutenant colonel said. "People were throwing names around and out of precaution they had you locked up to get to the bottom of it. I hear good things about you. But listen, some people are afraid of you. People aren't used to long hair in dreadlocks. The free people are intimidated by it. Judges and prosecutors will look at you the same way. You'd change a lot of minds if you cut your hair and dress more casually, like everyone else."

    I was listening to him. I wasn't surprised to hear white people tell us how to behave to prove that we were "civilized"; they thought Black people didn't have the right to claim any self-identity. I thought, no, I'm not doing that. "It's their problem, not mine," I said. "I'm not going to change my appearance just to please other people. Why can't they change their attitude and get to know who I am?" It was as if the two men had found out I didn't do what I was accused of but needed to let me know I was still a problem. I expressed how important it was for people to know the content of a man's character and not blindly judge him on appearance.

    The following morning I was released from administrative lockdown and returned to my living quarters. A few weeks later, they transferred me to the West Yard, to Cypress-4, a dormitory unit made up entirely of people who worked in the kitchen. I was excited because Ray North indicated that he would try to help me get into the prison GED program. But he was transferred to another prison before he could do so.

    Not long after this, I was in the *Angolite* office talking with Wilbert Rideau, the editor of the prison's newspaper. Wilbert was a wise man, one of the brightest prisoners I ever met while at Angola. Like me, he'd been sent to prison very young, at age seventeen, and had been sentenced to death. He's the one who taught me how to make my way inside the Main Prison. "You don't always have to be aggressive," he told me. "Listen to security and respond reasonably. Instead of rubbing it in when they're wrong, give them a way out, another option. They look at us as being far beneath them. In fact, most of the prisoners are way smarter than them. Try using their language."

Wilbert Rideau was a profiler, someone who talked to people and asked a lot of questions. He was good at reading people. That day he wanted to talk to me about how intimidated a lot of the free people were by the way I looked. But his focus was the expression on my face more than anything else. At one point, something he said made me smile.

"Gary, man, you got a nice smile," he told me. "If you smile more, you'll be surprised how people will warm up to you. It will change the way you look. When people see you with those long dreads and the African medallion around your neck, that intimidates them. You look too strong and dominant. People are afraid of someone like that; white folks especially are afraid of strong Black men. You need to soften up some, tone it down." He said it kind of jokingly and I chuckled, but I knew what he was saying.

Still, I wasn't going to cut my hair. But it dawned on me that I did need to change my expression. I didn't pay much attention to myself in the mirror. Yet I believe a person's smile shows a lot about them. It's a sign of brightness. I used to be someone who smiled a lot. I was grateful to Wilbert for making me recognize I had lost my smile. Afterward, I tried to practice smiling, but what I saw in the mirror wasn't genuine. I had to retrain the muscles in my face to get my smile back.

I DECIDED TO PARTICIPATE in certain prison organizations that I considered progressive. In 1986, I became a member of the Drama Club. And in November of the following year, I joined the Angola Special Civics Project (ASCP), led by my friend Norris Henderson, known as Saboor and by Biggy Johnson. ASCP aimed to change state prison laws, and I wanted to be part of that.

During those years, Jerry Wells, the free man who had dogged me while I was in the cell blocks, had gone to work at Camp J. Then he moved up in the ranks and came to the Main Prison. I don't know what happened, but once he got there, he was no longer exhibiting the brutality I'd known him for. After what me and this guy went through, I never thought we would get along. One day he saw me at the Control Center gate, on my way to the kitchen. "Wow, Gary Tyler," he said. "I can't believe it. You're not going to be down here long," implying that I would be sent back to CCR.

Weeks later, when he saw I was still there, he stopped me again. Wells was a lot taller and heavier than me. He looked me in the eyes. "Gary, you and I go a long ways back. Things change, things are different now. Listen, we're going to let bygones be bygones. If you need anything, you let me know. Don't be hesitant. I'll do what I can to help you. I ask you this, though. Don't come down here intimidating my free people. But if they mess with you, you let me know and I will *deal* with their ass." It was as if he were trying to make up for the wrongs he had done.

I realized that Wells had watched me grow up in prison. I knew I wasn't going to do anything to get myself in trouble. My character spoke for itself. But if security came up with something to harass me with, I needed defenders. Wells would tell other guards, "I know Gary. I'd think twice about messing with him." Sure enough, when we did need something to help a prisoner, I called on him and he took care of it. He'd pull a write-up, for example, to keep it from hurting someone who was going to court.

Throughout this time, I was reassessing my life and everything I'd been through, and recognized there were more changes I needed to make in myself. I was still in danger of becoming a product of my environment and operating off my emotions. I didn't want to reflect the degradation and dehumanization the system was designed to promote. That meant I had to start correcting some of the things I'd come to see as normal, like engaging in unnecessary pettiness that might aggravate another inmate. I had to let go of my rage at some people, including Jerry Wells. I had to listen to someone first instead of reacting and making assumptions that they were going to treat me in a demeaning way.

I was fighting to get out of prison and fighting with the challenges of being inside prison. It took a wake-up call, some friendly advice, and a new focus for me to make adjustments and begin to move away from bitterness. It sure didn't happen overnight. At the end of every day, I'd feel incomplete, like I hadn't accomplished enough no matter how much I did within that day or week. But I was on a path. I wanted to better myself and to find ways to help other prisoners as well.

CHAPTER 9

FIGHTING FOR THE RIGHT TO EDUCATION

I didn't realize until after I arrived in Angola how important an education would be for dealing with my situation. Nor had I realized how much my education had suffered because of integration as practiced in Louisiana. As much as I appreciated the help of my fellow inmates and what I'd already learned in prison, I knew I needed a more formal education to get off death row. I could no longer wing it. I wanted to fight my own battles, not have to rely on other people looking through legal briefs and helping me understand the legalese. I wanted to measure up to the brothers on the tier and understand the political world they were introducing me to. I was also getting massive amounts of mail from around the country, and I needed to better prepare myself to answer it. That meant I had to do some serious studying and work on foundations. Since I was on death row and had little to do, I figured I'd finish my high school education. So, early in 1977, I tried to enroll in the prison's academic program for a GED.

Mason L. Green was in charge of the prison education department. He sent me a notice that I was not eligible to enroll. It appeared the state thought it would be a waste of taxpayer money. It was not in the business of educating anyone condemned to die. I got the underlying message: "You aren't worthy. The state doesn't recognize you as a human being." It wasn't interested in educating me or anyone else on death row, only in killing us. No surprise that the majority of us on death row were Black.

My anguish over the policy only grew as I learned from my reading how enslaved Black people had been murdered when plantation owners discovered they could read and write. That injustice didn't end with slavery. I was living proof of Black folks still having to fight for access to equal education. It was no surprise that we were a disproportionate percentage of those locked up at Angola and around the country. The goal of the system was to keep us ignorant, feeling inferior and stigmatized, so we could provide free labor inside prisons and cheap labor outside. The power elite also knew that an educated prisoner is a threat. Reading and understanding might lead to filing complaints and petitions. They didn't want that. As long as they could keep inmates in the dark, they thought they didn't have to worry about us running wild in the light.

Vocational school was also off the list for anyone locked up on death row or in CCR. It was inspiring, but sad, that my educators had to be other prisoners. Learning from my friends in solitary and on my own were the only options at the time.

Despite the obstacles, I resolved to educate myself in whatever way I could. I read everything I could get my hands on—old newspapers, magazines, travel brochures, and books. I started receiving lots of books from people all over the country, sympathizers who heard of my plight and wanted to contribute to my endeavors. But this didn't go unnoticed by the guards. There were a number who despised me and did whatever possible to thwart my efforts. They shook the cell down repeatedly and confiscated books and materials they labeled as inflammatory and a threat to security. What they took to the property room, they destroyed. When you'd ask for your property back, the typical response was "That's all they had in the property room." I came to expect it. The guards did all kinds of underhanded things to get at the people they disliked.

Literacy wasn't my only focus; I also learned to play chess. My teacher was an inmate named Joseph Jenkins. After years at Angola, he'd been shipped off to a mental institution in Jackson. They transferred him back to Angola only a few days after I got there—he told me he'd organized a hunger strike among the other mental patients and started a fire. Jenkins was a very intelligent older guy, smart as a whip; he didn't appear to me to be crazy at all. During his hour out, he'd sit cross-legged on the tier in front of my cell on a towel or a pillow with the chess board between us, or vice versa, I'd be the one on the tier and Jenkins would stick his hands out the bars. I loved the game and saw how it taught strategic thinking. I learned how to concentrate and how to strategize, how to anticipate the opponent's next move.

Jenkins taught me other important lessons as well. I felt he and I had a lot in common, even though he'd entered the system in 1957, before I was even born. Neither of us should ever have been on death row. Jenkins had been convicted of murder for defending himself against a white guy who was attacking him. Four times he had an execution date set; twice he'd been within hours of the electric chair. Here was an individual who'd been fighting way longer than I had, and still refused to give up. "There were times I wanted to," he told me, "but I just couldn't, because I know I'm here only for defending myself."

I wouldn't give up either, not in my fight for justice or my fight to get educated.

IN 1979, MARY HOWELL, a civil rights attorney who'd joined my defense team pro bono, requested that a tutor be sent into the prison to assist me in my education. Warden Frank Blackburn denied our request. But on March 12 of that year, thanks to my supporters sending so many letters, the warden finally agreed to have me tested and to permit me to undertake what he called a "self-help" course in basic education.

That same day, Scott Tycer, a classification officer, came to my cell to administer the California Achievement Test. I got the results three weeks later from the prison school principal, Mason Green. My reading score was at the level of someone starting ninth grade and my English language skills like someone nearing ninth grade completion. In math I scored only at the fifth-grade level. I was twenty years old. While the prison officials considered the reading and English scores to be okay, I was not satisfied and began a regimen of studying each day, sometimes close to twelve hours. The department sent additional educational material to help with reading and math and told me I'd be tested approximately every three months. Unfortunately, that promise did not materialize, and I never received any tutoring assistance. Nevertheless, over the next few years in CCR, I stayed on my self-education program. I continued to receive textbooks upon request and help and encouragement from the brothers on the tier.

Every day, every chance I got, I studied. I read, and I talked with the other inmates to get an understanding of things. I had them test me on spelling, math, and comprehension.

We had political discussions on the tier, where we'd all read the same article or newspaper and talk about it. Those conversations helped me understand local, national, and world events. I learned about the movement for the Equal Rights Amendment for women, the fight against apartheid in South Africa, and much more. I also learned about young people like me who'd been lynched in this country. Willie James Howard was fifteen when he was murdered in front of his father because he gave each of his coworkers, including a white girl, a Christmas card. George Stinney, a fourteen-year-old Black kid from Alcolu, South Carolina, was the first person in the U.S. formally sentenced to death and executed. He'd been falsely accused of killing two white girls who had stopped by his yard on the day they died to ask where to find some flowers. I identified with those guys, like I did with the Scottsboro Boys. Their stories scared the hell out of me, but they also gave me the drive to keep going.

From my reading and conversations, I realized people in power hired police who were thuggish and cruel in order to make a statement. Police carried out indignities and terror to remind Black people to stay in their place, that they could never compete with white people. I learned that in the twenties and thirties, police power was also unleashed against union drives. Police shot and brutally beat both white and Black union workers to keep the working class under control. The violence was targeted, orchestrated, and controlled by the rich and powerful.

My education enlightened me and I wanted more. In 1984, the institution changed its policy and prohibited the education department from furnishing books or educational materials to prisoners in CCR. I wasn't about to let that discourage me. I just kept using what I already had and getting help from others. What I achieved during that time was mine, and there was no way they could take it away from me. That's the great thing about knowledge: Once you learn it, it belongs to you. I understood I was dealing with a system that was trying to keep me in the dark. But after being exposed to the light, I did everything I could to keep that light burning.

In May 1986, having spent time in the Main Prison and gotten positive comments on my work in the field and in the kitchen, I applied again to get my GED. I was informed by the education department that I was still not eligible because I had a life sentence. Angola wouldn't "waste" its time on anyone who wasn't going to get out of prison—as if education wasn't a goal in itself, as if no lifers or long-termers would ever qualify for early release. I wrote back explaining how I'd received materials from the department for a while in my cell and how my education had been cut short because of a change in prison policy. But I never heard back. So I continued with my self-education.

When I was upstairs on tier C, Angel Perez was in the cell next to me. He was one of the people incarcerated in Cuba who came over in the Mariel boatlift in 1980. This guy couldn't speak a bit of English. I introduced myself and he told me his name. The first thing I wanted to learn was curse words in Spanish. "How do you say 'fuck you'?" I asked him after I taught him the English phrase. I still have scraps of paper with the words he wrote out.

Once I made it to the Main Prison in 1985, there was a little Hispanic group I joined. Gilbert Guzman, who was a clerk for the chaplain's office and wrote for the prison newspaper, invited me. We had gotten to know each other and he liked what I stood for. In 1987, the group became the Latin American Cultural Brotherhood. I respected the men who headed the group, John Williams (Quabla), a Black guy who was fluent in Castilian Spanish, and Victor Vargas, a Puerto Rican out of New York who they called Julio. The chaplain's office sponsored the Brotherhood. That first year, I was appointed the sergeant at arms.

Quabla was upset about the language barrier at the prison. They were bringing Latino guys in and then giving them high infractions because they didn't understand what the guards were saying. These ignorant officers thought the Latinos were being defiant and deserved to be charged with "aggravated disobedience." The only thing the Latino inmates understood was that guards must be pissed off because they raised their voices and looked highly upset. In an effort to break the barrier, Quabla created an English language class and became the teacher. He also taught Spanish language classes as part of the club, which I took when I could.

As time went on, I wanted to learn other languages as well—French, Swahili, and German. I ordered material to help me do that and picked up a few expressions.

IN SEPTEMBER 1987, I applied again for the GED program but received no response. At the same time I learned that night classes were opening for inmates interested in trade school. The new program was instituted to help lifers and long-termers who were not eligible for day school because of the length of their sentence. I immediately wrote a letter to Mr. Tilghman Moore, supervisor of Jumonville Memorial Technical Institute, which administered the program, and requested to enroll. We had a choice of culinary, carpentry, auto mechanics, graphic arts, and horticulture. I asked myself what I really wanted to do. My friend Norris Henderson chose culinary and that interested me, too. But I knew a couple guys who were taking graphic arts and they sold me on taking that course.

I was accepted into the nighttime vocational program and got the assignment I wanted. For three years, I worked days in the kitchen and then attended vocational classes at night. The funding was allotted short-term, and those who ran the program had to keep applying for more. So each year I had to apply again for the program, and was accepted each time.

In the graphic arts program, I learned to work on multiple printing, offset, and copier machines, as well as stripping and platemaking for the printers. As I learned how to operate and maintain the equipment, I had the opportunity to help train other students. I also taught them the principles of offset printing and the importance of taking pride in your work. I consistently received good marks for conduct, discipline, and job performance at the school.

It was an interesting trade and I really enjoyed it, but once again I had second-class status. As a lifer, I wasn't allowed to graduate as a certified printer. I felt wronged, since it had nothing to do with my performance as a graphic artist. But I wasn't going to throw up my hands and say, "To hell with it." For me, the rule was one more example of how the prison system worked against us, especially those of us who were Black. It wanted to relegate us to a lower standard so we could never be as good as or better than white people. The more it kept us down and defined us, it believed, the better it would be able to control us. I refused to let them define me. I felt linked to a long line of Black men who'd been excluded from attending trade school and managed to learn bricklaying and masonry and other trades by watching skilled men at work.

In October of 1988, I wrote again to school principal Mason Green after a memorandum was posted on the dormitory bulletin board inviting prisoners who were interested in school to write regarding enrollment. To my surprise, I got a response that December with an academic school application to fill out and send to Mr. Coco, the instructor in the Main Prison school. I did as I was told but didn't hear anything back until the following May, when I was scheduled for testing. That happened in June. Finally, after twelve years of trying, I was accepted into the GED program. Within three months I was reading at the twelfth-grade level. I finished my GED on May 6, 1991. For me, now thirty-two years old, the sky was the limit.

Once I completed my GED, Tilghman Moore helped me transition into daytime vocational trade school full-time. Although I already knew the material and had gained the skills, being in this program allowed me to break through the bureaucracy. Against all odds, on October 27, 1992, I got the diploma certifying me as a printer.

I FELT AMAZED THAT I had been able to accomplish so much in the years I'd been in prison. At the same time, I knew I had a lot more to learn. One of the most important lessons of my life came when Nelson Mandela was released from prison in South Africa on February 11, 1990. I was in Cyprus-4 dormitory, where mostly kitchen workers lived. That was a day of celebration. We had read so much about Mandela, and now he was finally free and we could actually hear him speak. What's the marching order now? I thought. Whatever he said, I believed people were going to follow it. He had become an icon.

I sat on a bench in a packed TV room in Cyprus-4 and listened to that speech. After the horrible things that had happened in his life—being incarcerated for all that time, being accused of terrorism and robbed of his youth, knowing hundreds of thousands of young Black people had to fight for liberation, and many, like Steve Biko, had died for it—I expected him to exit prison a bitter man. What I heard instead for the first time in my life was the word "reconciliation." Mandela expressed how he forgave those who oppressed him and was implementing a Truth and Reconciliation Commission. I thought, how could he do this? Who could say "I forgive my enemy for what he did to my people"? Not a normal human being—they'd be wanting vengeance. But Nelson Mandela's words resonated throughout the world. People heard him, even whites who wholeheartedly supported apartheid and were panicked that the African people were going to go on a murderous rampage. Mandela's speech and his actions were a huge relief to them.

I knew I was listening to a true revolutionary. It wasn't like hearing a preacher say, "God says you must forgive those who commit sins against you." To me, statements like that were sterile. It was easy for someone to quote a few religious lines and make a proclamation, but did they really practice it? Here in the U.S. they were using religion to oppress and enslave people. That turned me off from religion, people speaking of peace and happiness and, at the same time, ready to devour you and tear you to pieces. They were wolves in sheep's clothing. I saw how organized religion had become one more tool of those in power.

Hearing Nelson Mandela speak so eloquently gave me strength and motivation. What set him apart was that he was a man of humanity, knowing the only way for his country to carve a path forward was for them to work together in a new system free of apartheid. Those who caused great harm needed to ask for forgiveness, and the country had to root out the legacy of colonialism that allowed this oppression to happen.

I wondered how I could apply these lessons—especially the role of forgiveness—in my own life.

CHAPTER 10

MAKING CHANGE FROM THE INSIDE

A big part of my education was learning how not just to survive, but to fight for change inside one of the worst prisons in America. Like me, many individuals were challenging sentences of life without parole and indefinite confinement in the cells. Some of us were reaching out to the public for support. But in time, I also realized that it was important to take on the inhumane conditions that were forced on us, together.

When I was transferred to Angola in December 1975, I quickly got caught up in the protests that Colonel Bolt, Bockaloc, and others were organizing on the tier. The problems were obvious. When the orderlies slid the food trays under the door, rats and all kinds of filthy things were running around the building. Feeding us this way was completely unsanitary.

There were mosquitoes, lice, and large rodents that felt they had just as much right as we did to sleep in our beds or eat our food. When we complained, the guards became hostile or were indifferent. They claimed it was out of their control.

We were also struggling to stave off the sweltering heat that engulfed each cell day and night because of poor ventilation. It was really bad in the summer. Because the building was old and made of concrete and steel, it got incredibly hot and humid, sometimes over a hundred degrees. It wasn't outfitted with any air-conditioning. Instead, it used antiquated exhaust ventilation, where a fan supposedly pulled the hot air out through a vent in the cell. There was a fan at each end of the tier, one blowing opposite the other down the hall. That was it. Like the vents, the fans made no difference whatsoever. In most cases, we'd be in the cell just in our underwear, wetting towels in the sink and draping them over our heads. We tried to get relief from little hand fans we made out of cardboard cracker boxes or the back of legal pads.

On top of that, we had to put up with horrible medical care. "Doc" Slater took sick calls for death row and CCR. If someone complained about chest pain or a headache or stomach problems, Slater would take the name down and submit it either to Dr. Kash or Dr. Butterworth. Dr. Kash was an out-of-state parolee from Florida doing community service at Angola for malpractice. He'd lost his license, the equivalent of a lawyer being disbarred. Prison work was the only form of employment open to him. If you were sick, even if you were vomiting or running a fever, he'd give you a Tylenol or a valium. Dr. Butterworth, a psychiatrist, would dope prisoners by giving them valium or shooting them with Prolixin or Thorazine, two strong drugs for schizophrenia and other serious mental health issues. I remember what it was like to see Jesse Washington come out of the cell next to mine. He was a big, old guy. Instead of being flexible, he'd move as if his whole body were in a cast, from the doctors keeping him on Prolixin.

Later, when I was in the Main Prison, there was a nurse at the prison hospital we called Pink Paper Pete. If an inmate had a problem, Pink Paper Pete would write them up on a slip of pink paper for an aggravated work offense, saying they were pretending to be sick to get out of work, and were "stealing time" from the state. Some inmates died because they were misdiagnosed and sent down the walk with that kind of write-up. Any other place would have fired him for incompetence and malfeasance.

FOR THESE REASONS AND more, and in spite of the backlash, inmates always found ways to demand change. When I first arrived, they were waging that hunger strike over how the food was delivered and demanding that prison officials put slots in the doors. "It's a just cause," Colonel Nyati Bolt explained to me. "We can't tolerate this. This is what we're doing. If you don't like being treated like a dog, then you'll be part of it. You know when it's right to stand up. You don't want guys to feel you're betraying them. To change conditions here, we must unite." Of course, I joined.

When the prison officials knew we were on a hunger strike, that's when they fixed better food to entice us to break the strike. They'd get the kitchen workers suddenly cooking the best meals, like chicken or fish. We had to be strong and turn it down. Most of the guys joined in and wouldn't eat anything. Some people threw the food down the middle of the tier. Some just kicked the trays out. Others left the tray untouched, and the orderlies would come back and see they hadn't eaten a bite. When the guards came on and tried to flex their muscles, prisoners would yell at them to get off the tier. Eventually the prison officials relented and said they would cut slots in the bars where they could put the food. They put up screens over the windows to stop the mosquitoes, and started putting rat poison in the pipe chase. The guards also gave us little kits to trap roaches and rats in our cells.

Our tier was kind of isolated from the others, reachable only through corridors of locked doors. To get the guards' attention you had to rack the bars by shaking them to make a lot of noise. We'd do that when a prisoner was about to hang himself or was having a heart attack, or if a guard was seriously harassing someone. Imagine being in a cell block and hearing nothing but doors being racked. Everyone on the tier would join. You could feel those vibrations through the whole building. When guys on other tiers heard or felt the racking, they'd start doing it, too, even if they didn't know the particular reason—they understood it meant some kind of emergency. The first time I heard that noise, I had no idea what it was. But as I figured it out, I realized it was a powerful way to get the guards' attention when something was wrong. It really showed solidarity and support.

We also made use of petitions and lawsuits. If a free man was causing a problem with prisoners on the tier or keeping us from using the phone, we'd start a petition to get him moved out. Inmates would sign because they realized that if he was causing that kind of problem for someone else, he could do it to them, too. To get the word out, we communicated through the vent and the walls. We'd give the petition to the orderlies, who were prisoners themselves, to bring a kite around without knowing what was in it. I heard guys use a form of Pig Latin to get messages across to each other. The guards really didn't understand it.

For some of the most widespread problems, prisoners used lawsuits. As of 1978, they still wouldn't give guys in the cells recreation in the yard. A man named Big John Fulford in CCR filed a suit about that and he won. Big John was known for filing lawsuits against the prison. The new rule applied only to death row prisoners, but eight or nine months later, they extended it to CCR. At first it wasn't every day. But it was really good to feel the sun for forty-five minutes, to toss the football or jog around the yard.

Back in 1971, before I got to Angola, a guy named Hayes Williams, with help from another inmate who knew about the law, had filed a suit about the medical treatment there. Angola didn't have proper staff or equipment, and there were many examples of people being misdiagnosed or written up for coming for help. When there was a stabbing, an inmate often was the person who sewed the victim up. I hadn't met Hayes Williams yet, but I heard he was serving a life sentence after he and a friend were convicted of robbing a gas station where someone was killed. In 1975, Hayes and the others won a victory when courts placed the prison under federal control. But medical conditions didn't really improve for most of us.

When I first went to Angola, whatever they cooked from morning to evening had pork in it. That's what drove me to stop eating pork altogether. They had pork in the grits, pork in the eggs, pork in the biscuits. At lunch, it was pork in the greens, the beans—everything they gave you had pork bits in it. Angola was huge. It had a slaughterhouse on the grounds, raised its livestock, and inundated the place with pork. Two Black nationalist prisoners I got to know, Gary and Dennis Ledbetter—Damu and Sabour—

and a Muslim named Keith Mohammed, gave me material to read on how pork caused high blood pressure and strokes and contributed to violence in prison. Muslims working in the kitchen had filed a suit against being forced to eat pork. Eventually, the cooks had to make some non-pork dishes.

IT'S NO STRETCH OF the imagination to say conditions on death row and in CCR were horrendous and unbearable. But those who survived under these conditions, and especially those who fought to change them, turned out to be better men with a strong sense of human worth. I know being part of these actions strengthened me. I saw the results of working together. The system's goal was to oppress us by any means it could and make us feel powerless. Organizing was a way for us to get conditions changed. We got people who were rebellious as individuals to join together to stick it to the system.

Seeing who would join was also a big part of figuring out who I could trust. I came to see that trust was based on a man having principles, being someone who did the right thing when it was needed. I learned to judge an individual by what they were willing to stand firm on. When we went on a hunger strike, filed a suit or a petition, they were the guys who were right there with you. As I got older, I had more judgment around reading people. If someone said, "You can trust me," and I saw he'd been in the trenches with me, stood up for me, that person became a trusted ally.

By the time I got out of the cells and was released into the general prison population in 1985, administrators were taking some steps to comply with court orders regarding food and medical treatment. But conditions overall were still horrible. Down the walk, we had a wider range of tactics to deal with them.

One of the most effective approaches was a work stoppage. In the field, the conditions were brutal, inmates working in hundred-degree heat. The guards didn't care about how many prisoners fell out, but if a horse fell out, they'd stop the work. They claimed prisoners who collapsed were faking, playing games. We had guys from cities like New Orleans, Baton Rouge, Lafayette who had never done field work and weren't used to it. Sometimes everyone would just stop working until the guards showed some consideration. Every now and then, there would be sabotage by an individual. Someone might blow out the tire of the cotton wagon. Once, when I was on line 4, a guy set a trailer of cotton on fire. These were isolated incidents. We'd act like we were surprised, but like everyone else, I got a real sense of satisfaction from someone rebelling.

There was a lot of protest in the seventies and eighties in various work areas. The major work stoppage when I was there took place in July 1991. I had just turned thirty-three. The Loyola Death Penalty Resource Center in New Orleans challenged the constitutionality of the electric chair at Angola, which malfunctioned on several occasions and left prisoners with bad burns on their face and head. Officials decided to replace the chair by having inmates in the metal fabrication shop build the death gurney for prisoners sentenced to die by lethal injection. I was in graphic arts school at the time. The inmates at the shop got a notice that the prison had won the contract and they were the ones to build the death gurney. They refused to participate in creating something that would kill their fellow prisoners. All of them got locked up in the dungeon. Several hundred inmates in the field did their own work stoppage in support of the metal fab guys. The National Guard were stationed to the outer perimeter of the prison with tanks, armed personnel carriers, and more. That was definitely overkill. It wasn't like anyone was burning the place down. It was just a work stoppage, and it was successful. The death gurney never got built at Angola.

What was more common than work stoppages was self-inflicted injury to get out of the field. People would drop weights on their foot or hand to break a bone and get what they called duty status, which meant being off work. One day Gregory England, who'd been on death row with me, used a hypodermic needle to shoot spit into his arm, which got infected. He wound up getting gangrene and lost a portion of his arm. Eventually he got a medical pardon, but his condition got so bad that he died a year later.

His experience reminded me of something I learned that had happened at Angola back in 1951, when thirty-one prisoners slashed their Achilles tendon to call attention to harsh conditions. One of them, George Elliott, was the oldest member of the Drama Club. At the time, inmate guards were brutally beating other inmates. The self-mutilation attracted a lot of media coverage and got the attention of lawmakers in Louisiana—who in 1966 made self-mutilation by prisoners a crime.

Over the years I also heard talk about the rebellion at Attica in 1971 and others that happened at San Quentin and Sing Sing. It was inspiring that prisoners were able to come together and make demands. But Angola was never radicalized like that. We had just a small group of prisoners who were politically aware and sometimes got the others to join in.

WHEN I WAS IN CCR, we always talked politics and I became actively involved in those conversations. So when I got moved to the Main Prison, where we had greater resources, some of us wanted to see what we could do to make concrete changes in our conditions, things that could make our lives better. We were tired of free people harassing us. The idea was to get involved and stay stimulated. We recognized we had to educate ourselves about how legislation worked. We were already members of CURE (Citizens United for Rehabilitation and Errants—an old-fashioned word meaning people who "behaved wrongly"), a group of formerly and currently incarcerated individuals and their families that worked to reform the criminal justice system. Thanks to Norris Henderson (Saboor), I got involved in the ASCP.

I met Saboor when I started working in the kitchen a year earlier. He was a well-groomed guy of medium build, brown-skinned, who had become a Muslim and always wore a kufi. In 1980, he'd been sent to Angola with his brother after they were falsely accused of killing a woman in New Orleans. Saboor was truly one of the good guys in prison. He was a mover and a shrewd thinker, working in the interests of the prison population. He was not judgmental and believed in giving people the benefit of the doubt. If he didn't like what someone did, he kept his distance but he didn't talk bad about the person. He'd help someone if he could, even if the person was a bad actor. Saboor operated as a humanitarian defender, making things happen inside the Islamic community, where he became the imam, and also outside it.

The Angola Special Civics Project began inside the Social Community Association (SCA), run by Melvin Tyler, which was one of biggest clubs in Angola. We had meetings in the education building on Mondays.

Saboor understood the dire need to work together to change state laws. The Republicans wanted to imprison more people and for longer periods of time, keep us on the slave plantation and under their complete control. They had started coming up with three-strike laws and mandatory sentences, "lock 'em up and throw away the keys," making it harder for people to get parole. Louisiana statute 15:574 said you couldn't get paroled unless the pardon board commuted your life sentence to a specific number of years, but the pardon board was resisting recommending people for pardons. A lot of inmates were losing hope. Guys were committing suicide, attempting to escape, getting in trouble for the first time out of despair. Many had been sentenced to life under the 10/6 law, which allowed those with good behavior to get out after ten years and six months. That law had been overturned in 1973, and the new version, life without parole, was applied retroactively.

My friends and I wanted systemic change, an end to racism and exploitation everywhere. But we also wanted an end to the warehousing and inhumane treatment of inmates. We wanted to give hope to the prison population. We wanted to get out. Our objective was to grow power within our communities by organizing our families and friends.

ASCP members started learning how to develop a legislative agenda, write laws, and find state champions to sponsor the legislation. We decided if we wanted to change anything, we had to do some organizing, and that had to start with organizing among ourselves. As convicted felons, we could not vote, but we realized our families and friends in Louisiana could. Together, they could become a significant voting bloc, a real source of power. We got packets together for prisoners with family in New Orleans, Baton Rouge, Lafayette, and Shreveport, telling them how to set up meetings in churches and homes. My family and many others got involved. And we started inviting community leaders like State Representative Naomi Farve and Ted Quant, head of the Twomey Center for Peace through Justice at Loyola, to our Monday meetings in the A Building.

Our top priority was making parole possible for long-termers. Most prisoners at Angola, Black and white, had that one thing in common: long sentences with no hope of getting out. Access to parole would make a real difference and restore hope to those who had lost it. It would also help bridge the gap between white and Black prisoners. We did have Black and white inmates who got along, but those divisions were always there, even though the prison had been desegregated before I got there. Even so, with struggle, people who don't like each other can still become comrades, because they realize that otherwise, they probably won't survive. Whites thought they were privileged and would be able to get out despite the change in the law, and under Governor Edwin Edwards many did. But things had changed. Governors came in who wanted to look tough on crime. Buddy Roemer was elected as a Democrat but changed to Republican. Of course, some whites still had a problem with Black people. They were too narrow to see that the slogan "free all our brothers and sisters" included whites. Still, white prisoners wanted to get out. Many realized ASCP was working for everyone and got involved. I worked with guys like Lane Nelson, who got his family involved and helped get other white guys to see that this was how we could effectuate change from prison.

One amazing thing about ASCP was the leadership from prisoners. These guys were tenacious and committed to the cause. Our responsibility was to organize prisoners inside to be on the same page and to give advice to people on the outside on how they could help. We wanted people from our communities and ally organizations to demand of candidates, "What will you do to help my loved one in prison become parole-eligible?" We showed that spending money to lock up more people for longer times while cutting social services was detrimental to everyone. What we wanted was immediate change and also to spread the word about our agenda, which included shorter sentences, alternatives to incarceration, and more educational programs, in addition to expanded parole eligibility.

From reading and discussions over my years in CCR, I'd learned a lot about the problems with democracy in our country. Big money determined who ran for office and who had the ears of the people who govern. Big money still blocked many people from voting. Thanks to mass incarceration, millions of people who'd been locked up couldn't vote and couldn't run for office. We had to expand the power in our own communities, Black and white, to change this. We had to fight power by building power.

State Representative Naomi Farve agreed to spearhead the parole legislation. What passed was less than what we wanted, but more prisoners were able to get a specific numbered sentence rather than "life." However long the sentences were, having a certain number of years made people parole-eligible.

I recall several key events held by ASCP, including a press conference at Angola on September 22, 1987, and the first penal symposium held at the prison in March 1990, where people like Norris Henderson and Checo Yancey presented a fifty-page report on sentencing and parole laws. We had discovered that Louisiana had more people serving life without parole than any other state. At both events, my case was one of those highlighted to show the injustice of the criminal legal system. At the symposium, Quabla (John Williams) from the Latin American Cultural Brotherhood, who was the moderator, spoke about the cruelty of sending a kid to death row. He made a blistering attack on how unfair the system was and how it caused long-term harm to the community.

At some point ASCP adopted a committee structure, and I joined the current events committee. We kept up with news around the state and the country and collected articles that dealt with prison reform and prison conditions.

WHILE ASCP DEALT WITH the bigger picture, we also needed help with everyday conditions. Once Buddy Roemer became governor, he got rid of the warden, Hilton Butler. The stated reason for his removal was that they had found out he was raising fighting cocks on prison grounds. In fact, prisoners had been taking care of those cocks for a long time; everyone knew about it. They wanted him out of the way for political reasons. In July 1989, we were surprised when Governor Roemer appointed Larry Smith as the first Black deputy secretary of corrections and interim warden of Angola.

Smith called a meeting with all the club heads and wanted to know what he could do. "We're civil servants meant to serve you and tend to your needs and interests," he told us. That was the first time we'd heard any talk about serving or listening to us. Larry Smith set up the Inmate Welfare Fund Board and inmates started electing representatives from each of the units: Cyprus, Spruce, Ash, Magnolia, Oak, Pine, Walnut, and Hickory.

I was chosen to represent Cyprus unit, which had four dorms. I felt honored the guys thought I would represent their issues with justice.

The eight unit representatives met once a month with the head warden, the warden of security, the colonel, and the classification head to talk about prisoners' needs and what could be done to address prison conditions. Sometimes we had emergency meetings. In general, the meetings were very contested and vocal.

Sometimes they'd give us what we wanted, mainly fixing specific things that weren't working and that they could address immediately. If the water was cold in the unit, they'd get a maintenance person to go take care of it. Problems with the toilets got dealt with relatively quickly. They addressed some problems involving security—like if the security man on the boot was not letting guys inside the dorms or not letting guys use the phones on the walk. Larry Smith would call an emergency meeting if there was an issue where they needed input from the prison population to avoid division among prisoners, like when white security personnel fomented allegations that Larry Smith favored Black prisoners. He wanted us to know this was happening to see how he could make clear he was fair and treated everyone the same.

On the powers of the purse, though, prison officials wouldn't budge. We specifically wanted inmates to be in control of the Inmate Welfare Fund and to designate how the money should be used, rather than having it be a slush fund for the administration. Why pay an employee to run the board when the inmates themselves should be in control? Why put fans in the dorms when you could outfit them with air conditioners? Why make us use phones outside on the walk when you could put them inside the dorms? Every year we got Christmas packages—we said, "Let us, not the prison officials, designate what prisoners should get, something practical and useful in our lives." They'd just tell us, "That's not plausible."

THE VARIOUS FORMS OF organizing inside meant a lot to me, but I knew there was one thing I had to be prepared to handle on my own. I had become an adult at Angola, but I never forgot when I was this little sixteen-year-old kid and the white police officers in Destrehan beat the living hell out of me, slung me around like a rag doll. That physical beating used to haunt me. The whole time V. J. St. Pierre was telling me to eat my blood and trying to force me to do that, I was saying to myself, If I become strong enough, this will never happen to me again. I will fight them back.

In the mind of a young kid, that meant I wanted to get big to the point where I could fight an army. When I was in the cells, I did a lot of push-ups and running. I used to watch Mid-South Wrestling, guys like Junkyard Dog, Dusty Rhodes, The Great Kabuki, and others. When they opened the yard in 1978, I started running outside and growing. As soon as I got out of the cell blocks, I began lifting weights. A powerlifting team came into existence in 1989. Guys like Stuart Mayweather, who competed, said to me, "Gary, you need to join the team. You're one of the strongest guys in the prison." At first I said no, because by then I was involved in the Drama Club as well as work. Then my friend Kenya joined and he got me to do the same. Powerlifting became a form of discipline as well as body strengthening. We called our team Raw Power—No Pain. No Gain.

You know the physiological effect on goldfish. You put them in a little bowl, they stay small. But if you put them in a big aquarium, within months to a year, the goldfish will grow, because they have vast areas they can travel, exercising their muscles. The powerlifting team trained every day except Sundays. The team competed three to four times a year against other Louisiana penal institutions, like Dixon, Hunt, Avoyelles, and Forcht-Wade.

Guys who showed me techniques were telling me about a white guy named Pompano at Dixon who had set a record of bench pressing 400 pounds. He was in the heavyweight section and our team didn't have anyone to compete against him. At the time, I weighed 217 pounds and I was thirty-one years old. My teammates told me I was stronger than that guy and to get in that weight group. So I did. My first competition, I bench pressed 445 pounds. He did only 405. I broke his record. After that, every lift I did broke records. In fact, judges determined I was the strongest inmate statewide. I became Angola heavyweight champion four years in a row, from 1990 to 1993. Winning was exhilarating.

The guys wanted our prison team to go professional and compete with people who weren't incarcerated as well. But in the mid-nineties, Warden Burl Cain came in and changed all that. Conservatives were yelling, "Lock 'em up and throw away the keys. Prisoners live better than everyone on the street. They got AC and cable TV. They're going into prison and getting stronger and stronger, then they come out and victimize people." Cain was a political man. Among other things, he put restraints on *The Angolite*, trying to control information. He also decided to take the heavy weights away from the prison population. He abolished the powerlifting team.

I was really disappointed about losing the team. We were making a difference in many inmates' lives. People looked up to us and came to the gym to learn our techniques. I hated that Burl Cain caved to those reactionary legislators. Still, I'd accomplished my goal. Big as I was, I felt strong and invincible. I was no longer that young kid who was vulnerable and could be manhandled the way I was. People also knew I was a fighter for change and had friends and comrades I could depend on inside and outside the prison.

CHAPTER 11

WHAT KEPT ME GOING

While I worked to make changes in prison, I never gave up on my fight to get free. At my trial, I had listened to all the testimony, not knowing what was relevant and what was not. But I had plenty of time to reflect in solitary.

After my resentencing in 1977, I started diving into the details of my trial so I could be a help to my new legal team. The more I did that, the more I realized how many things didn't add up. I wasn't an expert in the law, but I had common sense.

My new lawyers, Jack Peebles and Lolis Elie, visited often and kept in close contact with me and my family. It gave me a sense of hope to finally have people who were capable of representing me, notable civil rights attorneys, in my corner. We would meet in a room set aside for maximum security inmates and their attorneys next to the Visiting Shed.

During the trial, the defense had established that the bus was packed with three people to a seat and some standing in the aisle. Yet Natalie Blanks had claimed to be with me in a seat by ourselves. No one else said that's where she was sitting. Loretta London had also testified that she'd passed the alleged gun around the bus, tried to hide it in her sock, and then given it back to me. The deputy said he picked up the gun without wearing gloves. So why were there no fingerprints on it? And what about the weapon itself? The .45 automatic the prosecution presented was large and flat. How could I have hidden it if I had tight clothes on and got patted down by a deputy sheriff before I even got on bus 91?

The noise we heard on that bus was a pop sound. It wasn't much louder than a firecracker, but it was enough to rile the students to feel like we were being shot at. The driver, Ernest Cojoe, testified that the bullet that killed Timothy Weber couldn't have been fired off his bus, because it would have been much louder and he'd have recognized it. No one ever refuted that.

The AG claimed I was the culprit behind the race riot at school that day, which had actually kicked off after I had been suspended and was far from Destrehan High. That just goes to show how flawed the prosecution's argument was. None of their allegations made sense. But my attorney at the time, Jack Williams, hadn't called them on any of these glaring contradictions.

I finally understood that this was why the state had kept my whole family out of the courthouse—so they wouldn't see what the prosecution was up to. Those in charge did what they always do, hide things and engage in scandalous acts. As one of my lawyers, Mary Howell, later said, my trial was a legal lynching. I was just a kid at the time. I didn't know they had all this underhanded stuff going on.

At Angola, I'd learned a lot about injustice. And I came to understand that it had been easier for the prosecution to pull this off because, like so many other people caught up in the legal system, I was from a poor family who couldn't afford decent representation. In the months leading up to the trial, Williams kept calling my parents to say he needed money for this, for that. But during those days in the courtroom, he produced nothing, no expert witnesses, no independent ballistics or forensics tests. He told my parents he wanted this case. Yet the only work he did was read the grand jury minutes and interview the bus driver. He hadn't talked to any of the students on the bus. He hadn't arranged for any independent experts. At a

1977 state hearing, Williams described his preparation for the trial. He said he "relied on friends out on the street . . . that kn[e]w some things about the case," including an officer he talked to at a football game. I was present at that hearing, though I couldn't speak. When Williams had to testify about the judge's instruction, he said, "I did object in the judge's chamber." But incredibly, he claimed he couldn't remember whether or not he had also objected on the record in the courtroom, and if he hadn't, why not. I shook my head in disgust and disbelief.

Like any other Black family who had never been in serious trouble, my parents thought having a white attorney meant the guy was going to do what was right. They paid him $3,000, and then he told them the total fee was $15,000. He never got any more than $3,000 because that's all they had.

NOW I HAD A new legal team that knew what they were doing. Of course, they were still up against the Louisiana criminal justice system. It hurt like hell when I heard from Jack Peebles in February 1977 that the state supreme court had denied our appeal for a new trial. My lawyers appealed to the state supreme court again after the resentencing. We got another denial, although this time a Judge Calogero dissented. It was the jury's job, he said, "to determine beyond a reasonable doubt that the defendant specifically intended to kill or do great bodily harm to more than one person, when he fired one shot." Being told they should presume that I did have that specific intent was a "transfer of the burden" and "a prejudicial and unconstitutional violation of defendant's right to be presumed innocent." This judge understood, but he couldn't convince his colleagues.

One more time, it felt like the cake was baked against me. But I had innocence on my side. That continued to be my beacon of hope.

My defense team kept going. In 1980 they took my case to the federal level, the Fifth Circuit Court of Appeals. The lawyers focused on two areas: the judge's faulty instruction to the jury, and the fact that there wasn't enough evidence to convict me of first-degree murder. And on July 24, that court said the words I'd been waiting nearly five years to hear: I had been "convicted on an unconstitutional charge" and the trial was "fundamentally unfair." These judges all agreed that Judge Ruche Marino's comments about intent denied me the presumption of innocence. Marino had flipped everything around, making it so I had to prove beyond a reasonable doubt that I was innocent, when actually it was on the state to prove I was guilty. Without specific intent, the charge would have had to change to manslaughter, which would have required them to acknowledge my age and send me to juvenile detention. The fifth circuit vacated my conviction and ordered the district court to hold a new trial! I jumped for joy when I got this news. Finally, the truth had broken through. I felt this was the decision that would free me.

Shortly after this decision came down, Peebles left private practice to become an assistant DA with Harry Connick Sr., in New Orleans. Mary Howell, Sam Dalton, and Pam Bayer became the lead attorneys in my case. That same year, 1980, the legal team got a big boost, an affidavit from an attorney named William Rittenberg about how the charge against me was a scam. Rittenberg happened to be in the Hahnville courthouse on November 4, 1975, and had spoken with one of the prosecutors in my case. "This attorney informed me that the state didn't really have a first-degree murder case against Tyler," Rittenberg said. "The most they had was a possible manslaughter." The prosecutor had admitted to Rittenberg that the charge decision was "politically motivated" because of "the publicity of the case." In other words, everyone knew that a white teen had died from a gunshot. Somebody Black was going to take the fall and they had to fall hard. This affidavit would join the other evidence we'd use in a new trial.

But the attorney general's office in Louisiana wasn't about to give up either. They appealed the fifth circuit court's decision and filed for a rehearing. The AG put the focus on a legal technicality: Louisiana's penal code has a provision called the "contemporaneous jury objection rule"—a lawyer has to make an objection to something at the time it occurs in order for it to be considered in an appeal. Williams should have objected to Judge Marino's instructions that day in the courtroom. He hadn't. Now the AG's office claimed it was too late. Joining him were the AGs of Texas and Mississippi, the other two states covered by that circuit court.

On April 27, 1981, my case was back at the Fifth Circuit Court of Appeals. I couldn't believe my ears when Mary Howell delivered the bad news: The judges overturned that court's earlier decision. Yes, they said, my trial was fundamentally unfair and those jury instructions were defective and meant I was denied the presumption of innocence. But they still ruled I was not entitled to a new trial because my trial lawyer hadn't objected to the jury instruction at the time and couldn't remember why he hadn't.

How can you say my trial was unfair, my constitutional rights were violated, but you can't do anything about it? What kind of technicality is that? The judge violated the Constitution—isn't that a greater law? It was bad enough that some Louisiana loophole stopped them. Apparently the U.S. Supreme Court also had a precedent that said a federal court shouldn't accept claims that weren't raised first in a timely way in the lower court. What really stung was a concurring opinion from fifth circuit judge James Coleman, a segregationist who was formerly governor of Mississippi: "Tyler has already escaped the death penalty to which he was originally sentenced. Leaving him to serve a prison sentence for taking a young life, as he did, is not a miscarriage of justice."

It sure felt like a miscarriage of justice to me. The decision set me back and made my uphill battle much more difficult, especially when the Supreme Court refused to hear my case in 1982. I had still been hopeful. It was a crushing blow not just to me, but to my family, especially to my mother. And yet, I knew I had to stay focused despite the disappointment. I saw how hard my mother fought to be strong for me, and I knew I had to emulate that.

I worked hard not to despair, because by now I fully understood the magnitude of my struggle. I was dealing with a system intent on suppressing the truth. But I knew I couldn't give up and I couldn't give in. If I became bitter and vengeful, they'd say, "See, it's in his character! That's just who he is!" I had to maintain my dignity, my belief in myself. I never forgot what I'd been told by many of my supporters: "Gary, the only thing we need from you is to survive prison life." So I continued to fight on all fronts: educating myself on the law, being involved politically, and organizing against the inhumane conditions of prison life. I couldn't just say the system was unfair, I had to understand why things were happening the way they were and what we could do about it. For me, it was about maintaining focus and purpose.

There was one more thing I needed to do in order to become complete and be comfortable with who I was: forgive those who were forced to testify against me in the trial.

WHEN NATALIE AND LORETTA recanted in 1976, I was still focused on what had happened to me. I was the one who got assaulted and sentenced to die. What exacerbated my resentment was that Natalie and Loretta had come to visit me in the parish jail, as though we were friends, with me not knowing they had lied on me at the grand jury and were going to lie on me in court.

But as the years went by and I understood more about how the system worked, I came to see that the people who had literally and figuratively beat me so bad were also capable of terrorizing these young ladies. We're talking about two girls being threatened with ninety-nine years in prison for something they didn't have anything to do with; one also risked having her baby taken away. My ordeal had humbled me. I came to see how terrifying it must have been for them. Hearing Nelson Mandela speak in 1990 also helped me understand that forgiving these people who had hurt me was essential for me to move forward.

Natalie used to stop my mother on the road when she was coming home from work and talk to her. I knew those were signs of how bad she felt about what had happened. Like me, my mother was really hurt that the kids had lied, but she saw how Natalie and Loretta cried and how they'd been threatened. "Their parents were so intimidated until they just told their kids to do what they had to do," she told me. When others came to visit me and said how cold it was for the students to lie on me, I found myself defending them. I realized the cops must have threatened Ulrich Smith, too. He'd never been in trouble before in his life. He had just got a job. He and his girlfriend had just had a baby. At the time of my arrest, he had charges pending against him because he'd called Officer Nelson Coleman an Uncle Tom.

Playing on the fears of young kids like that showed how low the state government would stoop. With the kinds of intimidation they faced, those kids would have said whatever people wanted them to. They would have sworn they saw me shoot the pope or John F. Kennedy if they had to.

My feeling about V. J. St. Pierre and the other officers was more complicated, but I realized I also had to set aside my rage at them. I wasn't only fighting for my freedom but for my sanity. In order for me to survive, to make it, there were some things I had to put behind me. I'll never forget how those officers physically abused me. I can't change that. They can't change that. I'm sure some of them went through life wishing they'd never been put in that situation. But it was a matter of how I was going to live my life, whether I'd hold on to bitterness or not.

Getting to that point represented a big transformation, and it took years. You don't just wake up one day with an epiphany and say, "I'm going to change my feelings." It's not like turning a faucet off. In fact, some faucets you turn off and there's still a drip. It was important for me to go through that process; it gave me a chance to think things out. Being in my feelings hadn't allowed me to see what my friends had been through as well.

I don't know how I could have gotten there without the tremendous support I had from all over the world—from strangers I'd never met, some of them celebrities; from my family every step of the way; and from some completely unexpected places.

***

THE MAIL THAT STARTED in January of 1976, when "A Letter from Death Row" was published, kept on coming. I got a boost in 1977 when CBS did a feature story about me being on death row. The quantity of mail was so great that the security guards were bringing it in boxes. Eventually they started forcing me to get rid of large numbers of letters on a weekly basis to avoid the clutter or to get a rise out of me.

But the support I was receiving helped me realize my job was to stay alive. Other people out there were fighting for my life.

"Free Gary Tyler" committees were formed around the country and held a lot of rallies for me, from New York, Boston, and Pittsburgh to Louisville, Cleveland, Detroit, and New Orleans. Rosa Parks spoke at a big event in Detroit on June 19, 1976, with my mother and Hurricane Carter. For a poor Black family, fighting the whole criminal justice system was both daunting and a big burden. We had tremendous support from my mother's congregation, Fifth African Baptist Church in St. Rose. When my family started getting local, statewide, and national support, it really made a difference to all of us. Local people like Marie Galatas, founder of the Grass Roots Organization for Women, visited my mother on a regular basis and helped her see we weren't fighting this on our own. Even at my high school, classmates both Black and white organized a group called the "Gary Tyler Freedom Fighters."

IN MARCH OF 1976, a fundraiser was held in my benefit at Southern University at New Orleans. As some of my supporters came out and started walking to the bus stop, a Volkswagen drove up alongside them. A guy with a shotgun rolled down the window and shot at them, killing Richard Dunn in cold blood. I learned that he yelled for his friend, Gus Givens, to duck and then pushed him down, saving Gus's life. I'd never met Richard Dunn, but his death was a gut punch to me. Here was a young Black man my age who cared about justice—who was there to support me. For him to have lost his life was a tragedy that should never have happened. What sick, callous individual would do something like that just out of pure hate?

Two white guys were arrested for his murder. One turned state's evidence against the other, Anthony Mart, who was convicted. A higher court later overturned his conviction and ordered a retrial, where he was found guilty again and sentenced to life. And after ten years, what happened? This white guy, the killer of a Black man who was an absolute stranger to him, got a pardon from Governor Edwin Edwards.

A year later, Tom Henehan, an activist in New York organizing demonstrations and getting petitions signed for me from labor organizations, teachers, and nurses, was shot in cold blood by a man named Angelo Torres. Henehan died in the hospital an hour later. He was twenty-six years old.

IN SPITE OF THESE real threats to their safety, the movement to free me kept on growing. In 1977, a dozen or more supporters went to Governor Edwards's office and presented him with over ninety thousand signatures asking for my release. Like so many politicians, Edwards avoided taking a stand. He said he would wait until the appeals process had been exhausted.

After every setback, though, we received new support. My mother and comrades in the movement were reaching out to anyone they felt could help. My mother wrote a letter to the musician Gil Scott-Heron, who had created a lot of music about struggle. Soon, he wrote a song about me called "Angola, Louisiana." I didn't get a chance to listen to that song until decades later, but I heard a lot about it from my mother and from letters I got from people in the Black community who had heard it on the radio. My mother sent me a copy of a picture of herself and Gil Scott-Heron, taken when he was in New Orleans. "I know a brother man doing time," he sang, "and he didn't commit no crime." He told me to stay strong, "you're not alone."

The song was a testament to the overwhelming support I was getting from everywhere.

Then, in 1980, British reggae band UB40 wrote a song about me, too, after hearing about my case in the British press. They called it "Tyler" and used it to urge people to appeal to Governor Edwards. The song highlighted the manufactured evidence—a planted gun, no prints, no proof—and the white judges who showed no mercy.

In 1979, a group of prominent judges and lawyers from around the world interviewed me and other people they considered "political prisoners." They told representatives of the National Black Caucus of State Legislators that they were "shocked" and "appalled" at the conditions they witnessed in U.S. prisons. A few years later, the Russian newspaper *Pravda* described me as a political prisoner. That helped keep attention alive, even after the fifth circuit denied me a new trial. Newspapers around the world rallied to my defense. News of support was good news; it meant a lot to me that people were still paying attention. While the death penalty had been removed, I still had a life sentence. In prison, anything could happen.

In the early 1990s, Amnesty International sent representatives from West Germany to interview me. They put out a report in 1994 that clearly stated their belief that I had been denied a fair trial "and that racial prejudice played a major part." For them, I was a political prisoner because of the "racial and political context" of the prosecution.

Some U.S. news publications, like the *Houston Chronicle* and *The Louisiana Weekly*, did updates on me from time to time. And in September 2007, marchers protesting the racist charges against the Jena 6 in Jena, Louisiana, carried banners to free me as well. That same year, a reporter from *The New York Times*, Bob Herbert, wrote not one but a series of three articles about the details of my case, the beating I took, the "fundamentally unfair" trial, and the "racial hysteria" behind it all. I wasn't allowed to meet with him, though I did get copies of his column. Bob Herbert injected new life into my case, twenty-one and a half years after I was sent to death row. It was a prime example that some cases stay on people's minds. Mine raised questions like "How can we talk about freedom and justice and democracy for other countries when we don't practice it here in America?"

That coverage led to a story on *Democracy Now!* with my mother, my sister Bobbie Nell, and Bob Herbert as guests. Host Amy Goodman aired part of an interview with me done by a graduate student, Maia Weerdmeester, who was writing a thesis on Angola. "My fight is to get out of prison," I told her, "not to be bitter, not to seek vengeance on anyone, not to hate anyone, but to get out of prison, hoping that I get out of here a free man, a man who is able to prove his innocence." I pointed out that enough had been done to exonerate me, but the system didn't want to admit it had made a mistake in my case, just like it had in so many other cases. "To release me now," I said, "would imply that they knew all along. They don't want to be labeled as the villain. But as long as I continue to be here, it will never die. It will be a thorn in their side. I assume that they expected from the beginning, 'Well, we can just scapegoat him and send him to prison, and we'll never hear anything else about him.'"

TO KNOW THAT PEOPLE watched this broadcast, heard the songs of Gil Scott-Heron and UB40, read articles and reports about me, and then wrote me letters was a reminder that my case hadn't worked out the way the system expected. I wasn't fighting this struggle by myself. It was invigorating to have supporters locally, nationally, and around the globe. And at the heart of that support was my family, the ones who kept me strong from the beginning.

My mother, who comes from a very large family, had four children from a previous marriage when she married Uylos Tyler and gave birth to eight more; I'm the seventh of the eleven who survived and who Juanita and Uylos raised together.

Once I was arrested, my parents and siblings had to put up with a lot. My father was fired from one of his three jobs by someone he'd thought was a friend. He'd been working there a long time, was known to be the best employee, and was devastated by the betrayal. It didn't take a genius to figure out what the real reason for his firing was. One of my brothers was let go for missing work to attend one of my hearings. After passing around a petition to free me, my sister-in-law Jackie also lost her job.

Then there were the arrests. My brother Terry and Donald Files, who testified for me at the March 1976 hearing when Natalie recanted her testimony, were arrested on charges of burglary. The alleged crime happened on May 16, 1976, while Terry was in Detroit speaking at a rally on my behalf. Terry and Donald were charged with stealing a $2 bill and a pack of cigarettes. Judge Marino set a $5,000 bond for each of them. Terry said while they were being held, a white cop put two shells in his .44 Magnum, "spun the barrel of the gun, clicking the trigger at us, playing Russian roulette, I guess." In June of that year, Marino held my brother Steven on a $2,700 bond for a charge of "disturbing the police." Jack Peebles got involved in all these cases and eventually got them off.

In those years, Klansmen would drive openly through my hometown of St. Rose. Police stopped a number of them and found guns when they searched the cars; having firearms in the car was perfectly legal as long as the gun wasn't on their person or stolen. Other Klan members stalked my supporters and members of my family until community members sectioned off the area we lived in and announced to the KKK, "If you enter, you will not find an exit."

On January 21, 1977, at 10 a.m., my family got a knock on the door. Police busted into the house with a warrant looking for my brother Steven on trumped-up charges of robbery. DA Norman Pitre was involved. A male police officer patted my mother down, called my father all kinds of names, and snatched him out of bed—he had just gotten out of the hospital after having a heart attack. My brother was never charged. They prioritized harassing my family over actually stopping the Klan. They didn't like that my mother was so active at the time publicly trying to save my life.

THROUGHOUT MY ORDEAL, MY mother was my rock. I knew how hard she worked, speaking, meeting with people, cooking and selling dinners to raise funds, always driving to see me and doing everything she could to keep my spirits up. She used to tell me, "I come visit you because you give me peace. Of all my children, you turned out to be in the worst situation, but you don't give me heartache. When I come here, you uplift my spirit. That's why I come, because you give me strength." But it was my mother who gave me so much.

That doesn't mean things were always easy between us. In 1995, my mother became distrustful of a lot of people and reverted back to her religious beliefs: "Don't trust nobody but God," she'd say. "God is who will make it possible." But by then I had become politicized. In my mind, if there were a merciful God, He wouldn't have let this happen. I had become disillusioned with Christianity, and that caused a conflict with my mother. "You were baptized," she told me. "Your aspiration was one day to become a preacher. You were always the first one to go to church, and now you don't believe in God no more?" For a while we couldn't see eye to eye. I kept pushing back. One day, when my mother was telling me something, I told her, "I disagree."

"Boy, you're my son," she said.

"I'm not a boy," I told her. "I'm a man."

"I'm still your mother."

"Yeah, but you gotta treat me like a man."

She got up from the table and started walking away. Something told me, You've got to stop her or something bad will happen. I followed that voice, ran behind my mother, and apologized to her. After that day, I stopped arguing with her, even though I didn't always agree with what she was saying. She'd lost her son once to the system and now she was at risk of losing him again over a disagreement. After that, our bond was even stronger.

My father had a hard time coming to visit me in prison, first because of the long hours on his jobs, and then because of his health. When we were kids, my father was an apartment manager and a gas station attendant supervisor. He spent the weekends cutting grass, painting houses, fixing air conditioners. Then in 1987, after he'd had two heart attacks, the second one a massive one on the job, the doctor told him he could no longer work. My father was a proud man, who'd provided support not only to his immediate family but also to our extended family. He was the first one to move out of Tallulah and get a house in the New Orleans area. He helped some of my mother's siblings to move out there, too, having them stay at our house and finding them a job. I remember when my father and my uncle James decided to go to Tallulah, run water to my grandparents' home, and build a bathroom so they didn't have to keep using an outhouse. It was unbearable for my father to be told all of a sudden that his health wouldn't allow him to do the work he'd always done and provide help to loved ones.

One day in 1988, my mother visited me and said, "Your father is grieving." I asked what was going on. She told me my father felt he had abandoned me, failed me because he didn't visit as much as he thought he should have.

"That's not true," I said. "He's here with me today. He's the one who made it possible for you to come see me. He bought the car you drive here, he buys me clothes. I know he's with me. Next time you come, bring him here."

So she did. That day I entered the A Building and saw my mother standing at the concession. I walked up and embraced her and gazed around for my father. "Where's Uylos at?" I asked.

"There you go, right there." She pointed at this little man with a big old Stetson hat. My father loved wearing that hat. I had to take a second look. Even though my father, who'd always had the build of a defensive lineman, now looked frail, I noticed his smile, sad but genuine. I bent over to hug him, then sat next to him and told him how much I loved him. "Uylos, you have always been there for me," I told him. "When this incident happened, it wasn't no different. When Madea"—that's what we all called my mother—"comes, you are here in spirit. I know you have worked hard to make it possible for her to be here. She couldn't have done it alone. You always made sure I had what I needed in prison. You didn't have to be present physically for me to see you and know you were here for me. I appreciate you. I'm grateful you're my father."

It was like a light was turned on inside him. My father needed to hear that. "I love you, son," he told me. That was the first time I heard him say that. He'd seen how I'd grown up in prison. I was no longer that child bloodied and hurting he'd seen in the New Sarpy police station. I had become a man, in large part thanks to the support of him and my mother. "I'm proud of you," he said. "Stay strong for your mother."

About three weeks later, they had to rush my father to the hospital. His heart was giving out on him. My mother later told me that my baby sister, Jennifer, was there, and he told her she was pregnant. She was. My father smiled, and then he died. He was fifty-six years old.

I was able to go to his funeral, but the guards put me in shackles and handcuffs. On the way there, with those cuffs on, I wrote a poem for him called "Stranger." It included these lines:

Not really knowing you, alienated the greatest desire in most kids' hearts,
To know their father.
After all the childhood fears and insecurities,
I realized who you actually were.
But then, again, a stranger, as always, in my life.

I read the poem when I spoke at the service, and then I placed it in my father's casket. The church was packed, standing room only. That's how many people loved him. It was a big loss for all of us.

Gary (far left) and other students from bus 91 strike a pose for state troopers searching their bus. This photo was introduced as evidence in the trial.

Among Gary's guardians at Angola were Herman Wallace (Hooks) and Colonel Nyati Bolt. Photos taken in the maximum-security cellblocks at Angola in the 1980s.

Some of the books read by Gary at Angola.
PHOTO BY ROBIN FONG.

Defiant, a quilt made by Gary Tyler, shows him leaving the courthouse in St. Charles Parish on April 23, 1976, after being denied a new trial.
Defiant, 1976, 2023
Quilting fabric, thread, and batting
47 x 38 in
119.4 x 96.5 cm
PHOTO COURTESY OF LIBRARY STREET COLLECTIVE.

SUNO and Tulane students protesting outside the courthouse on April 22, 1976.
PHOTO BY H.J. PATTERSON, COURTESY OF HISTORIC NEW ORLEANS COLLECTION, 2020.0084.27.

Juanita Tyler with activist Kalamu ya Salaam after Gary's resentencing in March 1977.
PHOTO BY ROBERT T. STEINER, COURTESY OF HISTORIC NEW ORLEANS COLLECTION, 2020.0084.17.

These buttons were among those made by Free Gary Tyler committees across the United States. PHOTO BY LARRY MILLER.

From right to left: Singer-songwriter Gil Scott-Heron handing a check to Gary's mother, Juanita Tyler; brother Terry Tyler; and a friend.

Gilda Parks, who corresponded with Gary in the early years and visited for three days in 1980.

Gary and his mother, 1984. Photo taken at Angola.

Gary Tyler (bottom left) and other members of the Angola powerlifting team. Gary was heavyweight champion from 1990–1993.

Gary with two of his postconviction lawyers, Majeeda Snead and Mary Howell.
PHOTO FROM THE ANGOLITE, JANUARY/FEBRUARY 1990.

Deborah George Hardy, who helped train the Angola Drama Club members, shares a laugh with Gary Tyler (center) and Clarence Matthews.
PHOTO BY LORI WASELCHUCK FOR THE SUNDAY ADVOCATE IN BATON ROUGE, OCTOBER 10, 1991.

Gary and his six-month-old son.

Gary Tyler in the Angola hospice quilting shop, Stitch in Time, beneath curtains made by hospice volunteers. PHOTO COURTESY OF LORI WASELCHUK.

Gary speaking at a 2016 rally in support of Prop 62, to end the death penalty in California.

Gary working in his L.A. studio, made possible by a GoFundMe account begun by friends in 2020.
IMAGE BY DORIAN HILL, COURTESY OF THE ARTIST AND LIBRARY STREET COLLECTIVE.

The Tree of Life, a quilt made by Gary Tyler in 2012, now hangs in the Historic New Orleans Collection.
PHOTO COURTESY OF HNOC, GIFT OF LORI WASELCHUK, 2016.0298.8.

THE SUPPORT FROM MY family uplifted me but did not surprise me. Some support I got, though, came from places I never expected. One example was a white nurse who came to Angola in May of 1995. Karen Braud worked with the Louisiana Bone Marrow Donor Registry, a nonprofit that matched bone marrow donors with patients. She was hoping to find a volunteer donor for Nicholas Carter, a fourteen-year-old Black youth from Baton Rouge with a rare form of cancer. Norris Henderson connected her to club heads at Angola. Those of us who volunteered to be tested came over to the A Building on a Sunday. Some of the guys pointed at me and told Nicholas, "You know, Gary was on the powerlifting team. He's the strongest man in Angola." I gave Nicholas a Drama Club shirt and hat. He and I really took to each other. I wanted to be a match, but, sadly, none of us was.

A week earlier, Karen Braud had approached Wilbert Rideau and asked if he knew me. Wilbert acknowledged that he did, and said he'd encourage me to participate in the testing. The day she came back, Wilbert pointed me out and this woman started to run up to me. At first I froze—I wasn't sure if she was coming to attack me or what. As she got closer, I could see she was eager to say something. She was only about five feet one, but she reached up and gave me a bear hug, just kept hugging me real tight. Her eyes were teary, but she still had a wonderful smile. "Gary Tyler," she said, "I want to apologize to you for all the white people in St. Charles Parish, for what we've done to you. Never did we treat you as one of our own. You were one of our children."

That declaration from her took a lot off my shoulders. I thought all the white people in St. Charles Parish hated me. David Duke got a lot of votes in that parish when he ran for governor of Louisiana. After that, things started falling into place for me. In the early years, white guards would say, "He's the one who killed that white kid," not realizing I was a kid, too. But later, some white guards bringing prisoners in would see me and say, "We just came from Hahnville and we met a couple of deputies there. They asked how you were doing. We said, 'He's doing well, he's well respected.'" Several white guards at Angola—Sergeant Wayne Crayer, Billy Baggett, and others—started calling me "*Mister* Tyler."

I first met Billy Baggett in the late 1990s when he was assigned to guard the paint crew. He looked me over and asked, "Are you one of those Black militants who hate white people?" I made it clear to him: "I do not play with security." As time passed, we got to know each other. One day I shared a news article with him about my case. Baggett did his own research and eventually became convinced I was innocent. He was appalled about the criminal justice system and turned into a staunch advocate for my freedom. He'd bring his young daughter Tayler with him to watch the Angola rodeo and leave her with me at the Drama concessions booth. "I wouldn't leave her even with my coworkers," he told me. "You're the only one I trust."

All those people supporting me provided the lifeline that kept me going. It was like a force watching over me. I had seen the ugly side of white America, unspeakable acts committed against Black people, Black men accused of just looking at a white woman, me accused of murdering a thirteen-year-old white kid. There was no guarantee that I would survive this. It made the difference to have people I got to know and others I didn't know at all, had no inkling they existed, white, Asian, Hispanic as well as Black, people of all walks of life, saying "Enough is enough. You're talking about killing this kid or locking him up for life when the evidence shows he didn't do it. This is the legacy of slavery. We say no."

I was proud my case was something people wanted to fight for.

CHAPTER 12

PARDON ME

After the blow from the fifth circuit court in 1981, Mary Howell and her legal team began looking at other grounds to call for a new trial. A year earlier, when they had filed in court to get ballistics tests done on the gun and the bullet, they found out the gun had "gone missing" from the property room of the parish clerk's office. Mary knew there was more exculpatory evidence her team could uncover, evidence that could have gotten me acquitted, but they needed resources to hire investigators. Finally, in 1988, when I was thirty years old, she had the time and the funds she needed. Among my biggest supporters in this effort were the Neville Brothers. Various unions, churches, and other organizations raised funds as well.

In 1989, investigators found Larry Dabney, who straight up recanted just like Natalie and Loretta had done. The investigators also located Michael Campbell and Patricia Files Sims, who gave more detail on how the police had pressured them.

Larry's statement was detailed and graphic. He said officers picked him up at his parents' house late on the night of October 7 and drove him down to the sheriff's office. "I'll never forget what happened next," he said in his affidavit. "It was the scariest thing to ever happen to me. They didn't even ask me what I saw. They told me flat out I was going to be their key witness. They started telling me what my statement was going to be. They told me I was going to say I saw Gary with a gun right after I heard the shot, and that a few minutes later I had seen him hide it in a slit in the seat. That was not true. I did not see Gary or anyone else in that bus with a gun." The police told him he had to sign that statement and read it at the grand jury hearing and in court or he'd be going to jail for ten years. "I was just a kid," he said. "I had never had any trouble with the law. I was terrified. I was going to do whatever they told me to do and say whatever they told me to say." But clearly the lie had bothered him. In the affidavit, he said, "This has been over my head for 15 years." In fact, when the investigator came, Larry told him, "I've been waiting for this knock at the door for fifteen years."

At that time, I was still transitioning in the forgiveness process, but I was glad to hear that Larry finally was coming forward and admitting what the system had done. It substantiated what I had been saying all along.

Michael Campbell, who shared that bus seat with Larry and me and had become a staff sergeant in the army in 1976, also gave an affidavit: "I know that Gary didn't fire that shot," he said. "He was sitting next to me and would have had to put his arm in front of me to fire right by my head. It would have busted my eardrums. It didn't happen. . . . I didn't see anybody else on the bus with a gun either. No one was passing a gun around on the bus or talking about it. . . . There was not a slit in the bus seat or a gun hidden in the seat. I would have seen and felt it if there were." And then he said something I had not known—that he had gotten scared from hearing my screams at the police station. "The police . . . had Tyler in one of the back rooms and we could hear them hitting on him," his statement said. "He was hollering like he was hurt, and I could tell they were obviously beating him up. . . . The policeman scared me and I said things that were not true. The police told me they were going to give me 99 years as an accessory after the fact if I didn't tell them what they wanted to hear. . . . I didn't want to hurt Gary, but the police were acting crazy." It turns out Michael had already recanted at the time of his grand jury testimony. He had told them that he hadn't seen a gun and that police tried to put words in his mouth.

My first attorney, Jack Williams, had supposedly read the grand jury transcript, but he never mentioned this to me or used it to pose questions to Michael Campbell when he testified for us at my trial, or followed up when Michael made these points again on the stand. This was one more reminder of how Williams had botched my case. It was overwhelming to hear this; my emotions were raw. Of course, I was glad the additional evidence was out, but it didn't immediately change my condition. The state had gotten a conviction from a twelve-member jury and it wasn't going to do anything to right that wrong.

Patricia Files, who'd also testified on my behalf at the 1975 trial, had married my brother Steve and was now called Patricia Sims. Mary Howell's team got an affidavit from her, too. "I never saw Gary or anybody else with a gun," she said. "I said I did in my police statement and in court, but it wasn't true. I said those things because I was scared and because police told me that if I didn't say them, I would go to jail. They were badgering us like we were animals."

The police's intimidation of the witnesses was just the start. That firing range in Kenner where the so-called murder weapon had been stolen just happened to be one used by the St. Charles Parish police department. How would a sixteen-year-old Black kid get hold of a .45 from a police firing range? And how did the gun then disappear from the property room of the parish clerk's office? That disappearance just reinforced how much of a cover-up had gone on.

The investigators also looked for someone who could shed light on the testimony given by Herman Parrish from the crime lab about my gloves. They located a former colleague of his, forensics expert Ronald Singer, who revealed that Parrish had been fired a year after my trial for lying about test results in another case. Parrish denied this, but it was confirmed by two other people: Richard Thompson, chief criminal deputy sheriff, and attorney Sam Dalton, who said Parrish had admitted in a 1979 case that he'd been forced to resign because of giving false test results. Singer also said that accurate tests for gunpowder require the presence of whole flakes, not just "specks" like Parrish had described. He pointed out that Parrish named one chemical in the evidentiary hearing before the trial began and a different chemical when he testified before the jury, and neither of them was the chemical the lab actually used to test for gunpowder. If Williams had been the least bit prepared, he'd have found Ronald Singer before my trial.

Then there were the inconsistencies about the bullet. Kenneth Gaillot, the firearms examiner, testified that the bullet they found matched the gun. We later found out more about his background. His mother was Una Gaillot, president of Save Our Nation Inc., an organization she created to oppose desegregation in Catholic schools. In April 1962, along with two others, she had been excommunicated for this opposition. Mary Howell's independent ballistics investigation showed that with a .45 automatic, bullets mushroom on impact. The bullet the police claimed killed Timothy Weber had no damage to it. In early 1989, we found out about a report from the crime lab written in December 1974 that showed the bullet had no blood on it, no trace of having entered a human body. The prosecution knew this was exculpatory evidence, but they didn't disclose it in court.

MARY THOUGHT ABOUT USING all the compelling points of this newly discovered evidence to go back to the Fifth Circuit Court of Appeals. The team brought in another group of lawyers, who specialized in wrongful convictions, headed by Clive Stafford Smith. After reviewing all the pleadings, they felt even with this compelling newly discovered evidence, it would be very difficult to get a court to reverse the conviction because there was a strong presumption that convictions were valid despite new evidence.

It seemed, no matter what we did, there was no tailwind. I was caught up in a system so egregiously unfair that there was no possibility of the courts addressing the injustice of what happened to me. I clung to the two main pillars in my world: that first opinion from the Fifth Circuit Court of Appeals that my trial had been "fundamentally unfair," and the fact that I was innocent. I knew I had to persevere no matter what.

There was another route to try, getting the pardon board to change my life sentence to a certain number of years and then recommend my release. In 1988, Mary Howell decided to go that route and make the case to them that I was innocent, that my conviction was a "travesty of justice," one that the Board of Pardons had the power to redress.

The petition for pardon covered all the major problems in my case. It pointed out that the deputies had done nothing to stop the mob of white students and others who were hurling objects and racist cries at the busloads of Black kids. One officer, Major Charles Faucheux, testified to seeing a Black student running toward the road and being chased by fifty whites; he took no action to protect that young person. The police also never followed up on a statement from Donald Files, who was on bus 91, that he saw a white guy on a porch across the street with what looked like a shotgun. Mary and her colleagues reminded the pardon board that no one on the bus except for Natalie Blanks said they saw me fire a gun, and Natalie herself had recanted that testimony. In addition to describing how I'd been beaten at the police substation and my mother's pleas ignored, the petition reviewed the problems with the physical evidence—the origin and disappearance of the alleged weapon, the bus driver's testimony that no gun was found on his bus during the first two searches, the lack of my fingerprints on any knife found on that bus or any of my fingerprints on the gun, the problems with the so-called test on my gloves, and the contradictory testimony about "smoke" coming out a bus window. Mary described the incompetence of my trial lawyer, Jack Williams, especially his failure to object to that unconstitutional jury instruction.

Mary also made a strong case for the role racism played in how I had been set up. She ended her argument by saying, "Why was Gary Tyler framed? . . . Gary Tyler was charged with murder not because he was guilty of the charge but because he was guilty of being a proud young Black man who protested the bullying and intimidation of himself and other students by deputies. To V. J. St. Pierre, he was a 'smart N-word.'" And she made the important point of what a "pardon" would mean in my case: "Gary Tyler does not ask that he be pardoned for a crime that he committed and now feels remorse and reconciliation. Gary Tyler asks that he be pardoned as he has been unjustly imprisoned for a crime which he did not commit." When I got that brief, I rejoiced. I was so grateful to have a lawyer like Mary Howell who really got the big picture of what was going on here.

A lot of people wrote letters supporting my application, including prominent leaders like Rev. Avery Alexander, a civil rights veteran and Louisiana state representative who had marched with Dr. Martin Luther King, and Dorothy Taylor, a state representative from New Orleans and civil rights activist who'd marched beside my mother and worked with Albert Woodfox on key prison reforms in the early seventies. The parents of Richard Dunn, my supporter who'd been gunned down in 1976, wrote a heartfelt letter as well. Gary Shafner, a businessman who owned a printing company in L.A., had come to Angola with a longtime supporter of mine, Bob Zaugh, to interview me and offered me a job at his printing company. We also handed in a petition with twelve thousand signatures.

On May 4, 1989, Yvonne Campbell, chair of the Board of Pardons, notified me they'd received my application and scheduled a hearing for October. I wrote back May 12 to thank them.

Despite everything that had happened, I hadn't lost hope. I thought I was going to be freed. I felt strongly that once the people read what happened and looked at the evidence, I would walk away—they'd recommend a pardon and Buddy Roemer would sign it. His family was well known, although his father was in prison for malfeasance. I thought he'd be empathetic, open, and receptive to the case.

The state tried to trash all of Mary Howell's arguments. How could it be racism, they said, when the assistant principal who agreed with my suspension from school that day and the officer who arrested me were both Black? But in early November of 1989, after several weeks of deliberation, the pardon board decided in my favor, three to two. All the Black members voted to reduce my sentence to sixty years, with eligibility for parole after twenty years served. I'd already been in Angola for nearly fourteen years. I was relieved to have their support. The two white members voted no on the grounds that I hadn't yet completed my GED. They were both criminologists who'd seen all the ways the evidence fell short. For them to deny my pardon because of a GED I had been blocked from pursuing was a real affront, a weak way of copping out.

BUT IN JANUARY OF the following year, Governor Buddy Roemer told the press he was not going to pardon me. He had the audacity to say incorrectly in a press statement that every reviewing court had found my trial to be "fundamentally fair by all legal standards." Plus, he said, he felt I wasn't ready for society. "I believe his efforts toward rehabilitation have not been sufficient," he said. Because I didn't have a GED, he claimed, the odds would be against me.

First of all, I was already enrolled in academic school and it wouldn't be long before I got the GED. I had tried for twelve years to enroll in the program and would have been finished if the system hadn't gotten in my way. Also, the governor had granted pardons to other guys without a GED, like Donald Gaines and a little guy they called Giant. The truth was, Roemer was running for re-election against David Duke. He feared a backlash from white voters.

My legal team tried again two years later. In an application accepted on October 30, 1991, they focused on all my accomplishments in prison, including the fact that I had gotten my GED that May and my trade school certificate and that I was active in the Drama Club and the Jaycees. Mary also drew comparisons with other cases where whites who'd been found guilty without any doubt of killing someone Black got a suspended sentence, like Ronnie Acaldo, or were released after a relatively short time, like Anthony Mart, the guy who murdered Richard Dunn. In their response, the attorney general and district attorney's office were particularly upset that I had indicted the entire justice system.

This time the decision of the Louisiana Board of Pardons was unanimous. On December 4, 1991, they recommended reducing my sentence to fifty years with eligibility for parole after serving one-third of the sentence, and they restored the concept of reducing a prison term for good behavior. That meant I'd be eligible for parole immediately. Roemer no longer had the GED excuse. And he had no political reason to deny me this time. He'd switched from Democrat to Republican, pissed off people in both parties in the process, and lost his re-election. But four days before he left office in January 1992, Buddy Roemer denied me that pardon again. He gave no reason.

That decision took a lot of wind out of my sails. The governor set things back for me and for all my supporters, who had been fighting an exhausting battle around my case. I was devastated.

Still, we didn't give up. The third pardon attempt was with Governor Edwin Edwards on June 10, 1995. The emphasis was on my involvement in positive activities and the fact that a print job was waiting for me in Los Angeles, along with a place to live with my sister Ella and her husband. The pardon request included multiple articles about Drama Club performances and certificates related to my organizational involvement and accomplishments. There was a support letter from former Angola warden John Whitley, who said I'd "matured into a leader, looked up to by inmates and respected by prison personnel." Letters also came from a long list of elected officials, including the mayor of New Orleans, two judges, the overwhelming majority of the Louisiana Legislative Black Caucus, a white state senator, and two white state reps. Prominent musicians like the Neville Brothers and Wynton Marsalis, a number of churches, and twenty-six other organizations also wrote in my support. And there was an excellent psychological evaluation by Dr. Beverly A. Howze, who had also evaluated me in 1989, and recommended me for pardon both times. The first time, she said I had "grown intellectually" since my arrest, because of "self-determination and drive" that was "imbued by family, community and cultural values." This time she wrote that although I was "devastated" by the denial of a pardon earlier, I remained "committed to personal growth," "exhibited pride" at all I'd accomplished, and was "in possession of leadership skills, combined with good values and self-resolve"—and "sharpness of wit."

This psychologist's words meant a lot to me. She saw how much I understood the destructive role of bitterness and how hard I'd worked to keep it at bay and maintain hope.

The board scheduled a hearing for March 13, 1995. The recommendation was again favorable with a vote of four to one, reducing my sentence to sixty years with parole possible after one-third of the sentence served. The board submitted their recommendation to Governor Edwards on June 19. Newspaper reporters asked him about me. First he mixed me up with Wilbert Rideau, the editor of the prison newspaper. When he was corrected, he said, "I remember that case. That kid's been in prison a long time. He should be home with his family." He made it seem that when my case came before him, he'd do something.

But when a Black state senator, Dennis Bagneris, came to talk about pardoning me, Edwards wouldn't commit, and afterward he denied the request. Later we learned from *The Morning Advocate* that Edwards was being investigated by a U.S. prosecutor for corruption and that L. J. Hymel, the prosecutor in my case who'd become a judge in Baton Rouge and was a friend of Edwards's, had tipped him off about it.

By this time, I was outraged. I saw what was really going on. These governors didn't want to be politically tainted by doing what was right. The experience only deepened my dissatisfaction and mistrust for the criminal legal system.

Whenever I came up for a pardon, L. J. Hymel always registered his opposition. Yet I found out he wrote a letter of support for one of the guys whose trial he presided over, Shelby Arabie—a white guy who killed another guy over a drug transaction—arguing that Arabie deserved a pardon and should have been convicted on a lesser charge. To me, that was just proof of his racial hatred toward me.

Mary and her team kept exploring other options. They talked to groups like the Innocence Project, but that team focused on cases involving DNA, which was not a factor in my situation. They also continued to research angles to take the case back to the fifth circuit court.

AFTER I GRADUATED FROM trade school in 1991, I had become part of the Angola paint crew. We put up buildings and fences, laid the foundation for basketball courts—we did it all. Our crew traveled outside the grounds as well. When I first got on there, I was one of the workers. As time went on, I became the paint crew clerk, taking care of the clerical tasks.

I was still on that crew when Hurricane Katrina hit in 2005. After the storm, a group of prisoners from Dixon were working at the main warehouse in Baton Rouge where people were sending donations of money and materials. Some of them got caught taking contraband back to Dixon. Deputy Warden Darrel Vannoy over at Angola told the authorities, "I know some people I can trust who we can send out there." They recruited six of us to go to Baton Rouge and sort stuff out in various bins to go out around the state. Then they sent us to New Orleans to bring water and other supplies, clean up the offices of police and fire departments, which had been flooded, and put up stop signs, since all the traffic lights were out in the city. The only people in New Orleans at the time were police, the National Guard, and some workers. Even the local parish prisons were empty—the authorities had sent everyone to Angola. For almost eight months, we commuted back and forth to New Orleans Monday through Friday. The situation there was bad. They kept finding bodies among piles of trash.

One day a guy—I wasn't sure if he was a worker or a deputy in plain clothes—came out and looked at me. "Man, you look familiar," he said. He asked where we were from.

"Angola," we said.

"There's a brother there named Gary Tyler. You know him?"

I said, "Yeah. Me and him are real close."

"Tell that brother we still support him."

"I'm going to let him know."

Afterward, a guy on our crew we called Turtle said to me, "You're cold-blooded. Why you didn't tell that guy who you are?"

I explained that I wanted to maintain my anonymity. Although I was widely known in the city, these law enforcement teams didn't know who I was, and I wanted to keep it that way. I just wanted to do the job.

Prisoners were essential during the Katrina recovery work in Mississippi as well. We found out that Governor Haley Barbour had commuted the sentences of a lot of those inmates for their humanitarian work. That put pressure on Louisiana governor Kathleen Blanco to do the same for prisoners in her state who had helped so much in New Orleans.

In early 2006, Deputy Warden Leslie DuPont talked to me about going back to the pardon board. I had my doubts. I'd approached that board three times and gotten their support without things turning out like I wanted. I shared my disappointment with him. "The only thing they could do is tell you no or yes," he said. Reluctantly, I agreed. Word had come down to Warden Burl Cain to submit the names of some guys who'd been going to New Orleans in the aftermath of Katrina. It started with a dozen of us. Then they started chopping up the list. They didn't want people with certain charges coming before the board. They narrowed it to five—me, Louis Cruz, Shelby Arabie, John Floyd, and Dana Nelson. The board started reviewing our cases. Mine was the last case scheduled for review. The four other guys felt like they were being retried and persecuted because of the harsh way they were being questioned.

By this time, a new attorney had joined our team. George Kendall was working with Wilbert Rideau on his appeal based on the racial makeup of the grand jury that heard his case. In my case, too, both the grand jury and the jury were all white. Mary, George, and I discussed this, and we decided to ask the pardon board to set my case aside because I was in the process of working on a new appeal. The board granted the request and that was it. Louisiana had changed their procedures. Now, if you were a lifer, you couldn't come to the pardon board until you had served at least fifteen years. After that, you could apply, but if you were denied, you had to wait another ten years to come back. Anyone denied a third time had to wait an additional five years, and so on. That was how they stacked the deck against us.

SOME GROUPS TOOK IT on themselves to pressure Governor Blanco into taking action to release me. In May 2006, more than two dozen world-class athletes wrote to her as "Jocks4Justice," asking her "in the name of justice and racial reconciliation" to pardon me and free me from Angola. The signers included Rubin "Hurricane" Carter, gold medalists Tommie Smith and John Carlos, all-star pitchers Jim "Bulldog" Bouton and Bill "Spaceman" Lee, and NBA star Etan Thomas. They didn't understand that the governor couldn't just pardon me on her own; the Board of Pardons had to recommend it first, after a prisoner formally applied. But it was always a great feeling to still have people coming out to support me all these years later.

On February 12, 2007, Amnesty International, which had put out that report on my case in 1994, also issued a statement calling on Blanco to pardon me. It summarized what it called a "serious miscarriage of justice" in my case and made a direct appeal to her. "Amnesty International is calling on Governor Blanco to rectify this shocking injustice by granting a pardon to Gary Tyler with immediate effect," they wrote, "and by ordering a full, independent investigation into his case so that anyone found to have been involved in any cover-up or abuse is brought to justice."

I kept on hoping for justice, but I didn't hold my breath. I knew I had to be steadfast, but I'd learned to be realistic. To keep my sanity, I stayed involved in as many prison activities as I could. I especially poured myself into two projects that had come to mean a lot to me: the Drama Club and the prison hospice program.

CHAPTER 13

QUALIFIED TO DO ANYTHING WITH NOTHING

When Ronald Little first asked me to join the Angola Drama Club in the summer of 1986, I told him, "I'm not into drama." I was twenty-eight years old; it had been a year since I'd been released into the general prison population. My focus was getting out of prison and furthering my education. But Ronald had been my friend since childhood. He told me that Herman Smith, the president of the club, was interested in me getting involved and wanted to know if I'd meet with him. I said I'd do that. Herman put my name on the "callout"—those happened on a Saturday and allowed you to go to any part of the prison where programming was happening.

Herman invited me into his office, told me about himself and how he'd established this Drama Club a decade earlier. "I've gotten a break in the court and am expecting to go home," he said. "This is a rebuilding time. I want good people to carry on the club after I get released." He said he really respected what he'd heard about me and thought I'd be a great asset to the organization. I wasn't keen on getting into acting. I also thought my real-life drama was way more important than make-believe drama. But Herman asked me to come to one of his meetings, and out of respect, I obliged. I went one Saturday and talked to some of the members. Besides Ronald, my close friend Lawrence Jenkins (Kenya) was getting involved. We'd known each other since meeting in Scotlandville. Kenya was also good friends with Clifford Doleman, who was very active in the club.

Before I attended that meeting, I hadn't realized that Herman was also teaching public speaking. That was something I had never done in my life. I found it awkward and intimidating to be up in front of people. I was fine with introducing myself or talking at the meetings Ms. Lemoine used to hold at my high school, but not getting up in front of a bunch of strangers. The first time I got up in the club, I felt exposed. I introduced myself with a very short statement, then sat and listened to other people, how they'd give different forms of speeches—introductory, informative, persuasive, motivational, and entertaining. I thought, Wow, this is something I'd like to learn. I started attending the meetings and taking classes every Saturday. After that I became a regular. In addition to public speaking, the club taught various life skills, including financial planning, parliamentary procedures, and how to conduct yourself in a meeting.

Herman let me know he wanted my support for his nephew Pat to become president after his anticipated release. I gave him my agreement. When the court date arrived, Herman didn't come back; he was freed that same day. All hell broke loose in the club. It hadn't dawned on me yet how treacherous prison politics could be, but I got a quick lesson. Since I'd already seen how politics worked in the free world, it wasn't hard to figure out. Some guys were going to try to take over the club—I realized that's why Herman had asked me to support his nephew. Sure enough, people tried to leverage connections with certain prison officials and get friends involved who hadn't been part of the organization, using them like fake electors. Me, Kenya, Clifford, and a few others stifled that. We used the Administrative Remedy Process (ARP) to file grievances with the administration. Herman's nephew turned out to be young and inexperienced. He wound up allying with the very people who were trying to take the organization from him. We put our support behind Clifford, who won the election.

But the conflict continued. The group who lost alleged we had people voting who weren't members. Assistant Warden Roger Thomas called for another vote and sent in a monitor, Big Brother Amin, a Muslim brother who worked on the Angola radio station and was well respected in the prison. Clifford won again. We thought Big Brother Amin would record the truth, but he didn't. For months we went back and forth. In the end, they ruled that neither Clifford nor the guy the assistant warden wanted could run. In November of that year, we voted for Vernon Chapman as president and Kenya as VP. The administration accepted that. I became sergeant at arms.

KENYA, CLIFFORD, AND I were like one person, close friends and comrades—we called ourselves the Three Amigos. We focused on what we were going to do together to have a positive influence at Angola. After assessing everything the Drama Club stood for, we realized it wasn't doing any drama at all. The three of us decided to use the club as a venue to educate both the prison population and the public. We started writing plays and doing skits. Mary Howell sent some material to add to what the club already had. We were studious, learning on the job, drawing from movies and television and whatever resources were available to us. It worked because we put our heads together. The plays we created collaboratively, and some people also wrote individual skits or monologues.

Our first breakthrough was a play by the three of us called *Execution: Who Has the Right?* After the prison carried out several executions, we wanted to raise awareness about just how cruel and unusual this was. To prepare, I described what had happened to me, how the police manufactured a case and accused me of a capital crime. Other members shared stories of being charged with first-degree murder that carried an automatic penalty of death. We had some inmate lawyers among us who helped with terminology. Glen Hebert created a perfect set with a model of the courtroom, electric chair, and execution chamber. The chair resembled the real thing, with straps and wires and a halo that went over the condemned man's head. The character kept professing his innocence, but nobody would listen. On the set we had a red phone waiting for a call from the governor's office. The phone rang right after the execution. The governor was one minute late.

We performed the play in the Visiting Shed on October 3, 1987. Over a hundred inmates and their outside guests saw it. The message was so powerful that some people in the audience cried. They hadn't understood the impact of capital punishment until we gave them this close-up view. After that night, our group developed a following among prisoners and their family members. We had established ourselves as being a politically astute organization that dealt with matters of importance.

As the Drama Club started taking off, we recognized we had something that could be very powerful. Our plays could send a message to the prison population without offending most of security. The following year we wrote *Just Us*, which we later performed for a Black History Month program on February 28, 1988. The play focused on the inequities of the criminal justice system, a system designed to protect "just us"—white folks—not all of us as a nation. The set showed performers in masks sitting in cells, wearing all black. The response was really positive. The year after that, we took one monologue from that play and turned it into its own production called *The Actor*. It shared the thoughts of a man in a prison cell who had already spent fifteen years in solitary. "I made a mistake, I got caught," he said. "Is that technical enough for you? You're fighting corruption with corruption. This kind of punishment accomplishes nothing."

In August of 1988, we faced another change in leadership at the Drama Club. Vernon was a good guy, but he did some underhanded things, not listening to members and allowing the organization to be used for shady operations, including misappropriating funds. Club members were alarmed and told him he had to go. Vernon resigned in anger. Kenya moved up to president and wanted me to be vice president. I told him no, I didn't want a position of responsibility. I was happy being sergeant at arms. But he kept on insisting until I said yes.

That wasn't the end of it. Every club had to have a sponsor, and the guard Jerry Wells happened to be ours. Sponsors had to sign off on whatever happened in the organization. Kenya did something that pissed Wells off, and he forced my friend out of the president spot. Clifford knew Wells and went to talk to him. Wells said he didn't like Kenya's attitude and didn't want him running the organization. "What about Gary Tyler?" Wells said. "That's who I want."

When Clifford came to me, I thought about it and said yes. My plan was to do it for a few months, then step down, hopefully get pardoned, and give Kenya his position back. After some time passed, I met with Wells myself. "I'm going to bring Jenkins back into a leadership position," I told him. "I need him. We have each other's backs." Wells still didn't want Kenya in, but I did.

"Okay," Wells told me, "just because of you, I will agree to that." It was amazing how things had changed, that he trusted my judgment and felt I was working in the best interests of the members in the club. I think he wanted me to see he wasn't the same person he'd been in the past. I remained president and brought Kenya back as VP.

We were proud of our accomplishments, but we also knew we had a lot to learn. In June of 1990, we invited a group of professors and writers from Baton Rouge to conduct a writers' workshop with us. Mary had introduced me to her close friend Deborah George Hardy, a poet who'd attended LSU with her. Deborah was quite influential, married to a movie producer, and had deep connections at LSU. The night she and the other speakers came in for the workshop was stormy. I was at the podium reciting Alice Walker's poem, "First, They Said," when the power went out. The room fell into total darkness. By then we had learned never to depend on the prison sound system. I was nervous, but I projected my voice and continued to recite to the end of the poem: "And now, the people protected, we wait for the next insulting words coming out of that mouth."

Deborah was incredibly helpful to the inmates who attended. Many of them had never written anything creative before. She returned for a second workshop in October of that year, along with Barry Kyle, a British producer who'd set up a theater company in Baton Rouge, and Pinkie Gordon Lane, the state's first Black poet laureate. Their process was to put us in groups and lead us in writing drafts. We'd read each other's pieces and give feedback. Deborah also helped us figure out ways to change sets quickly, putting up props for the next short play as we entered and exited the stage. With her help, we learned about blocking and ways to make scenes clearer. Barry Kyle taught us how to make violence on stage look realistic, how to cry for an audience, how to create what he called diagonal centers of action to make an argument even bigger. These techniques would make us more effective in achieving our goal: have people leave every play with something impactful to think about. Deborah wanted us to reach people outside of prison as well. She let us know she was trying to arrange a performance for us at Louisiana State University.

ON THE NINTH ANNIVERSARY of the Drama Club, in December 1991, we premiered two plays. *Unheard Cries* told the story of inmate despair and hopelessness because of the violence in prison. It showed guards and administrators turning a blind eye to guys being raped, beaten, and murdered. The second play, written by Clifford Doleman, Kenya, and myself, we called *Who's Killing African-Americans?* The sketch involved drug-dealing by guys who were boastful, sadistic, and abusive to drug users and women. A friend comes to see them who has just been released from prison after fifteen years and is now a changed person. "This is where the money is," they tell him, urging him to get back in the life. But the man refuses. "How can you blame the white man for pushing drugs if you're doing it, too?" he says. "You're part of the conspiracy, acting as if lives are disposable."

That night, Angola warden John Whitley sat in the front row. Afterward, he praised the plays in *The Angolite*. "I was impressed," he said. "It's obvious they worked very hard at putting on these performances, which showcased some of the untapped talent we've got here." Warden Whitley talked about us "taking [the] show on the road." This was the support we'd been waiting for. On January 15, 1992, Warden Whitley appeared before the Classification Board, and they made me a minimum class A trustee. That meant I was able to travel statewide to perform our plays.

We finally set our first engagement at LSU for February 18, 1993. The question was, were we ready? In addition to Deborah, we worked with a woman named Charlotte Nordyke, wife of attorney Keith Nordyke out of Baton Rouge, who did a lot of litigation for prisoners. Warden Whitley knew Charlotte and made the connection. When she came up to see us, Charlotte was amazed at how advanced we were and was glad to help with the areas where we still needed guidance. Always face the audience when you speak to them, she taught us. Never turn your backs.

That first performance at LSU, we put on *The Actor, Who's Killing African-Americans?*, and two other sketches, both about parenting. *A Day Between Friends* shows prison comrades confronting an inmate named James who doesn't want to admit he's been a neglectful father and contributed to his son getting in trouble with the law and his daughter becoming pregnant at a young age. Finally, James does what he can from prison to connect with and support his kids. The second play, *Concerned Parent Child Abuse*, begins with a guy entering a jail cell. He uses his one phone call to reveal how he became violent with his daughter for skipping school and afterward was unable to revive her. Just like with our prison performances, the audience—this time students and college personnel—loved the plays and gave us a standing ovation. A photographer named Lori Waselchuk from *The Morning Advocate* out of Baton Rouge captured highlights of our performance.

Over time, I acted in all our productions. I played one of the jackers in *Who's Killing African-Americans?*, a powerful play about the harm of drug dealing in our communities that we felt prisoners needed to see. I started playing James in *A Day Between Friends*, a role I really liked as an actor. Being in *The Actor* was a good opportunity for me to perform a monologue and get in touch with my own emotions, to transform myself on the stage.

We started to travel to schools and universities to perform, places like Southern University and University of Lafayette, high schools like Woodlawn in Shreveport and Clinton High School in East Feliciana Parish. It got to the point where we were traveling two or three times a week. After each play, we had a Q&A session. And at every performance, we had young people who would come up in tears saying how the plays had impacted them and how they could identify. They were often shocked to learn how long we had been incarcerated. Sometimes girls would tell us they had been victims of abuse. Audience members would ask if we knew their father, brother, cousin at Angola.

We traveled on a prison bus and returned to Angola after each performance. Generally we had two guards, unarmed, who traveled with seven of us. Warden Whitley trusted me to choose prisoners to participate. Eventually Clifford Doleman and a couple of the other main actors left Angola and went home. I recruited new people to take their places. We had a professional musician, Kevin Hayes, who we called Writer; he had gotten into trouble and wound up in Angola. Writer was a gifted keyboard and guitar player who had played with Charmaine Neville and scored each of our plays along with Myron Hodges, Robin Pork, and Samuel Bickham.

Our work was popular, but not everyone loved us. In November 1994, *Reader's Digest* ran an article called "Must Our Prisons Be Resorts?" The author named Angola's Drama Club and me—who they called "a convicted murderer"—as part of the problem, criticizing our travel to colleges and schools. It wasn't the first time a news publication had taken a swipe at us. I stopped doing interviews with *The Times-Picayune* and *The Morning Advocate* because of the way they had distorted my case. One day a lieutenant decided to play a game with security down the walk. Our props at Drama Club included toy guns and a toy MK-16. The lieutenant gave one of those guns to an inmate to scare another guard. That made the newspaper. The lieutenant got fired. "The inmates [in the Drama Club] didn't cause the problem," Warden Whitley said. "If I had more like them, I wouldn't have as many problems."

WHILE WE LOVED SHARING our work with a broader audience, that didn't change our focus of bringing new members into the Drama Club. We always had an open-door policy. When we realized that we had guys who wanted to be a part of the group but couldn't read or write, we had to address that. We devised a way to determine someone's literacy level—by using our club motto.

Kenya, Clifford, and I wanted to come up with a motto guys could feel proud of saying, that would help people feel like a family. Clifford got us started: "We should be willing to do what we can," he said. We said, "Yes, we are the willing." To that we added, "We are the willing, doing the impossible for the ungrateful. We have done so much with so little for so long, we are now qualified to do anything with nothing." Even working with the bare minimum in prison, we believed we could make things happen. To us the motto was about trusting in ourselves, uplifting our humanity and sense of worth.

The Drama Club met every Wednesday and Saturday evening from 6:00 to 9:30. When new inmates joined, we gave them the motto to learn. We'd see if someone could end the meeting by reciting the motto from memory or reading it out. Of course, we never put anyone on the spot. Our method was each one teach one. If a new guy needed help, someone would volunteer. "I got that," they'd say. "Don't worry about it, he'll know it next time." As time went on, this approach encouraged the guys who couldn't read or write to learn. They started writing about their experiences and what they thought about things, and many became functionally literate. Every meeting someone would start by writing two or three words or thoughts of the day on one of the chalkboards on the walls and say why they put those words up there. We watched people light up as they made their contributions. One of the finest qualities of a person is the ability to express themselves. In the Drama Club, people got rid of their internalized fear of doing so.

After a while, we started getting guys with mental problems who'd been isolated by others. Gay people joined and we let them know they were part of the family. The Drama Club was a place where we were all going to treat one another with respect. Any member who left Angola to go home or to a satellite prison or an out camp, knew one thing: If they came back, they could return to the Drama Club.

For us, Drama Club was far more than playing with fictitious characters. It was a means of helping our fellow prisoners better themselves by letting their guard down, talking about their issues with people they could trust. We involved hard-core inmates who had difficulty listening and often acted out. Seeing people like themselves on the stage was inspiring and made them want to do it as well. That lifted their self-esteem and got them to do more. It worked because we took on subject matter drawn from inmates' reality and their traumas.

In many ways, the Drama Club was therapeutic. We worked with members who needed to acknowledge what they had done to hurt others and make amends with themselves in order to start healing. "Don't allow what you were convicted for to define you for the rest of your life," we'd say. "Your life didn't end when you entered this place, because you had a chance to change." For those like me who were in prison for something they didn't do, being able to articulate what had happened and gain support provided relief.

Even those who had done something that caused harm often faced injustices in treatment and sentencing. "I'll tell you the truth: I am guilty," someone might say, "but the crime didn't happen the way they said it did." Or, "Look, man, the guy came at me and I was only defending myself." Or, "By being an ex-felon and having a gun when you're not supposed to, automatically they're going to say you're the perpetrator." We heard people describe how the state hadn't shown any real evidence or had manufactured some. Many faced longer sentences and worse treatment because of racist assumptions and unfair laws. In 1995, I shared that my baby brother, Richard, had gotten twenty years for stealing a radio out of a car. Initially they offered him five years, but he refused. He was on drugs at the time. The Jefferson Parish police officers beat him so bad, he filed a suit against them.

Crucial to our approach was guaranteeing that whatever we disclosed in meetings was for ourselves and no one else. Breaking that pledge would be seen as breach of trust, a cardinal sin. No one ever broke it.

As the club developed, I did, too. At first it was a facade, but after a while, I grew into someone who was interactive and caring. I realized the road the organization was traveling was making a difference in many of these guys' lives. It worked because we were always active and persistent. The members inspired us. They trusted us to lead them. Each person who came in, we gave him a Drama Club packet. The packet included fourteen rules of conduct, including: "Don't allow members to deal with personalities during meetings; don't fail to take part in debates if you have a viewpoint to express or want information; don't come inside the organization unkempt or unfit unless there's a valid reason." The guys knew this was an organization where they could be themselves and really talk. It was like a union.

Their trust helped me take on the characteristics of those who had protected and mentored me, the leaders I'd met in CCR and also the ones I'd read about. I became a big brother, an uncle, a mentor myself. People started telling me, "Gary, you got all these youngsters trying to run up behind you." If guys who ran organizations had a problem with someone, they'd send them to me. Together with Kenya and Clifford, I taught discipline, responsibility, focus, how to be a man and a leader, by setting an example. When I gave a person my word, I tried to live up to that, to make sure I checked on people and showed them I cared about them.

As president, I would let other people conduct the club's business to give them a sense of how leadership is formed. If anyone said, "I don't listen to nobody but Gary Tyler," I'd call the individual in charge aside and say, "If you're leading, I expect everyone to listen to you and respect you as though you were me."

Most of our members were Black, but we welcomed white members as well. In 2008, John Valdez, who had participated in the killing of Scully in the dungeon when I was still on death row, was moved to Pine dormitory. After Scully's death, I had refused to be a witness against Valdez, knowing that the murder was a hit perpetrated by a high-ranking officer on the hill. In that dorm, John Valdez heard some white guys trying to dissuade another white guy who had joined the Drama Club. "It's a Black club," they told him.

Valdez said, "You talking about the Drama Club that Gary Tyler runs? That guy is solid. You want to learn something, Gary Tyler can teach you. He's a good guy."

I learned the story from that white guy who remained a member of our club.

EVEN AS I MADE new friends at Drama Club, I never forgot about my old friends, especially the guys in CCR. I didn't see Fox or Hooks again until 1988, when the prison closed CCR for renovation and transferred them temporarily to the Mental Health Unit. I was still working in the Main Prison kitchen then, but they needed workers at that unit. I was selected to go as an orderly from July '88 until June '89 and help distribute food.

While I was there, I got to know and become friends with Daron Brown, a Black guard who had become a lieutenant. He used to let me go on the tier and holler at Hooks and Fox and Moja, now known as the Angola Three for fighting against inhumane conditions at the prison, their unjust convictions, and prolonged solitary confinement. I'd ask them what they wanted. "Can you bring some doughnuts?" they'd say. I'd buy boxes of doughnuts from the vets' organization who sold them in the Visiting Shed.

After Jerry Wells died of cancer in 1992, Daron Brown became sponsor of the Drama Club. If I wanted to come over to see my CCR friends, I'd call Brown, and for a number of years, he'd arrange for me to be able to do that. Fox, Hooks, and Moja would tell me about their struggle, how they were doing everything they could to get their convictions overturned. They were also interested in what was happening with my case. We were in contact with many of the same people. Being with them again was like a family reunion. Those three always thought positive; the energy stayed high. "Keep up the good work," they'd say. They were proud of me for doing the work they would have been doing if they were out of solitary.

Being head of the Drama Club created other opportunities for me as well, including the opportunity to meet filmmakers. Thanks to big tax breaks, Louisiana was a cheap place to make movies. Directors of films that had prison scenes, like *Dead Man Walking* with Susan Sarandon, liked to come to Angola. At first they paid prisoners to play extras in those scenes. But after Burl Cain became warden in 1995, he put an end to that, claiming payment was illegal but the filmmakers could offer gifts like Moon Pies and cold drinks. It was common knowledge that Cain made private deals on the side. He could have been the model for that warden in *The Shawshank Redemption* or the one in *Cool Hand Luke*. Cain never went to jail, but he did come under investigation for loaning out prisoners to do free labor for rich friends in the community.

In 1997, a crew came to Angola to film scenes for the movie *Out of Sight*. John Hardy, husband of the Drama Club's friend Deborah, was a producer for that film. They came to Angola with director Steven Soderbergh and actors Jennifer Lopez, George Clooney, Don Cheedle, and Ving Rhames. The assistant warden for treatment contacted me to say the movie crew had requested that members of the Drama Club be part of the production. I talked to the guys. "If they aren't going to pay us, we're not going to be part of it," they said. "If we want Moon Pies and cold drinks, we can go to the canteen and get them." I shared these sentiments with Deborah, and she understood. They were shooting the basketball scene out of the Main Prison cell block, but me and my guys didn't show up.

At some point, Deborah requested that Wilbert Rideau and I come on the set and explain these feelings. They were filming a scene back by the old church, where John Hardy introduced us to everyone. When that group saw my T-shirt, which had "Angola Drama Club" on the front and "We are the willing" on the back, they asked where they could get one. "From the Drama Club," I said. Major Sam Smith brought me back to our office in the Main Prison, and I grabbed a bunch of shirts. The actors bought them all.

Deborah told them about the work we were doing in the club. When they weren't shooting, we'd spend breaks and eat meals together. It was surreal sitting among people of such stature. After the movie came out, we saw it on the prison TV station.

I enjoyed meeting talented people like these. Things had certainly changed; I was no longer subjected to the harassment I endured during my years in CCR and immediately after moving into the Main Prison population. But I knew anything could happen, and occasionally it did. On August 23, 2001, I was called from work on the paint crew to report to the Main Prison office. The lobby officer told me a shakedown crew wanted me upstairs in the office of the Drama Club. To my surprise, the room had been torn up and everything thrown around. One of the shakedown officers who I knew told me they'd found an X-rated videotape. At first I thought he was joking, but he showed me where they found it in an open file cabinet and asked me who it was for. Of course, I didn't know, and if I had, I wouldn't have told him. They put me in administrative lockdown for nineteen days for having contraband in the office.

On September 12, 2001, the day after the 9/11 attacks—which I found out about that night from an inmate counselor—I was released and received an apology from Sam Smith. Turns out the film had been shown on a local TV station and wasn't sexually explicit at all. If Assistant Warden Kalone had just reviewed it, he'd have seen it was fine, but looking at it was against his moral principles. Still, the whole incident could have been worse. I needed the rest and I lost twenty pounds.

CHAPTER 14

PROMISES KEPT

The vast majority of prisoners at Angola die there. Friends of mine would eventually get sick and be moved over to the Treatment Center (TC). That would often be the last we'd see them unless we got a pass from a colonel or warden, which was like trying to get an act of Congress. The treatment was callous, as if that inmate had never been a person. It was no different from how slaves died on the plantation, thrown in a hole with no regard and no time for their loved ones to mourn them. They were disposable and replaceable.

Things got even worse at Angola when AIDS and HIV hit the scene in the late eighties. Prisoners were dying at a disproportionate rate. In fall of 1993, when I was thirty-five, a public health nurse named Shannon Hager came to one of my Drama Club functions and asked if my group would be willing to take a class and become HIV and AIDS counselors. I talked to the guys and they said yes. That October, a group of us spent thirty-six hours training with Nurse Hager and William Crawford from the Department of Public Health. Afterward, we became counselors and started teaching guys in the prison about HIV and AIDS prevention. It was news to folks that the disease was transmitted by sex and by sharing needles—and that it wasn't spread through mosquito bites or toilet seats.

Nurse Hager and Mr. Crawford were part of a national program that decided to hold its HIV/AIDS Prevention Conference at Angola in October 1994. They asked the Drama Club to put a play together. We liked the idea, and the whole group collaborated on writing *The Enemy Within*. It showed a group of inmates meeting and talking with an HIV/AIDS counselor. I played that role. A guy who had forced someone to become his sexual slave came in and tried to disrupt the class. My character used that moment to inform the group that this guy's behavior with other prisoners was one way HIV and AIDS got passed on. Our cast got a standing ovation from the over one hundred participants. I still have the clip from the *Baton Rouge City Advocate* that described the conference and our play.

People saw how this kind of storytelling could help educate the public. That network held a follow-up conference at Angola on November 14, 1995. Nurse Hager said we had been the highlight of the program and invited us to perform again. Our club VP, Percy Tate (Baki), wrote a new play called *HIV Exit vs HIV Entry: The Unwanted Hitchhiker*. We wanted to dispel the myths the prison population had about the real causes of this epidemic. Once again the audience loved it.

At that event we met Carol Evans and Rhonda Herzog, both social workers, who told us how much they'd liked our production. They came back in March 1997 and approached a group of us, including me, Norris Henderson, and Wilbert Rideau, about whether Angola had a hospice program. We told them no. "Would the prison population be open to having a hospice?" they asked us. We told them they needed to approach Warden Cain. They did, and he thought it was a great idea. At first, inmates were conflicted. Angola had a program where someone who was terminally ill could apply for a medical parole. Guys worried that starting a hospice would impede those paroles. But in time, most inmates warmed up to the idea, seeing that hospice gave easy access to visiting friends who were ill. People also realized how hard it was to get a medical parole unless you had a highly publicized case.

I had heard of hospice before, but I understood it to be a place where knights who sustained grave injuries would go to recover from their wounds or eventually die from them. As I learned what hospice really meant, I associated it with care common in the Black community; when someone became very ill, family and community members would step in and go to their home to help.

TO GET THE PROGRAM started, they needed volunteers. I was one of the inmates in leadership positions selected to be in the first batch. In October 1997, we underwent two weeks of intense hospice training, learning about death and dying, ways to communicate with hospice patients, how diseases progress, and some things about the bereavement process. Our volunteer group held their first meeting on November 19, 1997. The person in charge was Tanya Tillman, RN, the inmate volunteer care coordinator. At the time, she was not well liked. Most of us perceived her as being too sympathetic to security. But after working with her, I saw how she really cared about the patients. Tanya won everybody over, me included. She was one of the most beautiful and caring people I met at Angola. The guys called her Mother Goose.

The training we got was very detailed and arduous. Sometimes when you first volunteer to do something, you have no idea what you'll have to go through to prepare. And no matter how hard you train, when you start the activity, you find that you're not actually prepared. Still, you have the tools—in this case, how to change a diaper, how to bathe someone, help them get dressed, feed them, change their bed. When it gets down to helping an individual out of bed and onto the toilet and then cleaning him afterward, the work can become quite challenging. You're talking about one man delicately taking care of another because he's not able to do any of these things himself. You trained for this, but you may have reservations. Men touching each other was a big taboo at Angola, and touch was a key part of hospice care. Some people backed out. A few quit when the first person assigned to them died. They cared but still had a complex about death.

I certainly felt challenged when I took care of my first patient in May of 1998. Lawrence Charles was in his late fifties, diagnosed with terminal prostate cancer. We didn't know each other, but he had asked for me based on what he'd heard about me. I was called upon to do a job, but I still lacked self-confidence and wasn't sure I'd be able to deal with his impending death. When I introduced myself, I tried to hide the fact that I was nervous and kind of lost. But I soon realized what was most important: this was about him, not me. He was facing the end of his life and I could help ease that process. It turned out Lawrence had lived in St. Charles Parish across the river in Killona, Louisiana. That connection allowed us to have conversations and break down our apprehensions about this relationship. We became friends. Lawrence Charles died two months later. It was surreal watching how his life left his body, knowing I'd never see him again. He was there one day and then he was gone.

Each patient is different. Some people are resigned that they're going to die, and some fight like hell. We learned to listen and to be open and honest. We saw that dealing with the first patient does prepare you to move on to the next. I understood the importance of making sure no one died alone.

When we cared for a patient, we were on twenty-four-hour call. We could automatically leave if the Treatment Center called for us in the dormitory or on a job site. Each of us chose our shifts and the number of days we'd do our time of caring or of vigil. I got off my paint crew job at three in the afternoon, and might volunteer between ten at night and two in the morning. How many days I kept that schedule depended on how close the patient was to dying.

In late November of 1998, my two worlds, drama and hospice, overlapped when the hospice program held its first annual banquet and invited the Drama Club to perform a skit. We wrote one about the transitional stages people go through when they're dying. Even though it was a serious subject, we managed to make the play humorous, like showing the struggle to turn a patient over to prevent bedsores and having the guy worry you're trying to hurt him. The audience needed a laugh, and they loved it.

My next patient, Leroy Rayford, was only forty-three years old. I sat with him for several months. His cancer had metastasized, and the pain was intolerable. I saw relief in his eyes when he passed in June of 1999.

That was how I learned that some patients in the final stage of dying welcome death.

Sometimes a patient wanted a medical parole as well as hospice so they could die at home. Melvin Lewis was a good friend I took care of in early 2000. Like me, he'd been sent to prison young and given the death penalty, and he'd fought hard to get his conviction overturned. His mother died on the same day Corrections Secretary Richard Stalder denied him a medical parole. I saw Melvin's world crumble and there was nothing I could do. On Valentine's Day, I got a call in the middle of the night to come to the Treatment Center. I had made a promise to him that he wouldn't die alone.

I made and kept that promise for many people, but I generally avoided funerals at Angola. Before hospice, when a patient died, they placed him in a plain pine box and put him in a hole with no real ceremony. After the hospice program began, leaders of the Angola Special Civics Project, the Human Relations Club, and *The Angolite* convinced Warden Cain to give more dignity to those who died, with nice coffins built by prisoners, placed in a refurbished hearse pulled by horses. I still stayed away, with one exception.

Charlie Hamilton was an inmate who hadn't liked me at first, when I was a graphic arts student and he worked as a clerk in that department. He was under the impression that I hated white people. One day I tipped him off after I overheard security saying they were going to bust him for making gambling tickets. I did that because I understood there were people who didn't have any support from the outside and did whatever was necessary to survive. Guards pulled Charlie aside in a shakedown booth and went through his belongings, but they never found any contraband. He thanked me afterward and apologized for judging me wrongly and not finding out for himself what kind of person I was. When he was in hospice, Charlie made me promise that I would come to his funeral. It was the only one I ever attended in Angola.

THOSE EARLY YEARS WERE a time of growth for the hospice program, which had gained financial support from outside the prison. The resources made it possible for the paint crew to build a special place for hospice volunteers, known as the New Hospice Chapel. It was adjacent to the Treatment Center, where an area on Ward 2 along with four rooms had been set aside for hospice patients. We built that chapel using raw strength. The yard couldn't take heavy equipment, so we got up on a scaffold and were lifting beams to put the building together. People watched us and were amazed.

The dedication ceremony for the chapel was held on November 10, 2000. Ronda Herzog and Carol Evans were the backbone of the Prison Hospice Project and oversaw the fundraising and construction along with Jamey Boudreaux, executive director of the Louisiana Mississippi Hospice & Palliative Care Organization. Thanks to them, donations came in from all over. The program was a novelty that many people thought was a good thing.

Still, more was needed. Our volunteer group wanted to know what we could do to help. Our goal was to make the patients comfortable and also give them something that wasn't sold in the prison canteen, like a nice bathrobe. After all, these would be their final days. Family members were also driving long hours to come to Angola to see their loved ones. We wanted to help them get good food and a hotel stay. The guys started kicking around ideas to raise money.

We needed something practical, so at first we sold sno-cones in the Visiting Shed. Each time someone ordered a cone, we would fill out a ticket and they'd take that to the cashier booth and pay. At the end of the day, the cashier would calculate the totals, put the money in a bag, and send it to the Administration Building on the hill, where it would be deposited in the organization's account. When we needed to buy anything, we'd fill out a purchasing form requesting it.

Then we came up with a bigger plan: making and selling quilts. After the first group of hospice volunteers finished our training, the prisoners celebrated by making a signature quilt we all contributed designs to in teams, a collage to hang in the Hospice Chapel; one of the nurses sewed it together. One of the guys, Ted Durbin, had a sewing machine; inmates who were hobby crafters were allowed to have materials and equipment. Afterward someone said, "Why not keep making quilts and sell them at the hobby craft concession booth in the Visiting Shed and also at the rodeo [a public event that took place at Angola every April and October]?

We could raise a lot more money." All of us liked this idea. I wrote a request to the warden to build a hospice booth at the rodeo. As soon as he approved it, I found a spot for us in the old arena and started hustling blocks and cement. The guys went to work making quilts in the Hospice Chapel. Every dollar made went back to the program.

The prisoners were using the Hospice Chapel as the place to do their sewing. And then in August of 2002, Warden Linda Miller, who'd come from the Louisiana Correctional Institute for Women to oversee Angola's hospital, falsely accused hospice volunteers of playing rap music in the chapel. She used that as an excuse to shut down the quilting work. It was hard to imagine how anyone could confuse Aretha Franklin with rap, but Warden Miller insisted that's what she heard.

That meant the hospice volunteers had nowhere to make quilts. My office as Drama Club president was in the back of the gym. Next to it was a room used to repair wheelchairs and beds for the hospice patients. I had taken over that shop when the previous guy in charge got released. People approached me about using that space to sew quilts because they were pressed for time; the rodeo was coming up in October. I told them, of course. That's not all they wanted, though—they needed me to help finish a quilt. I was reluctant. To me, quilting was not a manly thing to be doing. But one thing led to another and I said I would. Kenya had become part of the quilting crew. The guys showed me what they wanted me to do, how to cut out material, what instrument to use, how to sew. I started putting pieces together and saw how it became one quilt. And much to my surprise, I got really interested. I decided to make a quilt of my own to see how it would feel.

At first, I cut out patterns and sewed together pieces. I definitely got satisfaction, knowing it was something I created from beginning to end. I was making shapes and windmills. The more I understood about the process, though, I began to feel our quilts were too commercial. People were using printed fabric of cartoons and the like from the store. I wanted to make something traditional, adding more intricate details. As I wondered how I could enhance my work, I thought about the technique of appliqué I'd learned in graphic arts school and whether I could use it in quilting. And that's what I started doing. I made designs, stars, various African symbols, a giant Spiderman, then put those on quilts and sewed them up. The more I worked with appliqué, the better I became. Everything I made, sold!

I found myself reflecting back on times I would go to the country in Tallulah to visit my grandmother, and how I would see her making quilts. They kept us warm. She made them out of rags, with the stuffing put together from old clothing, newspapers and moss. Also, I remembered how my mother would use the patterns in the Sears and JCPenney catalogs to make dresses for herself and my sisters. Those memories gave me comfort, knowing I was following the tradition of my grandmother, my mother. At the age of forty-four, it seemed like my life had come full circle.

For our hospice quilts, we used prison materials like chambray shirts and blue jeans. Then we entered a contest in Baton Rouge and created a quilt with an Abraham Lincoln image. The women quilters couldn't believe guys in Angola were making quilts. They came to the prison and brought us quilting magazines and various fabrics. After that, we'd have the hospice coordinator go and buy us material and threads. We gave our quilt shop a name: Stitch in Time.

I began to love quilting, especially when I saw the results for hospice patients. We'd make a quilt for the patient, and when he expired, it went home to the family. They felt honored and loved, that they had something their loved one had wrapped himself in on the ward.

The quilts we sold went for $35 to $100, depending on the size. I decided to start making signature quilts with special rodeo themes that would be raffled out, so they would raise more money and get a fairer price for all the hours and hours of work that went into them. The next time we needed to make a feature quilt to raffle off at the rodeo, I took on that project.

THE SPRING RODEO FELL on a Saturday and Sunday in the third week of April. They also held a rodeo every Sunday in October. Thousands of people came to watch prisoners compete in events involving broncos and bulls or horses. In addition to the competitions, there were food concessions from popcorn to jambalaya, hot dogs, fried chicken, and alligator balls. Inmates and free people organizations used those concessions to raise money. Hobby crafters would sell various kinds of artwork. Those guys could keep the money to support themselves while in prison. Since most inmates were from poor families, they usually sent whatever little money they made to support their children.

One major rodeo event called "Guts and Glory" involved putting a token on the bull's forehead and awarding $500 to the prisoner who grabbed it. Up to a dozen inmates would get out in the ring while others in the chute shocked the bull with an electric cattle prod until it came out raving mad and began attacking everything in front of it. If no one snatched the token, the prize went up to $1000 and kept going up until someone succeeded. Another event was called "Convict Poker." Four guys would sit at a table that had been painted red, in chairs painted red, while a bull weighing two to three thousand pounds was being held in a chute and hit with an electric cattle prod. The bull would come out of the chute raving and charge at that table. The last person remaining at the table when the bull came in contact would win a money prize.

I saw guys get killed, paralyzed, mauled, or left with a broken arm or leg at those rodeos. There were always inmates with no family support or other ways to access money who were willing to put their life or limb on the line to win a cash prize. People also liked the attention. The public would hear each contestant's name announced and what they were in prison for. Whoever was successful would become very popular. The audience would cheer for them at the next event.

It was just like a gladiator sport. I knew guys who did this, but I was not crazy or suicidal. I had fought too hard to stay alive to risk my life like that. Still, it was a good place for us to sell things and raise funds for hospice.

The quilt I created for that rodeo featured a bull with a gold token in the middle of his head and a prisoner reaching for it. The quilt was raffled off. I was still president of the Drama Club, so I had to sit at our concession booth, where we sold tacos and taco salads. What really made me feel good was when people stopped by and told me, "Man, everybody wanted your quilt." The hospice group sold a lot of raffle tickets, $30,000 or more, and it all went to the hospice program. People came to me wanting me to make one just like it for a wife or associate. I told them, "I don't do duplicates, only one of a kind."

WHILE I WAS IMMERSED in the hospice work, an extraordinary change had happened in my own life. On September 20, 2000, I became a father. My child's mother had started to visit Angola for a research project. She was a graduate of Texas A&M who became valedictorian there. Unlike my feelings for Gilda Parks, this was a platonic relationship. One day she asked me whether I'd ever thought about having children when I got out.

"Yes," I told her.

"Do you want a girl or a boy?" she wondered.

"I love girls," I told her, "but I want a son to carry on my name and my legacy."

"What if I told you I'd be willing to make that possible, give you a son?" she said.

I was blindsided by this. She encouraged me to think about it and let her know. The more I thought about it, the more serious I became about the possibility. We found an opportunity to be together and she became pregnant. I made a baby crib with my coworker, Roy Jones, who was a carpenter. Security suspected this woman was pregnant by me. When they saw the baby, they were happy for me, friendly to her and my son, and kept it to themselves.

One guard came to me and said quietly, "Gary, I know that's your son because he looks just like you." I could see the boy had my facial features.

Another asked me, "How did you make that possible?"

"Immaculate conception," I replied, "like Mary was impregnated by the Holy Spirit."

My son, Damaryos, and his mother visited me until he was six months old, when they moved outside the U.S. Every chance his mother got, she'd bring him back to see me.

I felt really good about having a son. The first time I held him after his mother got out of the hospital, I smiled at him and I swear, he smiled back.

"He did not smile!" his mother said.

"I'm telling you, he did," I told her. I was giddy. I was a really proud father.

When the boy was three, I made him a Spiderman quilt and unveiled it in the Visiting Shed. At first, he acted like he didn't like it. Then people started coming to the table asking who sewed the quilt. "I did," I said. They all wanted one like it.

Damaryos immediately grabbed it and said, "This my quilt." He loved it.

The next year, I bought him a nice bike. Angola has a bicycle shop where they repair bikes and give them to kids. I brought the bike to the Visiting Shed and he took off on it. I could tell security was beginning to get agitated. I stood in front of him and held on to the handlebars. "Get your hands off my bike," he told me.

I looked him in the eyes. "Son, if security takes this bike away, I won't be able to get it back for you. But if you give it to me, you can take it home with you."

"Okay, Daddy," he said.

When he was about six, Damaryos came and stayed with my sister Jennifer in Destrehan for several months and saw me quite often. I was thrilled to have him there, but I asked my family not to say he was my son. I didn't want him to be in harm's way.

On one of those visits, he pointed to a slightly older Black girl, dark-skinned with dreads. "Dad," he said, "when I'm older, my girlfriend is going to look like her."

"What you know about girls?" I asked him. He just gave me a big smile. This was the same kid who told me when he grew up, he wanted to join Special Forces and then become an action film star like Sylvester Stallone and Arnold Schwarzenegger.

During those years, I drew a lot of satisfaction from my child and from my work in hospice. No one messed with me and my son. But the hospice program experienced its share of trouble from the prison administration.

ON APRIL 22, 2004, Hospice Coordinator Tillman called us to the chapel and told us she was resigning. She claimed it was for family reasons, but we had our sources and knew who was working to undermine her control of the program. We threatened to quit if she left. The people in charge started to panic. Nurse Tillman got up and asked us to stay, reminding the volunteers we had a responsibility to patients and the prison population to keep the program going. For the time being, she stayed as well. A few weeks later, however, there was an incident with a volunteer trying to walk off with some tennis shoes she had purchased for one of the patients. She had a run-in with security over it and didn't bite her tongue. Security escorted her off the prison grounds. We never saw her again. I really felt disheartened by her departure. So did everyone else.

Less than six months later, I received a call from the security supervisor informing me that I was being taken off the list of hospice volunteers by orders of Assistant Warden Donnie Barr. I felt totally blindsided. I was committed to my patient and I had no idea what had happened. That same day I went to the supervisor's office to find out what was going on.

"It's a security matter," he told me, "nothing you did."

That made no sense to me, so I went to see the program coordinator, Monica Saizan, who fought to get me back in the program. This woman was small in size but no pushover. It felt really good to have her stand up for me the way she did, but I also knew security wouldn't like having a free person, especially a woman, speaking out like that. I told her so. "I don't give a damn," she said.

Eventually we found out the real story. Weeks earlier, some volunteers had complained to Warden Cain that security was giving them a hard time and interfering with the functioning of the program. Cain sent Chaplain Tony to meet with us in the Hospice Chapel. The chaplain told us to take our hats off. I raised my hand and politely said, "With all due respect, it's always been understood that no religion takes precedence over others in this chapel. The chapel is nondenominational and everyone is welcome regardless of their religious or ideological persuasion. Some faiths require wearing a hat."

Major Ronnie Constance interrupted and ordered me to take off my hat. I complied and thought nothing of it.

A month and a half later, the chaplain was on vacation with Warden Cain out of state and told him about this incident. The warden had security investigate. They concluded I did nothing wrong, but decided it was best to remove me anyway. From my past interactions with Warden Cain, I knew that in his mind, prisoners had no right to disagree with free personnel.

Warden Cain met with our group and Chaplain Tony and agreed the punishment was too severe. I was proud to know that the hospice coordinator along with the volunteers had threatened to resign unless I was put back in. Still, he said I should have some punishment and made it a ninety-day suspension from the hospice program. Chaplain Tony apologized for making a big deal out of nothing. Even though it was unfair, I knew the nature of the beast I was dealing with. But Nurse Saizan resigned over it. She felt she couldn't trust these leaders and didn't appreciate things they said to her for supporting me. That was another big loss to hospice.

In May 2007, we had an opportunity to meet with Corrections Secretary Stalder and a California commission to stop prison rape. There was a special callout for all inmate counsels, *Angolite* staff, club presidents, and inmate ministers. Some hospice volunteers agreed to meet with commission members later that night in the Hospice Chapel. Cathy Martinez, president of the commission, hoped to find answers from prisoners. Thanks to Albert Woodfox, Herman Wallace, and others, some great work had gone on at Angola. Instead of letting us share that, Warden Cain bombarded the visitors with praise of Jesus Christ. Cain went on and on about how God made it possible for him to show everyone compassion and mercy, which had changed the environment at the prison. Because of his compassion, he said, prisoners had forsaken their evil ways and turned their lives over to the Lord Jesus Christ. No one was allowed to answer the woman's questions about stopping rape. I tried, but my efforts were thwarted. People were looking for viable solutions, not to be proselytized and preached at.

We made sure that never happened in the hospice program, where listening to the patient guided our work. I know that every patient I tended left an impression on me. I was honored to be able to ease their passing. After five years working in hospice, I had also become a bereavement counselor to help hospice volunteers and other inmates and their family members deal with losing someone. I was one of seven people chosen for the training that began in September 2002 and lasted for nine weeks. In addition to dealing with the grieving process, we learned how to create an environment where it felt safe to express grief. When guys sit with someone who's dying, they learn some intimate things about that patient, who often becomes really close and dear to them. After the person expires, they need time to grieve, to cry, to express their feelings about this person who existed in their life but was no longer with us. The guys who had taken someone else's life were especially changed by the experience.

In September 2006, I was asked to help train new hospice volunteers. I was glad to share what I'd learned. The most important thing, I'd tell them, was to put the patient's interests first. Our responsibility was to tend to that person and be there for them. It was important never to lie or give false hope or inject our own views about God or anything else. If the patient shared something private, we needed to keep it private. "Listen attentively," I'd say, "and always keep your word. If you can reflect back on a time when your grandparents got old and couldn't do much for themselves, and your mother would go visit to feed them and clean the house, and you were there as a little kid, taking out the trash and wiping things down, you were doing a form of hospice care whether you realized it or not." In a family, we understood when it was our time to render care for people who cared for us and now needed us. In hospice, we needed to bring that kind of care to each patient.

In all, I provided assistance to approximately one hundred men who died at Angola. Every death was different but memorable, and the work was rewarding. Through my work in hospice and by becoming a father, I found a profound appreciation of life and of caring for others at every stage of their lives. Warden Cain had noted at the beginning of our hospice program that at least 85 percent of the inmates at Angola would die there. I made a solemn promise to myself I was going to be part of the 15 percent who did not.

CHAPTER 15

CAST THE FIRST STONE

The idea for prisoners to perform a passion play came from Cathy Fontenot, an assistant warden who'd gone to Scotland in 2009 and seen a production of *The Life of Jesus Christ* at a castle there. Later, she urged the head warden, Cain, to have this play performed at Angola. Cain wanted to change the mindset of the prisoners by proselytizing Christianity, so she reminded him that this would help. Angola had a large religious community and a Bible college, the New Orleans Baptist Theological Seminary, right on prison grounds. Warden Cain agreed the play would be a good thing. They had the land, the manpower. He told Assistant Warden Fontenot to put the idea into effect. Of course, they weren't considering the logistics and the work that would have to be put into such a production.

In early 2011, Fontenot called a meeting with the heads of all the religious groups at the prison. She showed them the script and told them the warden wanted the religious community to come together and make it happen.

"That's above our pay grade," they told her, reminding her they didn't know much about theater. When the assistant warden asked who could possibly do this, my name came up.

"Would Gary be willing?" she asked.

"If anybody can get it done, it's Gary," they said. "He has the respect of the prison population; people listen to him. He gets along with everybody. And he has the Drama Club. They do performances all the time."

With that recommendation, Fontenot got security to call me to meet her in the A Building. She was one of the wardens people felt they could go to. I had done a play at her request some years back about the Board of Pardons, for a meeting that took place at the Training Academy. I selected a few guys from the hospice program to portray pardon board members debating a prisoner's fate. At the time the board was packed with victims' rights advocates who favored harsh treatment for inmates. We wanted to show how that board essentially put the people who came before them on trial instead of listening and rendering mercy. Our performance was done in front of corrections officers, state police, and other agency recruits, along with parole officers and judges. Some of those judges were fed up that they didn't have more discretion, that people in Louisiana were having to receive far longer sentences than elsewhere, and that the pardon board wasn't helping. They liked the performance. For others it was controversial, but Fontenot had been pleased with it.

She filled me in about this "marvelous production" she'd seen in Scotland and the support from Warden Cain. Would I be willing to make this happen? Sitting next to her was a big old stack of paper. It turned out to be the script, which included information on how to set up a promenade production, where the audience walked among the actors while they were performing.

"This would be really good for the prison population," she said.

The script looked like a couple law books on top of each other. I didn't want to touch it.

"Why are you coming to me?" I asked her. "You have a religious community that I'm not a part of, because I'm not a Christian."

I am a spiritual person, but not a religious one. I was born in a Christian family, baptized, and aspired to become a preacher. But I had become disillusioned about religion. Why would Jesus forsake me, a kid? Over time I came to renounce my faith. I tried to become a Muslim, but I wasn't satisfied with that either. Finally I realized I was going in circles. Why run from one religion to another when I could become a truth-seeker, someone who aspires to do right and avoids getting into a war about which religion is better than the other? My fight was to get out of prison. I had decided I didn't have to be a member of anyone's church. I didn't have to become an ordained minister to prove my beliefs. If I stayed true to myself, then people would appreciate me for who and what I am.

Still, I had respect for the religious groups at Angola and worried this would be an affront to them.

"They're the ones who sent me to you," Fontenot said.

That took me by surprise. Knowing the men in the religious community, though, I realized they didn't have the ability to organize auditions and the other steps necessary to make something like this happen. They knew I was focused and a disciplinarian. They'd attended many productions I had done down the walk and saw the people around me who loved performing. But their support wasn't enough to stop me from wondering, Why me? At the age of fifty-two, I had other things I wanted to do. Besides, I didn't want to go down a religious road. I had a negative view about how Christian crusaders had plundered and murdered and colonized and destroyed countries. And I was apprehensive about Warden Cain, the way he'd prevented us from talking with the California commission trying to stop prison rape and filled the air instead with talk of Jesus. This guy was also an antisemite. He wouldn't let one of the hospice volunteers, Ted Durbin, establish a Jewish inmate organization. Once, Cain called all the club leaders and religious groups to meet Daniel Bergner, who wrote *God of the Rodeo*. Cain said, "The guy is a Jew but don't hold it against him. It's not his fault that he was born that way."

I told Fontenot about my reservations. She reiterated that the inmates in the religious community thought I was the ideal person. Eyeing that stack of paper, I tried to find some way to discourage her. I told her I needed women to play the women's roles.

"Women?" she said. "You can get the guys to do it."

"This is not a Kabuki play," I told her. "If we're going to be true, we've got to have women."

"We'll get the women who work here to play the women," she insisted.

"This is by prisoners for prisoners," I replied. "If we took an ad to promote the play and said free people were in it, how would that look? No, I need women prisoners."

"Where are we going to get women from?"

"St. Gabe," I said, referring to the Louisiana Correctional Institute for Women (LCIW), about an hour and a half away in St. Gabriel.

"You must be out of your mind." I could almost read her thoughts about how all this could go terribly wrong.

I wasn't out of my mind at all. I thought this would be the way to forget about that play.

Less than two days later, I got a phone call to go to the office of the East Yard warden, Perry Stagg. He was in there with Warden Kevin Benjamin. I walked in and Warden Stagg said, "Sit down, Gary. You want a drink?" I told him no. "What time do you want to go to St. Gabriel to audition the women?" he asked. They told me they were acting on the orders of Assistant Warden Fontenot.

What finally convinced me, however reluctantly, was the Drama Club members themselves. They really wanted to do this. Every time I had something I needed them to do, they listened and did it. I felt I owed it to them, despite my differing views on religion. They wanted to be in the production, they told me, even if they had to play the women. They knew me and they trusted the direction I'd go in.

I had tried to convince the prison administrators not to do it; they went against me. I had tried to convince my guys not to do it; they went against me. Finally, I looked at it and said, "Why not?"

IN ADDITION TO THE LCIW women, there were several things I insisted on with Warden Fontenot: I had to have the autonomy to rewrite the play, since it was much too long as it was to prepare and perform. I also wanted some incentives for my cast, so the actors wouldn't have to work in the field all day. The warden gave her approval.

I knew I needed to take ownership of the script. First, I had to cut it from three and a half hours to under two. The play as structured was too long and redundant. I went back to the Bible, drawing from things I'd known when I was into it, and feeling there were some significant areas that needed to be highlighted. Judas had just a cameo in the production. I wanted a bigger role for him so, as villain, he could serve a purpose. If God knew all things and set things in motion and sent John the Baptist ahead of time to pave the way for Jesus, then what Judas did was also preordained. If this was something he was born to do, who's to say that Judas was not standing right now next to Jesus? Also, the play needed to show the role of outside influences. Even when parents and other loved ones give good guidance, kids become exposed to so many things, economic pressure and peer pressure. Judas needed money and was used by the Pharisee gang to carry out acts they didn't have the power to do themselves. Jesus was falsely accused and condemned by a corrupt system. I wanted the audience to see that we should not be so quick to judge.

I wrote most of the changes before we started, literally transforming the story. My goal was to make each and every character stand out. Above all, I wanted to highlight that the story of Jesus is a story of unfair allegations, with Pontius Pilate convicting an innocent man. It's also a story about the importance of redemption and forgiveness. I wanted to magnify the lives of these prisoner actors in the characters they took on. And I wanted to expose the power dynamics. Even though the Romans were the conquerors and subjugated the people in their land, they were also manipulated by the Pharisees to do the dastardly deeds they wanted. The Pharisees weren't allowed to take the law in their own hands, but they were able to make Pontius Pilate feel threatened by the power of this new movement and carry out the Pharisees' wishes. I saw a lot of parallels to the way the police, courts, and prison authorities reinforced each other and maintained the status quo.

Once I had the rewritten script, I told the Drama Club, "If we're going to do the play, we're going to do it right. We'll give everyone an equal opportunity to take on the challenge of a role." We put a callout for the new Main Prison chapel and passed out flyers that we were looking for people who knew carpentry, electrical work, and sewing as well as people who could act and sing. I was confident in the Drama Club members, but there were more roles than people in our organization, and we wanted to involve the rest of the prison population as well. A lot of guys showed up for the auditions. Committees signed people up or held an introductory interview asking why the individual wanted to be in the production, whether they had any special abilities or experience. Then I'd talk to them, look at the recommendations. I recruited people from all walks of life, including a set designer, Peter Rubens, who used to build floats in New Orleans and would work with Kenya; musicians Quntos KunQuest and Calvin Lewis, to do the score for our a capella production; a sound person; singers; carpenters, plasterers, and more.

Some people came to us who had disciplinary problems. I knew these guys, people with a propensity to get in trouble. They said, "Give me a chance. Let me prove myself." It was like they were asking society for an opportunity to show they had changed. I heard their cries. Being part of something this big provided meaning and purpose for them. These guys turned out to be some of the most committed and dedicated actors in the production. There were other people I was reluctant to have involved, guys who had prison sex offense charges, "known 21s" we called them. At the same time, I didn't want to turn people down if this could be the chance to turn their lives around. I gave that group an opportunity to work on the set where they wouldn't be in rehearsals.

Every role had one actor and one understudy. I had the guys in the Drama Club judge each person on how they interpreted and projected the character they were trying out for. Our members gave notes so people could learn from one another. As director, I made the ultimate decisions on who best embodied each role, looking at likability, believability, and credibility.

In the end, we had Buddhists, Muslims, Jews, Christians, and nonbelievers filling the parts. Working with people from differing backgrounds certainly educated me. I told them, "You were acting a role when you were on the streets, and you were judged based on someone you were not. Use the same energy behind the deception for this role, one that you can control."

DURING THE TIME WE were selecting the men, I also went to LCIW in St. Gabriel to find women for the play. We met in the women's chapel. Our paint crew had worked at LCIW to build that chapel and also an academy. Men weren't allowed to go inside the facility. We'd worked there for months without coming into contact with the women. Male guards patrolled only the outside perimeter. When I went for the auditions, the women looked at me like "Who is this guy walking among us?" I didn't see any other men around.

I asked the women inmates who had come out to tell me a little about themselves and why they were interested in being in the production. Some of them had been part of a documentary called *Hard Time*. The producer was one of my former Drama Club members who got transferred to Hunt Correctional Institute and pitched a documentary about sentences related to drug dealing.

I told the women about this play. "I'm looking for quality, not quantity," I said, "people who know how to listen and follow directions." Then I passed out the roles for the women characters and extras, and I played the men's roles while they auditioned. I jotted down the ones who seemed strong and also ones who needed more work, and wound up selecting all eighteen of them. One woman who was born in Cambodia, Serey Kong, seemed really shy. Assistant Warden Mary Kennedy told me Serey acted like that but she'd be really good in the play. I listened.

Any man who says women are weak has something wrong with them. Let me tell you, I was a powerlifter in Angola, a heavyweight, but I felt intimidated by those women. "We're going to eat your men's lunch," they told me. "They're going to wish they never saw us."

They were very confident. They almost convinced me that they were going to make my men look small.

I told them, "I want you all to know. I could get this play done without you because I have guys in my organization who would take on women's roles. But I want women in the production, and I want to give you the opportunity to be part of something that's never been done before in prisons for men or women. This is a history-making event. It will help every one of you to make a difference."

I didn't narrow down which roles they'd have until they started coming to Angola. I had them study the various parts. I knew I wanted the quiet individual, Serey Kong, to study the role of the Virgin Mary.

BACK AT ANGOLA, I told the Drama Club members how strong the women were. I also told them it would be mandatory for each of the actors to learn two to three roles. Things were looking good except for one problem: Nobody wanted to play Judas.

One night I called in everybody in the cast. "What makes you think the Judas role is any different from anyone else?" I told them. "If I remember, many of you were choirboys in church, and still you did the things you did. What makes you think that you're too good to where you can't play Judas? When your parents brought you into this world, they gave you the best they could. They worked hard to provide you with a roof, clothing, to send you to school, to try to give you the finest things in life even though they had so little. They loved you, they nurtured you, they did everything for you, and you betrayed them. So what makes you think you're any different from Judas? I see most people here as Judas. You betrayed your family, you betrayed your neighbors."

That lecture made a difference. I had over a dozen guys who wanted to challenge each other for that role. I just wanted two, an actor and an understudy. I let them compete and selected Levelle Tolliver, a Drama Club member who'd been sentenced to life without parole for killing a loan shark in an argument over loaded dice.

Next, we needed a place to rehearse. I wanted to get the old Plasma Building down the walk, a building where inmates used to sell their blood plasma. But the prison was in the process of renovating it for hobby shop boxes. They had closed some of the dormitories on the East Yard. So I asked for Cypress-4 for our rehearsal space. Deputy Warden DuPont made that possible. We used the big room where the bunks used to be, setting up tables and chairs on the perimeter and leaving open space for making props and practicing our scenes.

In the early stages, we thought about having the performance at a small lake on the grounds. Warden Fontenot wanted to emulate the promenade production they'd done in Scotland. But she hadn't factored in that most of the actors were people I recruited from the general inmate population. To have people mingle with members of the free world, they would all have to be class A trustees.

Some in the administration wanted to restrict who I could have in the play, like people with escape charges. I told them, "When Jesus went out and selected his disciples, he didn't go to the synagogue and select the Pharisees. He went to the common people, selected people who were everything from thieves to tax collectors and fishermen. In Angola, we have a combination of all."

Eventually, the administration agreed. We decided to forget the promenade structure and do the whole play at the arena where the rodeos were held. I could have who I wanted in the production.

When the LCIW women first came to Angola, they were intimidated to get on stage with men. "We're not used to hearing men's voices," they said. I tried to have men and women practice in pairs, and the women froze. They were afraid of how security would respond if they touched a man. As they learned to trust me, the women told me they weren't even allowed to braid each other's hair at LCIW or they'd get a sex offense charge. That place was hard on the women. When they came to Angola, they had to be handcuffed and have their legs shackled each way on the bus. The women called it their "platinum jewelry." By the time we performed the play, though, the women and men had become really comfortable with each other.

WE WERE SCHEDULED TO perform the play in 2012. Over that summer, the Mississippi River crest rose every day. It goes through Angola to get to the Gulf of Mexico, which means a lot of pressure is put on a narrow stretch of land. Rising water can lead to levees bursting, which could threaten the prison. Warden Cain declared an emergency and evacuated the prison. Many prisoners thought it was a ploy by the warden to get more funding from the state, since the mass evacuation didn't include trustees, inmates in maximum security, the cattle, or the guard families living on B-Line. Nonetheless, they shipped a lot of prisoners out to satellite locations. I was sent to Camp F along with Bobby Wallace, the actor playing Jesus. I looked at it as an opportunity for me to really work with Bobby to get his role down. For the two months we were out there, I spent a great deal of time helping him learn the whole play, since his character was carrying it. He had to know all the actors' roles, male and female, so if they missed a line, he could put them back on track.

After Bobby and I returned to the Main Prison, I had to scramble to get back a lot of the guys who were still at satellite prisons. We had to work hard to get ready for the performance. Sometimes prison operations like the twice-daily count would interrupt us. At any given time, the authorities might close everything down. Fortunately, that didn't happen too often. We had access to the Cypress dormitory every day. Whenever individuals were available, they'd come there and rehearse with each other or with me. I was still working on the paint crew and sometimes had jobs outside the prison grounds. Security had a list of all the men assigned to the production who were allowed in that rehearsal space.

After I told everybody it was their responsibility to learn more than one role, some guys learned three or even five parts. Besides Bobby, two others knew the entire script: Brandon Robinson, the understudy for Jesus, and Michael Ellis who played Luke.

I tried to give useful advice about acting. "A good actor is flexible, innovative," I said. "The unique thing about us is we are gifted with emotions, and we've got to be able to utilize that to our advantage. The day of the performance, you are going to become one unit. We will all shine together." I reminded them that being in front of people is more than giving a performance—it's about educating the audience.

The actors were really into it. They worked hand in hand. To see guys walking around the yard in their roles, throwing lines at each other, was really something. Inmates called Bobby "Jesus" and called Earl Davis "John the Baptist."

IN APRIL OF 2012, Suzanne Lofthus, who had directed the play in Scotland, came over to help us. She was amazed at how skilled people were and showed us some helpful tricks, including how to have Jesus appear from the dead.

Other volunteers who didn't want to be actors worked behind the scenes on costumes and props, supervised by Kenya and Peter Rubens. I'd go to the Drama Club office and we'd have boxes full of stuff that guys had found dumpster diving. For example, the rec department had gotten new equipment in and was throwing away a lot of shoulder pads and football helmets. We used those for the uniforms and headgear of the Romans. We got big barrels that we cut in half for shields. Broomsticks from the mattress factory became the Roman spears. Peter designed sets from material like PVC pipe and bicycle tires. The whole play was scored from beginning to end.

The original script called for incorporating some animals, like sheep, cows, donkeys, and pigeons. The prison already had those. The administration asked us what else we needed. Goats, we said, and a camel. We were just being facetious, but lo and behold, a guy on a private farm in Shreveport had a camel and offered it to us to use. That camel walked alongside one of the wise men.

All our hard work finally came together. In early May of 2012, we put the production on three times, a Friday, Saturday, and Sunday, with more than seventy performers. Family members of the actors came from far and wide to see it, along with inmates, church groups, and some members of the public—over a thousand at each performance. The play was also shown through satellite to more than thirty countries around the world.

I SAT AT THE top on the opposite side of the arena. I wanted to get out of the way, so the actors weren't wondering what I was thinking. Before each performance, I gave them a pep talk. "Now it's on you," I told them. "I have no hand in it. You own this. You worked hard for it. Show the audience what you're made of." They didn't see me again until after the play was over.

Some wondered how the audience would perceive prisoners doing a religious production. "If you see yourself as a prisoner or convict, that's how the audience will see you," I told them. "But if you go out there and do a marvelous performance, the audience will see you as the character you project on the stage, people they envisioned when they read the Bible. So you have to convince them they're seeing Peter, John the Baptist, Judas, as well as Jesus and the town people." In fact, the audience loved it, even white Baptists. There were people crying during various scenes, like when the actors ran into the stands to break open the loaves and pass out bread, making the audience part of the event. After the play was over and I made it to the back, the performers wanted to know what I thought. "Why should you wait for approval from me when the audience itself loved you?" I told them. "What I have to say is nothing compared to that." The actors were proud of themselves and proud of one another. They laughed and hugged and recited the Drama Club motto.

I felt redeemed. We always hear that prisoners will never amount to anything, they'll always fail at any meaningful tasks. I'd been working with incarcerated men and women who could have chosen anything else to do but be in this play, who recognized the significance of what we were doing, that it could change the hearts and minds of people who saw the play and also how they saw themselves, people who had doubted they could amount to anything in life. It made me proud that these women and men trusted me to guide them in this journey. I was honored and grateful. At the beginning, I'd had no idea we would succeed, given the odds against us. But as long as I stayed focused, so did the actors. They trusted and depended on me. That made me determined that the production would turn out to be a success, for every individual incarcerated in Louisiana and around the world. It was a testament to the prison population that despite their fate, they were able to do something this monumental.

We were really fortunate that a lot of our work got captured in a powerful documentary about the making of this play, what it was like putting it together, what it meant for the actors. A film producer named Jonathan Stack happened to be at Angola during this time making a film about the flood preparation. I had met him several years earlier, when he made two award-winning documentaries pertaining to Angola, *The Farm: Angola, USA* and *The Farm: 10 Down*. Warden Fontenot told him about our production after she sat in on one of the rehearsals with the singing shepherds. Their harmony and talent made her cry.

Jonathan came to Camp F, where I was, and asked if he and his crew could watch a rehearsal. I told him that would not be a problem, once we got the actors back together. When they finally ended the emergency and shipped us back to the Main Prison, Jonathan came with his film crew to see the singing shepherds. He was blown away by their beautiful voices.

"Gary, can I follow you and create a documentary about the making of this play?" he asked. "Would the guys mind?"

I checked, and the actors had no problem with it. They wanted to be seen. A play on this scale had never been done before in a prison in the U.S. or around the world, especially with men and women prisoners coming together. "It's a watershed moment for us," I told Jonathan, "like the first stepping on the moon."

He agreed. "This is something no one can claim but you all," he told me.

Jonathan started attending rehearsals, joining the people who were creating sets. I thought about how this documentary could be an effective way to help those involved and give the women exposure. A lot of prisoner activities have come out of Angola, and the media had focused on that, not looking at the fact that there was also a women's prison and they were doing a lot of things, too.

JONATHAN NAMED HIS DOCUMENTARY *Cast the First Stone*. When he had a final version, he held a special screening at Angola on March 27, 2013, for everyone who'd been part of the production, people from the administration and churches, and some special guests. The next day, he did a public screening at LCIW. Those were the first times I saw the film. I was blown away by it.

I knew Levelle Tolliver, who played Judas, had really studied that character and used his performance to think about the ways his own crimes had hurt people. But I hadn't heard what he told the filmmaker: "I really do believe Judas was forgiven of his sins. I just don't believe Judas knew that he was forgiven."

Like Levelle, Sandra Starr, who played Mary Magdalene, had a sentence of life without parole, in her case for killing the boyfriend who'd beaten her for years. In the documentary, she said if she had to do it again, she'd take the beatings rather than serve time, so at least she could be with her kids. That really hurt to watch. No woman deserves to be beaten. I knew if Sandra hadn't defended herself, she'd be dead.

The film showed some other scenes I had not been privy to, like the women rehearsing together at LCIW and sharing their thoughts on themselves, their roles, what it was like working with men.

I listened as Serey Kong described how I had "fussed" at her to have confidence that she could be Virgin Mary. "God, I didn't like Gary at first, he was so arrogant," she said. "His belief in me—that's something he gifted me with."

And I laughed hearing Patricia Williams, who played the older Mother Mary, talk about the scene where they put Jesus on the cross "with not much on. I was like, 'Oh my God, I have not seen a man with not much on.'"

All of us were moved by the bond Patricia forged with Bobby Wallace. When she was arrested in 2006 for embezzlement, her family was ashamed of her and she lost touch with them. She told the filmmakers how she'd cry every time Jesus's body was put in her arms because it reminded her of her son serving in Iraq and how she worried he would come home in a body bag. "I have no say in his choices," she said. "These men treat me like a mother, and it's given me an opportunity to be a mom again."

Justin Singleton, who played Peter and was also a lifer, talked about the importance of the audience seeing the actors as people capable of change. "You want people to know you're not the same person you were out there. So to actually do something that portrays change is awesome. To do something of this magnitude and for people to respond the way they did, it's an amazing feeling."

I was proud Jonathan Stack included a shot of the gurney used for lethal injection—the current form of execution—when he showed the scene of Jesus's crucifixion. And I was also proud that near the end of the documentary, he included these words from me: "I just want people to know, when they see the actors on stage, that they see their neighbors, their sons, their daughters, they see their mothers, their sisters, their brothers, that they see themselves."

Shortly after *Cast the First Stone* came out in 2013, we did a public showing at a church in Baton Rouge. The guys in our van weren't shackled because we were all class A trustees. We got out to stretch and noticed the LCIW van was there but it was empty. Inside the hall, we saw the women in chains. Warden Fontenot was appalled. She immediately called the warden at LCIW. "That's not good publicity," she said. She got the shackles removed—at least for that night.

I had hoped the film would get broad distribution. But film festivals and distributors didn't pick it up. They thought the film was powerful but worried it was too religious. For us, this film wasn't about religion. It was about redemption and hope, about men and women in prison who acknowledge what they did in their lives and see all the ways they have changed. It was a film about love and compassion. And for me, especially, it was about avoiding a rush to judgment and punishment.

We performed the play again in the spring and fall of 2013. I attended those productions with a new sense of hope about my case.

CHAPTER 16

THE LONG ARC

People in prison want to get out. They stay on top of cases moving through the courts, especially ones that reach the Supreme Court. That was certainly true at Angola. We were always hoping and wishing that a decision would arrive to open the gates for us to leave. My friends Norris Henderson and Kenya were both inmate counsels who spent a lot of time in the prison law library. If a new decision came down, they'd let me know and also post it on the bulletin boards in the dormitories.

The cases I had my eyes on were ones that would be landmark decisions concerning sentencing, especially for juveniles. In 2002, the U.S. Supreme Court issued a ruling ending the death penalty for individuals with intellectual disabilities, which set the stage to eliminate it for other groups as well. A watershed moment for me came three years later when the Supreme Court said that it was unconstitutional to sentence juvenile offenders to be put to death, because that violated the ban on "cruel and unusual punishment." I had the feeling the court would keep going in this direction and say it was also unconstitutional to sentence juveniles to life with no meaningful possibility of getting out.

Cases on juvenile sentencing kept moving through the courts. In 2010, the Supreme Court ruled in *Graham v. Florida* that juveniles convicted of any offense other than homicide could not be given life imprisonment without parole. Next up was a case known as *Miller v. Alabama* that wanted to go even further. The attorneys for Miller argued that no crime should require automatic sentencing to life without parole for anyone seventeen or younger. In June 2012, the majority on the high court agreed. The justices struck down statutes in twenty-nine states—including Louisiana—that mandated life without parole for children. "Imposition of a State's most severe penalties on juvenile offenders cannot proceed as though they were not children," the decision said, because youth are less responsible than adults for wrongdoing and more capable of change. The lower courts would have to hold new sentencing hearings.

This decision meant a resurgence of hope. Out of three hundred juvenile lifers in Louisiana impacted by the ruling, I had been one of the first to enter prison. The papers mentioned my case as an example of those affected. Other inmates had newfound hope as well. They were saying if the decision applies to those age seventeen and under, it should also cover anyone who was eighteen when they were sentenced. Those inmates were considered juveniles in a number of states.

The chief lawyer for the case was Bryan Stevenson, who had also taken the lead in *Graham v. Florida*. He'd made the argument that sentences should take into consideration "the unique status of juveniles and their potential for change." You can't treat kids as if they understood the consequences of their actions when they weren't old enough to discern that yet, he said. He pointed out that the proper name for this sentence was not "life in prison," but "death in prison." I really agreed. No other country in the world but the U.S. was imposing death-in-prison sentences on children. Bryan Stevenson also felt youth had greater potential for growth and rehabilitation, and that they had special needs. He argued that juveniles need more "attention and protection" in the criminal justice system than adults.

Those words really struck me. I'd never heard them used about any inmates, certainly not juveniles. I was in an adult prison with a lot of violence where you had teenagers who'd been sentenced to life without parole. In my case, on top of everything, I was innocent. A young person is not physically able to compete in such an environment. It's a constant scene of action that always draws a reaction, often a violent reaction. How do you expect teenagers to defend themselves when they're much smaller and less mature? Often they're going to adapt to the violence and go to the extreme to prove their manhood, when really they're not men, they're children. Whether they convert to the violent ways of the prison or not, they become victimized by it.

Here was Bryan Stevenson recognizing the challenges young prisoners have, and how they end up serving more time than those sentenced at an older age. When I was on trial, no one had referred to me as a juvenile. This was a time when white Americans in the South never looked at young Black males as children. They always treated them as adults. In Alabama and the other Southern states that had nonviolent protests, kids were on the front lines. Police were just as brutal with those young demonstrators as they were with everyone else. When I first got to Angola, I thought I was the only young person there, but after a while I learned there were guys as young or younger than me who'd been prosecuted as adult offenders. For me, any "attention and protection" I experienced came from older prisoners who had children before they went to prison or who had been in the movement and felt it was important to protect younger inmates. That group understood the criminal justice system better than anyone.

Several weeks after *Miller v. Alabama* came down, Bryan Stevenson and a few other attorneys came to Angola to advise the juvenile lifers not to rush to file all kinds of briefs in court. Sometimes an individual makes a filing without effective representation and it winds up setting a bad precedent for the rest of the inmates. Over one hundred people were at that meeting. The attorneys were trying to come up with something that would help all of us.

When I introduced myself, Stevenson immediately recognized my name. He was familiar with my case and knew my attorney George Kendall, who had worked on getting amicus briefs in the *Graham* and *Miller* cases. The guy was thoughtful and clear in what he was saying. He was confident, as he should have been. He knew what he was talking about. I was impressed with him. He gave us a ray of hope.

Stevenson also made the point that the *Miller* decision wasn't as clearcut as some thought. Would it be applied retroactively? How broadly would it impact juvenile lifers? The Supreme Court didn't ban the sentence altogether, it just said it couldn't be mandatory. What about states that had a lower age threshold for who counts as an adult? This meant a ball of confusion that lawyers and courts would have to work through.

Louisiana and several other states were still trying to see what the impact of the decision would be and what they could do to get around it. They hadn't made any objection to *Graham*.

But soon state authorities declared that *Miller* would apply in the future but not retroactively. They would not re-sentence any of us who'd been given life without parole when we were seventeen or younger. This was the same set of people who'd been against me all along: the attorney general's office, the sheriff's department, and the political apparatus of St. Charles Parish.

AFTER WHAT I'D GONE through all those years, I wasn't surprised, but I was pissed. I felt this was a decision from the U.S. Supreme Court and they needed to accept it. The same ugly heads reared up: "We can't let Gary Tyler out, his case is old, it's over with." I knew it would take some time for the judicial process to straighten things out. But I didn't know it would take almost four years.

George Kendall was still working on the jury selection angle in my case when the *Miller* decision came down. He and Mary Howell and the others realized this was a door that had been opened for me. Several attorneys from New York, including Corrine Irish, Carine Williams, and Harmony Loube, worked with George to shape the arguments. Side by side with the New Orleans team—Mary, Majeeda Snead, and Emily Ratner— they helped explain why the court's decision in *Miller* was a substantive rule of constitutional law. It had to be applied to cases where mandatory life without parole had been forced on young defendants in violation of the Eighth Amendment. Louisiana was wrong to argue that the new rule was just a procedural matter, they said. States didn't have the right to deny new sentencing to those of us who'd been wrongly condemned to death in prison.

While the judicial process played out, I remained very active. I had a life at Angola that kept me sane and grounded, working on the paint crew, volunteering with hospice, continuing to lead the Drama Club and travel with the troupe. None of that stopped while we waited for a resolution. I kept having visits with my family.

The one thing I didn't have during that time was visits with my son. Living outside the United States made it too expensive for him and his mother to travel back and forth. I hadn't seen Damaryos in nearly six years, since he was six years old. I wrote him as often as I could. What kept me going were memories of him, how smart he was, and what a sense of justice he had already.

One of the last times I'd seen him was in the Visiting Shed. A guy named Vashon Kelly, who was also a hospice volunteer, was working the kiddie concession. When parents brought their children to the Visiting Shed, sometimes they'd lose sight of them. Kids would be running all over the place. There were signs on the wall saying, "Keep your eye on your child," but that didn't stop kids from taking off. My son had gone over to the kiddie booth. A young mother saw Vashon talking to her child, and she went ballistic. "Don't be touching my son," she said. Damaryos had seen everything and realized there was no touching. Nothing inappropriate had been said or done. Everyone who knew Vashon—including this woman's old man, who she had come to visit—thought he was a great guy. All the kids loved him. But the woman had a complete meltdown. My son came back to where we were and was telling us about the incident. I was concerned because they were talking about locking Vashon up.

I called to Lieutenant Samantha Angelle, an aide who was working in the A Building. "My son was over there," I told her. "He and the other kids were saying nothing like that happened."

Lieutenant Angelle asked me whether I could get Damaryos to make a statement. We gave him a pencil and paper, and my son wrote down everything he saw. Six years old he was and smart as a whip. He stood by the table and wrote it all out. When I brought his statement to the lieutenant, she couldn't believe that a six-year-old kid could be that clear. I understood: He wanted to do what was right, because he understood the concept of an unfair accusation.

IN SEPTEMBER OF 2012, my mother became too sick to come to Angola and had to be hospitalized for nearly a month. Doctors had to remove a large part of her intestines. The last Sunday of October, a rodeo weekend, my nephew Darrick came to see me. Although he visited regularly, something didn't feel right. I saw the expression on his face, and then he told me that they weren't expecting my mother to live. I had just talked to her that Thursday, and she said she was sitting up with her sisters and was going to be released in a few days. I was thinking I'd have her visit in a week or two—spending time with my mother was such a great help to me. The news really messed me up. I couldn't concentrate on anything. I wanted to scream and holler, but that wouldn't make things any better.

I left the concession booth and went looking for Deputy Warden Leslie DuPont on the rodeo grounds and told him the bad news. He had me come to his office the next morning and arranged for me to see my mother in the hospital on Tuesday. Two guards accompanied me. The warden gave them a $100 bill and said, "If Gary's hungry, get him whatever he wants."

The visit was disheartening. I didn't know how to deal with the situation. When I walked into my mother's room, my oldest sister, Ella, was there with a family friend. I heard the TV on and it was showing Hurricane Sandy hitting New Jersey. That was just how I felt. I embraced my sister and bent over to talk to my mother, who was heavily sedated for the pain. I wasn't sure she knew I was there, but she was giving me faint responses.

"Listen, Richard sends his love," I told her. "He's thinking about you and has you in his prayers." My baby brother had recently been transferred to Angola.

My mother said, "Fuck Richard," and started crying. I looked at my sister and the two guards—we were all surprised. But I understood, she was very angry at my baby brother for being in prison. My mother felt there was no reason for him to get in trouble; he had family who were really supportive. But he'd gotten on drugs and was out of control. Richard used to worry her all the time about coming to visit and sending him money. It really bothered her that he was still struggling to adjust to prison life. She was upset that he was not me. I had been reluctant to mention his name to her, but that was her baby boy. I wanted her to know he sent his love and kept her in his prayers.

My sister and I tried to make light of her reaction. I continued to talk to her, letting her know I loved her. To lift her spirits, I also reminded her about the *Miller* decision. She'd known about the case because I told her during a visit that this might be the decision that would get me out. That gave her hope that my ordeal finally would come to an end.

When hospital staff came into the room to change my mother's position, I could hear her pain. I knew they were moving her to prevent bed sores. Even though I'd been part of care like this so many times, I had to leave the room, and I cried. This was my mother. To me, she was invincible. She was the person I always kept on a pedestal. I never thought I'd see her in a situation like that.

Throughout the day, my mother was in and out from the medication. At one point, my baby sister Jennifer came in with her husband. She told me our mother preferred dying at home. "That shouldn't be hard to arrange," I said. I knew there was a hospice declaration for the patient's last wish. I talked to someone who was a hospice volunteer himself and was familiar with the declaration. He said they just needed family to agree. Ella was the oldest and all the rest who were there approved and signed the paperwork. My mother was home the very next day. They brought a hospital bed and made her comfortable.

I called every day to see how things were going. I'd talk to her and she'd faintly respond, but she knew I was there on the other end. When she did come around, she was really pleased that she was at home. She thanked my sister Jennifer for honoring her wish. "Gary's the one who made this possible," Jennifer said.

"Gary came?" my mother said.

"Yes, he was there for hours." My mother burst out crying. She hadn't remembered that.

My mother died just a few days later, on a Monday, November 4, 2012. That Friday, I was able to attend her funeral in St. Rose at the church where she was an elder. Unlike at my father's funeral, I was a trustee now and was not shackled. I requested to speak. My remarks that day were emotional. I was speaking from a son's heart, how my mother had comforted me as a child, assured and protected me and made clear how much she loved me. "I was my mother's son, and she made that known throughout her days," I said. "She was always proud of who I was."

Being able to honor my mother's memory and to get to see my son were even more reasons I wanted this sentencing case decided. But my wishing didn't speed up the judicial process.

IN 2013, THE DISTRICT attorney out of St. Charles Parish, Joel Chaisson, reached out to George and Mary. "Do you have a problem with me coming to Angola to meet with your client?" he asked them. George checked to see whether I'd be willing to talk with Chaisson, and I said, of course.

Soon afterward, I got a phone call from Warden Cain, who assumed I didn't know and informed me that DA Chaisson wanted to visit me. I'll never forget what Warden Cain told me next: "If you want to get out, give them what they want. Tell him you're guilty, you're sorry. Do whatever you can."

Like always, Warden Cain, like Boss Hogg in *The Dukes of Hazzard*, wanted to have his hand in it so he could say he had something to do with my release and grab the credit. This was a guy who stooped to playing the prisoners against his staff. Assistant wardens would implement some new rule Cain had ordered them to do, and when the prison population resisted and went to complaining, Cain would act like he didn't know anything about it.

"Who made that decision?" he'd say.

None of the assistant wardens would dare tell him, "You told us to do that."

One time Cain had called everyone, inmates and all staff, to the rodeo grounds and announced that he was the CEO of the prison. "I'm on top and prisoners at the bottom," he said. "Anyone in between can be replaced." His employees knew he wasn't playing and they didn't want to lose their jobs.

Warden Cain was even the reason we stopped learning other languages. After 9/11, he wanted English only. Inmates had to turn in any materials other than English or be written up for contraband and possibly get reclassified as maximum security. This warden was also why we stopped performing *The Life of Jesus Christ* after 2013. He started suspecting people around him were giving incriminating information to the authorities investigating him. Fontenot was among the people he stopped trusting. That passion play was one of her biggest projects. I didn't need Cain or his advice.

In the summer of 2013, I had my visit with DA Chaisson. We went to the Ranch House, a place designated for meetings with dignitaries and politicians. Mary and George were sitting behind me, but Chaisson talked just to me. He was a few years younger than me, a nice-looking fellow who still had a full head of hair. After all the vicious people I'd seen from the DA's office and the state AG's office, he was the first one who I can say was very respectful and polite. He was also a straight talker. I saw he came to get a feeling for who I was. He told me he remembered me from Destrehan High and that he'd known my younger brother Terry. He expressed condolences for the death of my mother and then talked about his career. From what George had told me, Chaisson always had problems with my conviction. He felt I should have had the lesser charge of manslaughter. First-degree murder and the death penalty were a stretch that he thought was clearly political.

"Several officials at Angola spoke highly of you," he told me. He said he'd heard about the positive things I'd been doing in prison and how those would be good for society if I got out.

To me, the DA came across as being understanding, open, receptive, and willing to do what he could to alleviate my situation. "I'm getting a lot of pressure not to touch your case and prepare for a re-sentencing," he told me.

Heat was coming from the AG's office and from the DA Association.

Back in 1974, they argued, the DA in St. Charles Parish brought them in to help prosecute my case, and the association felt they had authority over it still. They insisted they should make a determination on what was in the best interest of the state.

DA Chaisson looked at me. "I told them, 'I'm going to do what I'm going to do. The local office invited you back then. I'm disinviting you. It's my case and I'll do what I want.'" Despite the opposition he was getting, Chaisson made clear he was going to do everything in his power to help me get out of prison. "Gary," he said, "you've been here too long and you shouldn't be sitting where you're sitting. You should be free with your family."

If Harry Morel had still been in the DA's office, he would have invited the state people in and let them argue that I got exactly the sentence I deserved. Morel once came on a tour of the prison with his two grandchildren. Fontenot stopped him to point me out. He asked me how I was and wished me good luck—and then opposed me each time I went before the pardon board.

I thanked Chaisson for coming to visit me and expressing his condolences for my mother. That was the first time out of almost four decades that anyone from the district attorney's office out of St. Charles Parish had been willing to come talk to me. The past DAs were adamant about keeping me in prison. This guy was even willing to put his career on the line to do what was right. I saw someone sitting in front of me who felt not only compassion in his heart, but shame in how the system had been willing to treat me like I was nothing, not even a human being, how they threatened to take not only my life but my whole existence, hoping I would die in prison.

I was still processing everything and making sure it was genuine. Never before had someone from that office who could make a difference to my life seen that the system had been unfair in dealing with me. The secretary from his private practice had come with him and was sitting behind him. Near the end, I saw she had tears in her eyes.

I prepared so I could get out on any given day. If they said, "Gary Tyler, you're free to go," I'd be ready to leave right away. But I'd learned to keep my expectations low. I'd lived through the fifth circuit giving and then taking away an order for a new trial, the Supreme Court refusing to hear my case, three pardon board recommendations turned down by various Louisiana governors. In September of 2013, the Louisiana Supreme Court ruled that *Miller* was not retroactive. It would take another case making it to the U.S. Supreme Court to turn that around.

I stayed on my guard. *Miller* was a good decision and I was hoping it would affect me, but I wasn't going to set myself up for another disappointment.

CHAPTER 17

FREE AT LAST

No matter my intentions, those years after *Miller* were the most excruciating I can remember. It was like everybody's undivided attention was focused on what case on retroactivity would make it to the U.S. Supreme Court and what would happen then. We knew the decision would resound throughout the criminal justice system. Would that be the moment for me or not? I was still skeptical, worried something could happen to stop me from getting out. I always had my guard up. I didn't want to go through any more letdowns. By this time I knew what I had to do to deal with my situation: continue to stay involved, work with other people. That gave me the strength to keep my focus. I knew there were folks who had it worse than me, guys who were likely to die in Angola.

One case was already in the pipeline. George Toca, another Angola inmate, had been sentenced to life without parole as a juvenile out of New Orleans. Louisiana denied him a new sentencing hearing and the Supreme Court had agreed to take up his case. But before arguments were heard, the local DA offered a plea bargain. The deal allowed Toca to get out of prison immediately but he had to end his fight to make *Miller* apply retroactively. I know he was glad to be free, but he came to me to say he felt bad that this could set the rest of us back.

It appeared the next case would be Henry Montgomery's, also an inmate at Angola, who'd been convicted as a juvenile out of Baton Rouge for a 1963 murder. Many thought *Montgomery v. Louisiana* was a bad choice because he'd been convicted of killing a police officer, and also because his lawyer had never argued before the Supreme Court. At least the case didn't have to go through every legal hurdle, just the Louisiana Supreme Court and then the U.S. Supreme Court. In the fall of 2014, the high court agreed to hear *Montgomery*.

I was nervous. I got caught up in the hype that this case might hurt everybody. Montgomery had an inmate counsel as well as an attorney. The inmate counsel meant well, but he was keeping things secret and telling Montgomery that the lawyers who wanted to help were trying to keep him from getting out of prison. Montgomery, who we called Wolf, was a functional illiterate, traumatized by the life he had lived in Angola. He had come up during the worst time in that prison.

Eventually Montgomery did accept the help of our attorneys and others, who assisted with the briefs and organized several moot courts, or practice rounds, for his lawyer. But that guy wouldn't let any of the other lawyers argue the case alongside him at the Supreme Court. Then Bryan Stevenson used his persuasion skills with the Department of Justice and convinced it to come in on the side of Montgomery. George said this was the only case he knew of where the government made an appearance on the side of a convicted prisoner. When the Supreme Court heard the case in October of 2015, the counsel for Montgomery had his fifteen minutes at the podium, and then Michael Dreeben, the deputy solicitor general, came to the podium—without any notes. He knew it would be a close vote and he wanted to look at the justices while he was talking.

The decision in *Montgomery v. Louisiana* came down in January 2016, a pretty short turnaround. They reversed the Louisiana Supreme Court's decision in *Miller*, declaring—just like my lawyers had shown—that *Miller* amounted to substantive rules of constitutional law because it prevented states from imposing a certain type of penalty or "category of punishment." The justices agreed that life without parole for prisoners sentenced as juveniles was "akin" to the death penalty. In capital cases, the Eighth Amendment requires individual sentencing, not any automatic sentence regardless of circumstances. States did have to apply the *Miller* ruling retroactively as well as in the future.

This decision really opened the door for me and others. My attorneys told me, "You're going home."

I WAS THRILLED, ESPECIALLY because I had a home to go to when I got out. In November 2013, Pam and Steve White had come to New Orleans on vacation. They were a retired couple who lived in Pasadena, old friends of Mary Howell. When they asked how I was doing, Mary said, "You can go see Gary in Angola, and you're in luck—this weekend you also get to see the passion play he directed."

At the prison, they met another visitor of mine, Bob Zaugh, who lived in Los Angeles and had been looking for a place for me out there. Pam and Steve wanted to help. I got word that they were at the play and I sat with them in the audience. At first, I thought they were old radicals from the 1970s, like people from *The Big Chill*. Then I found out how deeply involved they'd been in my case and how they'd dedicated their lives to organizing and working for justice. When they told me I had a place to stay with them whenever I got out, it was like the stars lined up in unison with each other. Their kindness helped change the trajectory of my life.

Things looked good, but I still had to have a court hearing. The date was set by my attorneys and DA Chaisson in St. Charles Parish. They were trying not to make it public to avoid a media circus and crowds of people who didn't want me to get out. The DA was vehement that he was going to do everything in his power to get me released, but he was clear there had to be a compromise. He told George, "You've got to give me something I can lay my hat on and you'll come out as winning." Chaisson's idea was to drop my charge to manslaughter, which has a maximum penalty in Louisiana of twenty-one years. I'd already served forty-one and a half years. If there was an agreement, I'd be released the same day as the hearing.

I had been adamant to my attorneys that I would not get in court and say I was guilty. The DA understood that. He wanted me out of prison. He was not going to oppose me under any circumstances. If I didn't take the deal in court and went before the pardon board, he would not oppose me there either.

Chaisson did everything humanely and respectfully, given the constraints he was under, to make sure I could be released. I didn't have to get up there and make a confession, just express in my own words my empathy and sympathy for Timothy Weber's family, which I'd always wanted to do. I had hoped to reach out to them early on, but the prison had a rule forbidding any contact with a victim's family. Many people later thought I had to say, "I did it, sorry, I murdered the victim." It was nothing like that.

They proposed the deal to state district court judge Lauren Lemmon. She agreed to accept it. But they all recognized there was a glitch. How were they going to explain the extra twenty and a half years I'd spent at Angola? That would open the authorities to a lawsuit to compensate me for those extra years.

George came back and told me the problem. "You'll have to waive any rights to post-conviction relief and to pursue any compensation," he said. "It's up to you to go along with it or not. If you don't want to, we'll deal with it some other way."

I thought about it and thought about it. I had gone to prison when I was sixteen years old. I'd lost a lot in the time I was confined in Angola. I lost loved ones, starting with my grandparents—they were in their sixties when this incident happened to me. They used to come from Tallulah to visit me. I lost my father in 1989, my mother in 2012. I lost my niece and my brother Mac back-to-back in 2016. I'd lost other family members, friends, and supporters. I was fifty-seven years old. Would I be guaranteed that I'd still be alive in five, ten, fifteen years? Prison doesn't offer you the best medical attention. Herman Wallace only got out when he was terminally ill; he died three days after leaving Angola. My whole life flashed across my eyes. I was a hospice volunteer who'd witnessed people dying as young as eighteen. I knew that anything could happen. I could fall ill. It wasn't hard to imagine a virus spreading through the prison. I could be one of the individuals affected.

Here was an opportunity for freedom. Would I take it or walk away, go home or risk staying in prison the rest of my life? This was the only opportunity that had been given to me. I knew Chaisson could leave the DA's office, could drop dead. The system that had done this to me for forty-one and a half years wasn't going to give ground. This DA's offer was the first opportunity I had from someone sensible, who thought what happened to me was wrong and wanted to do what he could to help. Friends like Calvin Duncan and Norris Henderson had been given similar choices and had gotten out; they urged me to do the same.

So I made my decision. I chose freedom.

I TOOK THE POSITION Albert Woodfox took—this was a freedom plea. Sometimes you have to bite the bullet and make certain sacrifices to get what you want. After fighting for over four decades, I knew this was a quid pro quo—I had to give up something in order to get what I needed. I'm still disappointed by it—I should have been exonerated. Now I have to go through life with the stigma of being labeled an ex-offender for a crime I had been falsely accused of committing. But I also knew how many people had been put in those same shoes. Most never had a way out.

I told my attorneys, "I've thought about it. Tell them, don't worry about the twenty and a half years. Let them know that I served that time wisely." I could sense how relieved they were. If I hadn't been humble and methodical in my way of thinking, I probably would have said, "Fuck them. They did this to me." But I would have lost out.

During those last weeks, I had mixed emotions: dread not knowing how things would actually turn out for me in court; excitement at the idea of leaving Angola and starting my life all over; hope that my release would inspire other men in prison to feel they had a chance at freedom as well; concern that, once released, I might never again see some of my friends who had become like family to me. I talked about this with Kenya. "It's time, man," he would say. "You've been here too long. You deserve this."

Once that was agreed, Mary and George kept reminding me to be ready to go to court. I wouldn't have more than a couple days' notice. In April, I was going back and forth to New Orleans with a special work crew. The news came on Wednesday, April 27, that I was going to have a court order that Friday. I left on Thursday to work in New Orleans, and got up the next morning to go to court in St. Charles Parish.

I got word from Judge Lemmon saying, "You can wear whatever you want. I don't want to see irons or prison clothes." She made it clear to everyone that she didn't want heavy security, she didn't want guns in the courthouse, none of that.

My attorney said he'd never witnessed a day in court like that April 29 hearing. "Ordinarily, when inmates go back to court, they have 'jewelry' on," George told me, "hands bound and chained to the waist." Angola guards would take the person to the parish deputies, who have strict procedures for how to transport someone.

But Chaisson said, "Gary's not going to the sheriff. He's going right to my conference room in the courthouse." And I did, in regular clothes, no "jewelry," with one unarmed guard. The DA wanted some time with me before the hearing. "This is a great day for me and for St. Charles Parish," Chaisson said. "I hope it's a great day for Gary Tyler." Not long after that, the judge wanted to say hello as well.

Going to court, seeing that welcoming atmosphere, being able to talk to the DA, the judge, meeting the judge's family, seeing how the guards greeted me and smiled, was incredible. There was only a small group present, including the legal team and my friends Norris Henderson and Calvin Duncan. My lawyers had decided to keep the hearing quiet to avoid any publicity that might attract opponents. When the judge made her announcement, "You should be released today," everyone breathed a sigh of relief. People turned to each other and hugged as the reality began to sink in. Even the judge cried. It was a glorious, unforgettable moment. I walked up to DA Chaisson. His staff shook my hand and hugged me. I asked him, "Sir, if there's anything I can do to help, let me know." Chaisson's reply was: "The only thing I want you to do is go about your life, make the best of your life, put this behind you." I felt he was sincere and earnest. He, along with the judge, had put his career on the line. I was thinking, If I go to court, I'm going to get mass protests from people in the community riled up by those who oppose me and have harsh feelings about what happened—but I didn't get any of that.

Here's how George remembered it: "The way Gary was treated by everyone who came in proximity with him that day was as someone who'd been mistreated, had overcome that, and was a remarkable human being."

THE NEXT PART WAS easy. I was already packed. As soon as the *Montgomery* decision came down, Mary and George told me, "You're going home, start packing your stuff." All my things were centralized. I had a room in the gym where I had a locked cabinet with the important stuff—letters from family and supporters, my notes, photos, and other personal items, everything except for minimal stuff I kept in the dormitory. When Mary and others came to visit after DA Chaisson got involved, I gave them boxes I had packed up. The day of the court hearing, I put everything left on a wagon and told Kenya, "If they release me today, I'm going to come back for this."

I had been saying good-bye to people and gearing up to leave, cutting back on a lot of my responsibilities. Kenya moved up to become president of the Drama Club. I had my last hospice patient in 2015.

When they brought me back to the prison, I went straight to the hospital. You have to have a physical examination before you're released. People in the hospital had already heard that I was getting out. They knew me and were happy for me. Ms. Tillery, who was working the security booth, had known me since I was on death row.

"Good luck," she told me. "Your mother would be so happy to know you're getting out."

From there, I went to the radio station to give an interview to Prentice Robinson. I also had an interview with Kerry Meyers at *The Angolite*. And then I was ready to go. The prison truck came outside the gym, and Kenya and a few other guys helped put all the boxes on the truck. Darrel had replaced Burl Cain that year. Even though he got to the prison very early every morning, Warden Vannoy waited until I was ready to leave and was the one who drove me to the front gate. I knew him when I was young and he was a lieutenant in CCR. He always looked out for me. We basically grew up in prison together. But prisoners and security cannot fraternize with each other. At the front gate that day, he said, "Gary, I've been knowing you a long time. Since you're a free man, now I can honestly call you my friend."

There outside the gate were George, Mary, Majeeda, Emily, Corrine, all of my lawyers. They were helping Norris and Calvin move my boxes from the truck to people's cars. Some members of the Drama Club and other friends sent me off by reciting the motto: "We are the willing!"

Freedom refused to be denied. Even though I was no longer a religious man, I know the Bible well. When I left that prison, I dared not look back. Not that I was afraid I'd be turned into salt, but I didn't want to go back, so I didn't look back. Getting out of prison was less of a challenge for me than for many people because so many people had dedicated their lives to ensure I wouldn't have a hard time being free, despite what I went through, despite what I had lost.

The only painful thing about it all was that my mother wasn't physically there. But I knew she was with me, and that she would be eternally.

CHAPTER 18

STITCHING A LIFE TOGETHER

On April 29, 2016, I walked out of Angola a free man and got in a car with my New Orleans attorneys, Mary, Majeeda, and Emily, and filmmaker Chandra McCormick. As we pulled away, Emily handed me a flip phone and showed me how to operate it. They had taken the list I'd given them of names of family members and put them all in the phone. I was moved and amazed. With Angola getting smaller behind us, I started making calls. My family still didn't know I'd been released, given how fast things had happened and the lawyers wanting to keep the hearing low-key. First I tried calling Auntie Lady—the Louise to my mother's Thelma—but I couldn't get through. Next I tried my sister Bobbie Nell but couldn't get through to her either. Finally Auntie Lady picked up. She was so ecstatic, she cried and kept repeating her nickname for my mother, "Juanice." Then she told me she'd got word that Bobbie Nell had been rushed to the hospital in Jefferson Parish.

Emily took me there as soon as we'd dropped my boxes by her house in New Orleans. My sister had just come out of the operating room. We got the elevator and met my nephew Darrick and the others up in the lobby. They were really surprised and glad to see me. My three-year-old great-niece ran over. She was playing a game on some kind of phone. I felt so embarrassed and intimidated—here I had this flip phone and I had problems just making calls. When I was at Angola, I'd had the opportunity to get a cell phone, but it was contraband, and I stayed away from anything that might keep me from getting out. I pointed to the girl's hand and asked my nephew, "What's that?"

"That's an iPhone, Uncle Gary," he said. "Don't worry about it. The best ones to teach you are the children. They'll be so happy to show you how to use the phone and the computer."

Soon my sister was in her hospital room and coming out of the sedation. I bent over and told her, "This is supposed to be my moment, not yours. You're upstaging me." When Bobbie Nell realized it was me, she gave me a big smile. We stayed there awhile as more family members arrived.

The next day, George took me to Norris Henderson's, where I stayed for nearly two weeks. First, we made a stop to see Albert Woodfox and Robert King—Fox and Moja—at a hotel in Harvey, Louisiana, where Moja was staying. He'd come from Texas for the weekend. It was empowering being with both of them. The last time we'd seen each other, I was bringing them doughnuts while they were still in solitary. Since then we'd lost Herman Wallace, the third member of the Angola Three. A judge had ruled his indictment years earlier was "fatally flawed" because women were excluded from the grand jury. Being free now and able to see Fox and Moja free was exhilarating and surreal. These guys were my idols. Here I was, standing with men who'd given so much of themselves to me and made it possible for me to survive and thrive in that treacherous environment. They were older, but you could see in their faces, in their presence, that they were strong.

I told the lawyers I also wanted to contact Richelle McKenzie, the daughter of Richard Dunn, the supporter who had been shot and killed in 1976 leaving a fundraiser for my case. Mary made arrangements for me and Richelle to see each other at the law office the following week. After four decades I was meeting the daughter Richard never had a chance to meet himself. Richelle had written me a letter when she was a teenager, telling me she wanted to get to know me. She'd been raised all her life hearing my name and how her father died. Now she was married with twin daughters, Paris and Page, and a son in college who'd been named for her father. Even though I never had the opportunity to meet him, I saw Richard Dunn in her. I sensed her kindness and also her nervousness. Her father wasn't there to embrace her, but the man her father died for was. Richelle and I sat with her twin daughters and got teary-eyed as we talked. I felt her pain as well as her joy.

THOSE VISITS LIFTED MY spirits, but I also had a lot of work to do to get adjusted to the free world. I was sixteen years old when I went to jail. I didn't know anything about paying rent and having responsibilities for daily living. I knew I had to hit the ground running. Norris had started an organization called VOTE, Voice of the Experienced. He helped me learn some basics about how to integrate back into society. I had to get my paperwork straight, find my birth certificate, and get official documents, not carry around a prison ID. I also needed new clothing. Norris and I went to Costco and I picked out some shirts, socks, and underwear, what we call "street clothes." I felt strange looking in a full-bodied mirror and seeing clothing that wasn't prison-based. To me, I looked awkward, wearing a colorful shirt that wasn't chambray blue or white. It was like dressing for a whole other world.

Norris and I sat down and discussed my future. At fifty-seven, I had to start from rock bottom. There are people who retire around that age and live modest, comfortable lives. Here I was this old man with nothing to his name. How was I going to go about establishing my life? My longtime supporter Bob Zaugh had let me know that to get Social Security, I'd have to work for at least ten years. I was starting with a zero balance; the two cents an hour you earn at Angola didn't count. That was kind of scary. You think about life expectancy, especially of Black people. You hear about Black people not making it to Social Security, who've been working in the system for a long time. Who was going to want to take on the responsibility of hiring someone my age? I knew there wouldn't be great opportunities to make a decent salary.

Despite my worries, my family and friends made sure I had fun those first two weeks. My nephew Darrick got some tickets to a Katt Williams comedy event in New Orleans. It felt really good, my first time being at a live comedy show, although some of my guys in the Drama Club did comedy and they were outrageous. Darrick also got me a Samsung Galaxy S5 phone, which I quickly learned how to operate.

Before Angola, I had never gone out to a restaurant. In St. Charles Parish, those were exclusive places only for whites. In our community, we had "chicken shacks" that are now gone, taken over by chain stores like McDonald's and KFC. Darrick took charge of picking me up from Norris's place and taking me to different restaurants. The day after my release, Mary, George, and the other lawyers even took me to Landry's on Lake Pontchartrain in New Orleans. I always said, "When I get out, I want to get me a seafood platter." And that day, I had one. I used to tell Mary about the German chocolate cake my father would make. He baked one for me on my eighteenth birthday and brought it to the jail in St. James Parish, when I was waiting for the resentencing hearing. My father was the best baker I ever met. When you bit into that thing, you wanted to eat the whole cake at once, that's how light and good it was. Sure enough, Mary got the people at Landry's to bring me German chocolate cake. She'd never forgotten what I told her.

The two weeks in New Orleans zoomed by. Bob Zaugh arrived and flew back with me to Los Angeles. "What's the first thing you want to do when we land in California?" Bob asked me.

"Go to the beach in Santa Monica and wade into the ocean."

I had to wait, though, because it was evening by the time we got in. A few days later, Bob brought me to that beach. I took off my shoes and walked in. Was it cold! Still, I really enjoyed it, and I appreciated Bob making it happen for me.

The night of our arrival, Bob drove me to Pam and Steve White's in Pasadena, a city I'd never been to. They greeted me so warmly, it felt like a reunion with old friends or family members you hadn't seen in a long time. We embraced and they showed me around their really nice home. It was a large place built by the original owner a hundred years earlier, well designed with beautiful woodwork from trees in the neighboring hills. Even at night, I could see the house had a lot of flowers.

"Here's your bedroom," they said. This was the first time in my life I'd had a room of my own. At home, I'd shared a room with my brothers. On death row and CCR, I had my own cell, but it had bars; I was always exposed. The prison dormitories each held sixty men, eighty-six by the time I left. But here I knew I could shut the door and sit, my mind could wander in my own little world, I could talk to myself. I would have privacy.

Not only were these two providing me a place to live, Pam and Steve and other supporters, including Bob and Joan Anyon, who had actually named their son Tyler after me, had helped raise funds for me through the Liberty Hill Foundation. That meant I had some spending money of my own.

That first night Steve did the cooking, as he usually did. I assumed they knew I didn't eat meat, just fish. As they passed various dishes, I saw he'd made chicken and thought, I'll just eat the vegetables. I was in their house. But they figured it out and were gracious about accommodating me.

In the morning, we walked around the neighborhood. Every corner I went to, I noticed something I'd never seen before—mountains visible from the sidewalk, people riding on a bike trail.

We talked about what I'd need to do to get my life in order. There was so much, it felt like a monumental task. I had to wonder, could I accomplish this? No matter how much you learn in prison, out in society you realize you don't know enough.

I had to go to the DMV to get a California state identification card, and I had to sign up for various benefits like health insurance. In prison, they take your picture and give you an ID, show you where to go if you're sick. But out here there's a lot of paperwork and people looking at you in surprise. I didn't have anything to refer back to about what benefits I had been getting.

Pam and Steve had to show me how to navigate around the community. When I was out in California as a kid, I learned the bus system from South Central L.A. to downtown Hollywood. But when I came this time, I didn't know north from south, east from west. At first, I stayed inside or in the backyard. Walking by myself around the community felt like a challenge. Wherever I went, somebody would chauffeur me.

After a few weeks, Pam and Deborah George, my drama advisor at Angola who had remarried, taken back her maiden name, and moved to nearby Highland Park, told me, "We're going to teach you how the transportation system works." Pam got me a TAP card that covered the bus and the train. We caught the bus to the Gold Line train and went all the way to Union Station. From there, we went around Chinatown, got on the Green Line 7th Street and rode around different parts of Los Angeles, got on the Expo Line out to Santa Monica. After that, I started going on my own every Thursday to a job search place at Union Station on Orange Grove Blvd. for people who'd been incarcerated and others trying to get their lives together.

Steve brought me to LA Fitness, where I got a membership card. Pam showed me how to catch the bus to go there on my own. One day when Steve brought me to the gym, he said, "You're going to have to find your way back." That was challenging, too, but I was able to do it. When I came through that door, Pam was really relieved. They also showed me how to use the GPS on my phone. Pam had the energy to go on walks with me in different parts of Pasadena and Altadena.

A FEW MONTHS IN, Pam and Steve went to Hawaii for a week for a friend's wedding. They missed an exuberant fifty-eighth party thrown for me in Santa Monica by Jan and Jerry Manpearl, prominent donors and fundraisers for political events. They had a large birthday cake for me in the pool area of their home. The Chambers Brothers provided the entertainment; actor Mike Farrell was among the speakers. It was a heartwarming event.

I was staying in Pam and Steve's house alone, but by then I had learned my way around. Each week they took me grocery shopping at a store called Vons. I thought, I got this. I took a bus to Washington and transferred to another bus on Allen, where Vons was. I didn't write down what I wanted because I knew what that was. The supermarket door popped open.

I had been there many times, but that day when the door opened, I became discombobulated. I didn't know what I wanted to get. I stood near the door and people were walking by, minding their business. I started interpreting the looks on their faces: "Look at that guy, he doesn't know what he's doing." Finally, I mustered the strength to grab a cart and did a pretend shopping. I went down every aisle in that store. When I finished, I realized I'd gotten prison food—bread, peanut butter, soups, no more than five items. I didn't get any of the things I had gone to the store to buy. I was nervous while paying and almost fell out when I left. I shook my head and told myself, I got to get over this phobia. After I caught the bus, I was walking downhill when a guy pulled out of his driveway. He looked at me and asked if I needed a ride. We started talking and he wondered where I was from.

"Louisiana," I said, "around New Orleans."

"I recognize your accent!" he told me. "I was just out there a month ago." The guy was an undertaker at a funeral home. He gave me his card and told me to contact him if I needed anything. I still have that card somewhere. His kindness helped me get my bearings.

Two days later, on a Saturday, I decided to go back to Vons prepared with a list of the things I wanted. I reminded myself that when I went to the prison canteen, I always had a list.

That week was one of the few times in my life I'd been all by myself. The house seemed like it was alive. I could feel it breathe and move. I heard every little sound, the squirrels on the roof, avocados dropping. One day I was sitting in the living room watching TV, when I grabbed my phone to call my nephew and the phone wouldn't come on. I started getting panicky. How would I contact anybody? All of a sudden I heard a telephone ringing—it was Pam and Steve's landline. I remembered Deborah's number and called her. She said she'd take me to a phone store to get my cell checked out. But first I called my nephew on the landline.

"What's wrong, Uncle Gary?" his girlfriend asked.

After I told her, she said, "Uncle. There are two buttons on the side. Hold them down and let them out." I did that and the phone came back on. She had a similar phone and told me sometimes they just reboot with new software.

Other commonplace things were also brand-new to me. I'd never had a bank account in my name. The system required a user name and a pin number—how was I going to remember that? You have to come up with something you will remember but not too simple. I don't know how many times I had to change my user name or pin number to get things right. I had to learn to write checks, which I did by paying bills. Each month I would deposit the check I got through the mail from the Liberty Hill Foundation. That regular interaction helped me learn the banking system.

I'd also never had access to a computer. Warden Cain considered it dangerous for inmates to have a computer, like having a weapon. Prisoners could use it to file suits against him. He had a megalomaniacal perspective that involved banning books, typewriters, and radios in the cell blocks. Before Cain came to Angola, we had a computer room at the graphic arts school. I learned how to turn one on and off and how to print, but I wasn't able to learn any other technical skills. Pam and Steve slowly showed me how to operate a computer. In 2017, Deborah and her friend Margie Simkin bought me a Mac laptop.

One day Pam dropped Deborah and me near a restaurant in Chinatown that sold soul food. We walked down a side street. I never thought I'd see soul food in the middle of Chinatown, but the menu listed dishes sold in New Orleans. After we ordered, I started looking around, expecting to see somebody Black with an apron coming out from the kitchen, like Black cooks do in the South. That didn't happen. An Asian waiter brought out my fried fish and Deborah's fried chicken. The food wasn't spicy and didn't taste like any seafood I knew. Another new thing.

As a kid, the first movie I saw was *Bonnie and Clyde* in the old Kenner Theater, one big theater with a big screen. It was great. Then when I came to stay at my sister's in California in 1972, I saw *Planet of the Apes* in a drive-in. So I thought I was ready for a movie in Pasadena. I went with Pam and Steve. We got our tickets and I just stood there in the lobby. There were so many theaters inside this one building. Pam showed me that the theaters each had a number and how to tell which one was showing the film you wanted to see. I smiled and took a breath and walked in.

After some time, I needed to learn how to drive. Once I got a job, I took the train for the first year. It gave me a sense of freedom knowing I didn't have to depend on anyone. But eventually it took a toll. You met a lot of unruly people who wanted to get into altercations. Police wanted to scan your TAP card to make sure you were legitimately on the train, or stop people and shake them down, go through their bags. Sometimes the train had mechanical problems and you had to wait till they sent buses to pick you up and take you to the next station. That could last for hours. There were days I didn't get home till twelve or one at night. People would invite me to something, but I couldn't go because the transportation system stopped at a certain time.

So I realized it would be best to get a car. In prison, I had driven vehicles for the paint crew. I knew how to drive, but not on city streets. At Angola there are no stop signs or flashing lights. You don't stop when you come to an intersection unless you see a vehicle coming from another way. I had a lot of rules to learn. I took a computer test to get a learner's permit. Pam and Steve showed me the proper way of driving. After twice failing the test for my driver's license due to minor errors, I decided to take it in Glendale, and I passed. The guy at the DMV saw my age and said, "This is your first time getting this? Where the hell have you been?"

In 2018, I bought my first car, a charcoal-gray 2016 Camry. The day I walked out of prison, I knew how freedom felt. But when I got this car and was able to go wherever I wanted at any time, that was total liberation for me.

Thanks to Pam and Steve's connections, I had a lot of free dental and periodontal care. Dental care at Angola was mainly extraction. That's why I stopped chewing gum and eating a lot of sweets. People were surprised I kept so many of my teeth, but I still needed a lot done. The local optometrist also donated eye care and free lenses. I hung on to my Angola frames.

Those months at Pam and Steve's were one of the sweetest times in my life. They meticulously took time to help me in all the areas I needed, listening to me and being willing to move at my pace. This world was completely different from the one I'd left behind. I understood how Rip Van Winkle felt.

I really savored freedom. Those first months, I loved being able to get off the train or the bus wherever I pleased. I didn't have to rush, I could take my time to recalibrate and decide where I wanted to go and for how long and appreciate every moment of it. I thought a lot about how my ancestors must have felt after emancipation, about those who fought for freedom and were willing to die for it because they knew they wouldn't have to go back to bondage.

They came to know freedom. And so did I.

I ALWAYS TOLD MYSELF if I got out, I'd get involved in the fight against the death penalty. I'll never forget what it was like having an execution date. On May 11, 2016, the day after I made it to Pasadena, I was surprised to learn I was the honored guest at an event of Death Penalty Focus. Mike Farrell, Sister Helen Prejean, Jackson Browne, and Joan Baez were all there. The group was also honoring Albert Woodfox and John Thompson, another person who'd been sent to death row at Angola after being wrongly convicted of murder. He had sued the state and the jury awarded him millions of dollars. The case went all the way to the Supreme Court, where Clarence Thomas made the argument that the state was not at fault. John Thompson never got a dime.

In July, I joined a rally and press conference that Death Penalty Focus had in downtown L.A. with Mike Farrell and the former district attorney, Gil Garcetti. They were mounting a campaign called Yes on 62, to abolish the death penalty in California. Soon after that, Jackson Browne performed a benefit concert for the campaign in San Diego and invited me to open by sharing my story. One young lady in the audience began yelling for Jackson Browne. A lot of other people shouted, "Speak, Gary, speak!" Jackson Browne came out on the stage. "They want to hear you," he whispered. "Give them your story." When I was done, I got a standing ovation.

We didn't win the ballot initiative, but Death Penalty Focus has continued to do important work. Over the years I have participated in annual events and met other great people, including Michael B. Jordan.

With the help of Bob Zaugh, I began doing a number of speaking engagements. In September 2016, I was a keynote speaker for Susan Burton's Justice on Trial Film Festival. Susan Burton, founder of a reentry program for women called A New Way of Life, had also nominated me for a "Longevity Soldier Award" from Black Women for Wellness, which I was honored to receive. I spoke at colleges and universities, several churches, and the Rising Scholars program at Cal State Long Beach, for formerly incarcerated individuals. I had appearances at Tim Robbins's experimental theater, The Actors' Gang, and twice at the Long Beach Opera for their production about the Central Park Five. Later I got invitations to go out of state, to Wisconsin and Michigan and other places.

Because of my work in the Drama Club, I felt comfortable doing this. I had learned that audiences want to hear what you have to say. How attentive they are depends on your delivery. I knew how to talk about overcoming my ordeal in a lively style using humor. If I'd just shown resentment and hatred, people would have seen someone the system broke. That wasn't me.

When I first came to Pasadena, I thought I'd move to Fontana out in the valley to be near my sister Ella and my brother Jimmie. But eventually I saw there were a lot of activities happening in L.A. If I went to the Valley, I'd be far removed. So I decided to stay in Pasadena and find a job in the city. Joanne Michael, a neighbor of Pam and Steve's, had a guesthouse in her backyard and offered to rent it to me once I found employment.

The first job I got was in 2016 with GroundWorks Campaigns. Pam and Steve knew people there. Our team made calls encouraging people to vote for various propositions and amendments. My coworkers loved me, but the job took a lot of intestinal fortitude. I'd describe a proposition to increase taxes on the wealthy in California and people would say, "I'm a Donald Trump supporter," and curse me out. I knew it wasn't personal, but I knew I didn't have to take the insults either.

Deborah took me to Father Greg Boyle's Homeboy Industries. I liked its work hiring former gang members and people who were getting out of jail, but I wanted to be away from a prison vibe. Then I went with Bob to A Place Called Home, a youth group run by Debrah Constance. She had been a big supporter of mine and had even made a weaving of me. That place seemed ideal, working with kids I could help keep off a path leading to prison. When I was working with reentry programs at Angola, some of the men I mentored had mentioned how they wished they had met someone like me when they were younger. The kids and the instructors all liked me. But they couldn't get a response to the Live Scan procedure requiring people working with kids to prove they had no sex offense. Sometime later I found out that my records had been sealed and only I could give access.

In December of 2016, Bob brought me to Safe Place for Youth (SPY). The director, Alison Hurst, didn't have any openings. Bob handed her a disc with the *Cast the First Stone* documentary. As soon as she watched it, Alison called Bob and said, "I've got to hire him." I worked there for more than seven years. It was a young organization, with vibrant, sincere staff. I felt at home. I liked doing outreach work with young people who were homeless or had dysfunctional families, looking for a place where they could be themselves, be fed and be safe, talk with people who took a real interest in them.

In 2018, I started a drama class at SPY, which I really enjoyed. They wanted me to start a sewing class as well. I told them I'd help someone else if they started one. A young woman named Jasmine took the lead. Then Alison approached me about being part of a group going to the anti-lynching museum Bryan Stevenson had created in Alabama. After experiencing the museum and seeing me interact with people there who knew about me, Allison pulled me aside and said, "Gary, it's time for the kids at SPY to know who you are." We had made an agreement when I was hired for me to remain anonymous. I know how kids can glamorize someone who's been in prison for a long time. I wanted them to know who I was as a person. Many of them thought I was from the military or law enforcement because of the way I carried myself and said "Good morning" to everyone.

When we came back, Alison organized a showing at the Vineyard Church in Los Angeles of *Cast the First Stone* as the way to introduce my story. SPY had a lot of wealthy donors who want to help young people get off the streets. While the donors had good intentions, I saw how they ignored the homeless camps near the SPY office. I decided to have a couple of our young actors do a guerilla theater performance I called *Blindsided*. Even Allison didn't know what I was doing, but the kids did. The night of the screening, one of the young people, Gary, sat outside the door of the Vineyard with a guitar begging for money for food. Security knew he was an actor. "Remember the face of anyone who donates so you can give the money back," I told Gary. But every person walked by as if he weren't there.

The program opened with the documentary. After the credits, Gary burst inside hollering and pointing out the people who had passed by him.

"I asked you for some money to buy food, but you just ignored me like I was nothing," he said, "like I was a piece of crap." The performance was so good, everyone believed it. People were wondering, where was security? They were part of the plot! When Gary got to the front of the room, he dropped his bag, looked up at the audience, grabbed his guitar, and started singing—he was a great musician. And then he started crying. No one knew what to do.

Another actor, Isaiah, came out and asked if he could help. Gary told him, "I've been trying to eat all day. I thought someone would be kind enough to help me, but nobody cared."

"I'm here," Isaiah said. "Let's go across the street and get something to eat." They left the stage. Everybody was quiet. I had told Gary and Isaiah, "Go out through the side door and go backstage, count to 10 using one one thousand, two one thousand, then come back out then come back out and bow." They did that—and the audience realized it was a performance, a lesson in the difference between good intentions and good deeds.

That same year, I was honored that a short film about me, *Gary Tyler, My Neighbor*, by Mwï Epalle and Ming-Wei Fasquelle, won the Speak Truth to Power award of the Robert F. Kennedy Human Rights project.

MY DRAMA WORK AND other responsibilities didn't leave much time for sewing on the job. But during those years, I heard a lot of people say, "Gary, do what you do best." I'd always thought of quilting as hobby craft, but they were encouraging me to see it as something more. Then in 2020 a group called Art Matters named me a fellow. They knew my work because of Lori Waselchuk, who came to Angola in 2007 to do a photo essay about the hospice program. Lori returned in 2009 and photographed many of the quilts made by hospice volunteers. She got a grant from the Open Society Foundations to create a traveling exhibit about the program, which she called "Grace Before Dying." The grant included commissioning two special quilts. I started a piece and three others joined in and made their own sections for *The Blue Print*, which traveled with the exhibit all over the country and is now in the National Museum of African American History and Culture in D.C. For a follow-up grant, I made a quilt called *The Tree of*

Life. I wanted that piece to signify the continuation of life, people becoming seeds that cause new life to sprout as long as there is fertile ground. That one also became part of the hospice exhibit and is now in the Historic New Orleans Collection museum.

I told Bob I wanted to quilt but I couldn't do it where I was living because it wasn't big enough. So he decided to start a GoFundMe to get me a studio and equipment. The following year at a fundraiser for the studio, I met a woman who knew people at a spot called The Brewery. With her help, I got space there. At first I was just dabbling, to see if I still knew what I was doing. But then people around the country started sending me fabric and a sewing machine. One woman in the community donated $15,000 to the fund.

In the summer of 2022, a couple named Robert and Robin Moreland came to the studio to see me. Robin was Deborah George's daughter and had often come with her mother to Drama Club events at LSU. Robert was an artist. He looked at photos of my work that Lori Waselchuk had sent me. "Can I take pictures of these?" he asked. "I have some people I want to show them to." I said yes.

Robert sent those photographs to Anthony and JJ Curis from the Library Street Collective in Detroit, and then introduced me to them over Zoom. The two of them encouraged me to stop by the gallery if I ever found myself in town. That November, I had a speaking engagement in Detroit, and the gallery turned out to be right around the corner from the hotel where I was staying. Anthony and I walked and talked. He said something that really resonated with me: "Your greatest asset is yourself." And I knew then that quilting was a calling, that I had to get off my duff, stop making excuses about not wanting to do things I had done in prison. People knew about my case, I realized, but did they really know me, know that I was an artist? I decided to use my art to reflect on what I'd been through.

Back in the studio, I pondered how to approach this. I wanted to show I was more than a victim of the system, that who I am today was shaped by what I went through yesterday. I challenged myself to do something I'd never done before, put myself on fabric. Is that self-centered? I asked myself. Then I said, No, people really want to know who you are. They want to know "Why are you not insane, Gary, why are you not bitter?" I began embracing my identity as an artist.

To my surprise, the Library Street Collective invited me to do a solo exhibit beginning July 8, 2023, curated by an amazing Black woman, Allison Glenn. It said it had an unexpected opening; could I do twelve pieces? "No problem," I said. But I knew this was going to be a tremendous task. I wanted to do something different from what I had done in prison, something that would make an impact, show my transitions.

I decided to call the show, "We Are the Willing," after the Drama Club motto. I created six quilts based on photographs of myself taken at different points in prison. Something told me to do the self-portraits in black-and-white, because many people can identify with that as a way to see an individual's soul. For each quilt, I went to as many as ten fabric stores until I found just the right pieces. I always visualize what I can do with certain material. I can use that for the fences on the perimeter of the prison, I'd say. There's the color of the denim in Angola jeans.

The first quilt I called *Captivity*. It was inspired by a photo of me standing against a brick wall in the Hahnville Parish jail a few months after I'd been arrested, savagely beaten, and charged with murder. In the actual photo you can see my arms, but I wanted to show that I'd become immersed in the brick wall, overwhelmed by the forces controlling my life. I had no say whatsoever.

The next one I titled, *December 14, 1975*, the date I arrived at Angola. I used a still from a CBS News program about me in my death row cell. On either side of the image is my death row number and my cell number.

Defiant was based on a 1976 photo of me coming out of the courthouse after Judge Ruche Marino denied me a new trial. The large group of supporters outside chanting "Free Gary Tyler" gave me a sense of power. I wanted to throw up a fist, but I was handcuffed. So I made my cuffed hands into fists and used my expression to communicate: "I have not been beaten, I'm here no matter what."

Twelve years passed before the photo for the fourth quilt, taken after I was in the Main Prison population. I called this one *Unwavering*. Lines radiating out signify the sense of awareness I'd gained after my years in solitary confinement. I knew how and why I had been unfairly treated and why I had to stay strong and keep fighting. By then I was actively involved in organizational activities. My hair had gotten longer, my sense of culture more defined. I was evolving into the person that I've become today. At the time, there was no ray of light whatsoever, but I knew I couldn't give up because there were so many supporting me. In this quilt, you see me peering out through an open space in the prison bars, defying the odds. I made another quilt with a similar message, this one called *Emboldened*, from a 1992 photo.

Wilbert Rideau took the picture behind *Remembrance* when I was working on the paint crew with my friend Leslie Smith. Leslie was a lifer, sentenced in the seventies to ninety-nine years for selling drugs. He and I became good friends. That November, Leslie took sick. He was diagnosed with AIDS and died a few months later. His pardon—what we called the golden seal—came through just a week after that. I knew Leslie well, how decent he was, how caring, how he went out of his way to help other people. He's still a part of my life. I wanted to show the humanity of those incarcerated, whose lives touch so many others. When I went to prison, there were some three hundred thousand people locked up in U.S. jails. Now there are over two million. Imagine how many people are stumbling through grocery stores because they're just returning from years of isolation, or are missing a loved one who's shut away.

For the Library Street Collective, I also made quilts depicting butterflies—*Hope, Matriarch,* and *Rebirth*—and two called *Ray of Hope* and *Ray of Freedom*. Like those butterflies, I'm constantly evolving. I am everything good and bad that happened in my life. Despite it all, I came out on the good side.

Almost all my quilts sold the first weekend of the exhibit. Press about the show helped get word out about my art. In February of 2024, I was presented the Frieze Los Angeles Impact Prize. I can honestly say that this was the first time I won the lottery. I was honored and very humbled.

The quilts I made for the Frieze art show included one titled *Indignity*, about the "Guts and Glory" competition at the Angola rodeo. The Santa Monica Art Bank bought my *In Memoriam of an Ashanti Warrior*, made in honor of my friend Kareem, who died on the operating table six months before he was to be released. Kareem played the warrior in the Drama Club's production of *Water for an Old Ashanti Mother*, the story of a proud African warrior who'd been captured and sold into slavery. In the plantation field one day, he noticed an elderly woman and understood she was dying. The warrior rushed over to give her water. He could not save her, but this woman recognized him as a member of her tribe and lit up. Many years later, after winning his freedom, the warrior went back home and told his people about the Ashanti mother. Kareem's performance captivated audiences.

IN 2024, I WAS one of six formerly incarcerated artists to receive a fellowship from the Right of Return organization. It came with a cash prize and three one-month artist residencies. When I was notified that I'd won a fellowship, I was stunned. I'd seen the application as a long shot, and it became a blessing. It meant people studied and appreciated the significance of my artwork. To make time for the residencies, I had to make some critical changes in my life, including leaving my job so I could concentrate on my art.

That December, I was invited to show my work at the Untitled Art Fair in Miami; my display, "Grief Not Guilty: Reclaiming My Time," won the Last Resort Artist Retreat Residency Prize. I was also invited to speak at the World Economic Forum in Davos, Switzerland, in January of 2025, my first trip out of the country. It was amazing to meet people from around the world and quite moving to have my work and my story recognized there.

IN ADDITION TO MY work and my art, I've spent time since my release connecting with friends. A few months after I got out, I made it my mission to get in contact with Gilda. I was determined to return her high school graduation ring. An attorney friend knew an investigator who located her within an hour. I emailed her and we arranged to talk on Thanksgiving of 2016. We were both excited to hear each other's voice; we talked for over two hours. That Christmas I was able to see her and her son.

I also stayed connected to friends from Angola. I've made eight visits to the prison, beginning in 2017, to see Kenya—everyone knew we were like Siamese twins, with a steel bond between us. That hasn't changed. I'd also see Levelle Tolliver, Terrence Williams, and several others. I'd always wanted to know how it would feel to come and go through that door on my own volition. People were excited I was there—prisoners were hollering at me, security greeting me. I knew I'd made the right decision to go back. I was thrilled to see the hospice and the Drama Club still going strong.

COVID took the lives of a lot of people I knew inside Angola, including Michael Williams from the cast of *The Life of Jesus Christ*. I was well aware that I could have been one of them if I hadn't gotten out. In 2022, COVID also took Albert Woodfox. It was a real blow because I knew he'd had a bad bout of hepatitis in prison and they denied him proper medical treatment, as though they were trying to expedite his death. It affected his motor skills to where he talked slow, he moved slow. As time went on after his release, he became more mobile and energetic. I'd talk to him and tell him to take care of himself. He told me he'd gotten the COVID vaccine, but I found out later he didn't get the booster.

Whenever I went back, I also got to see friends in New Orleans who'd been released from Angola, including Calvin Duncan and Norris Henderson, whose organization VOTE kept growing, and Kerry Myers and Andrew Hundley, now leading the Louisiana Parole Project in Baton Rouge. One person I wasn't able to see was Joe Jenkins, my chess teacher on death row. Joe had become counsel chief for the Guardians of the Flame Mardi Gras Indians in New Orleans. They called him No Hum Bow. I was sad to learn of his death in 2020 in a nursing home at the age of ninety. I'd always catch up with Bobby Wallace, who played Jesus in our play. Recently he did a rendition of *The Life of Jesus Christ* in a big yard in Harvey, across the river from New Orleans. He told me a lot of people showed up, including some guys who'd been in prison with us.

I had really hoped the documentary about that play would get distributed and raise money for the actors. When I got out, I had a long talk with David Deniger, the guy who owned the film. Even though *Cast the First Stone* was not being distributed, David gave me the right to show it wherever I wanted. "Gary, what I want is for you to do showings and make money from it," he told me, "so you and others can get some pay for the time you spent in prison." My goal was to set up a trust for the men and women who were still incarcerated, so there'd be some financial support if they got out, instead of leaving Angola with just the $20 the prison gave you. Having an event for them is still something I'd like to do.

I also stayed in touch with Wilbert Rideau, the former editor of *The Angolite*, who's living in Baton Rouge. Both Wilbert and Albert Woodfox wrote memoirs after they got out. It was great that they shared their experience with the public and helped clear up misunderstandings about prison life. Despite the horrors of prison, inmates can help make it fertile ground for themselves and others to grow and create.

I was not able to see Loretta London, but I was glad I got to talk to her on the phone some months before she passed in 2023. I wanted to let her know I had no hard feelings and to give her family my love. I knew they had suffered as much as my family did. The ordeal brought our families closer together.

Unfortunately, I never had a chance to talk to Natalie Blanks because she had died much earlier. A few years ago at a gathering, I met her daughter, who didn't know who I was. I introduced myself and expressed condolences for the loss of her mother as well as her aunt. She was shocked and didn't say anything. Fifteen to twenty minutes afterward, she came up and hugged me. "Thank you," she said.

Among the people who made time to see me was Billy Baggett, the former guard now retired from Angola. He and his family came all the way from St. Francisville when I was home for a family reunion.

I CONTINUE TO HOPE to see my son. Always I wish him the best. I know that his mother has done whatever she could for him. Recently I also expanded my family by having Richelle McKenzie, Richard Dunn's daughter, christened as my goddaughter, a beloved daughter who should have been in my life all those years.

I've been thinking a lot about what it means to be a father. After my mother died, my sisters Bobbie Nell, Ella, and Jennifer used to visit me together in Angola. During one such visit, I felt they had something important to share with me, something unexpected. Finally, one of them said, "Gary,

Uylos was not your daddy. Your real father was a guy who lived in Texas." The only person who knew that was them and Auntie Lady.

But I know who my father is, the one who was there for me, who took time to show me how to work and how to play, who always treated me as his son, who died remorseful thinking he hadn't done enough to support me. He used to take me to work with him on the weekends, teaching me things about being responsible. To be willing to take in a woman with children and be willing to raise them, that's a very strong man, a man with a big heart. He went out of his way to prove to me that he loved me as much as the other children, even though many Black men at the time didn't use words to express that. I remembered the glow on his face the last time I saw him, when I told him how much I felt his support and how much I loved him. He was a true father.

EPILOGUE

REFLECTIONS

It used to disturb me when people at Angola said, "You must be guilty." For a long time I put more validation on what they said than on supporters who knew I was innocent. Once I stopped trying to convince people, I had individuals come to me and say, "I don't believe that you killed him—I misjudged you," or "Gary, you done spent too much time in prison, you deserve to go home."

Now, finally, I have shared my whole story. I understand how important it was for me to learn what Indigenous people went through here on their own land, what the Japanese experienced during internment, what Jewish people went through in World War II, what is being done now to Palestinians in Gaza. To learn how the system was stacked against people in so many countries during colonization, what Black people have lived through and continue to endure all these years later—and how members of all these groups were able to survive and tell their stories, giving others strength. I want people to know the injustice that was done to me. I want to be part of people speaking the real history of the United States.

I have learned a lot about how the system works. American elites tell whites who are living dirt poor that they're losing jobs and seeing their children go hungry because of Black people—all to keep attention off the ones who are really responsible. Fast-forward, now who's said to be at fault—people who come to this country as immigrants. Pundits whip up prejudice and hatred so when people see Asian, Latino, Black faces, anyone who speaks a foreign language, they say, "They're taking our jobs, bringing crime here in America." The power structure maintains control by making sure hardworking people don't look at *them* and say, "Wait a minute, you're the ones who've got the power, the money. You're who's determining my economic progress." This is an old playbook. I want my story to help disrupt that.

I saw young people who stood up for me and gave my family hope. I want to thank all those, young and old, who saw their own liberation in mine. And I want to applaud young people standing up today to police brutality, mass incarceration, systemic inequality, and hatred, and saying, "Enough is enough."

I also want people to know that despite what an individual's been through, they can come out of a dreadful situation whole and not be broken or bitter—if they can find community, engage in meaningful activities, and stay focused on the truth, on what is just and right. Don't think those forty plus years I spent at Angola were a waste. My friends there called me Nyeusi Kuumba, which means Black Creativity. Making art kept me sane and focused, able to pay attention and to bring a smile to other people's faces.

I'm still an individual walking around in daylight with a flashlight to find my way. I'm deeply aware of the four decades of freedom stolen from me, the limits on my life expectancy. It's horrible that Timothy Weber lost his life and that I had my life condemned by a racist system. What happened had a devastating effect on both our families as well as on our community. It's outrageous that I still have to prove my innocence. I also know that the systemic injustice I faced decades ago continues to happen every day in this country.

I'm not a policy wonk; I'm not laying out a detailed agenda. But I am someone who learned from his experience in life and knows that the criminal legal system is fraught with inequities and gross injustice. America prides itself on having the best criminal justice system in the world, while ignoring the systemic problems—which communities are subject to police brutality and criminality; who lacks economic opportunity; who gets locked up, beaten up, held for long periods just because they lack money for bail; who is sentenced to excessive terms, sentenced to die in prison through execution or a life sentence. Our country perpetuates a prison industrial complex that profits off prisoners' unpaid labor—their servitude. Men and women who spend long years in prison get out with no income despite the hard work they have done. They still have an X on their back, a mark that makes it hard to survive. Many formerly incarcerated people also have no right to vote. I left prison no longer a charge of the state, but at the age of fifty-seven, after decades of work, I had zero contributions to Social Security and serious hurdles to finding a job.

The criminal legal system has a devastating effect on poor and working-class communities, leaving them with economic and psychological trauma. Many organizations around the country, often led by formerly incarcerated individuals, are working to change this. The lawmakers of this country need to hear them and address all their proposals.

I FEEL DEEPLY ABOUT these injustices. At the same time, I know how to appreciate life. I cherish each and every opportunity given me. Exciting things keep happening. In May of 2024, I received an Honorary Doctor of Fine Arts degree from the Massachusetts College of Art and Design at their commencement. I met the actress and painter Kate Capshaw and got interviewed by the actress America Ferrera and the artist Jesse Krimes. One day on the sidewalk I met Frankie Faison, who played Emmett Till's father in *Till*. I told him how much that movie meant to me, especially the scene where Emmett's mother touches his limbs the way my mother touched me after the police beat me. A few weeks later, Faison and his partner, Samantha, took me to lunch to learn more.

During the Frieze awards, I also went to a private event at the home of Ari Emanuel, CEO of Endeavor. "Are you happy?" he asked me.

"Yes," I said. "I am happy. But I'm not thrilled."

"Why not?"

"Because my mother's not here," I told him. "My mother was the rock of my life for a very long time, and she needed to see where I've come. I wish she was here with me."

When I got ready to leave, Emanuel told me, "I'm always going to remember what you said about your mother."

I hope my experiences and thoughts will also stay with you. I hope you remember me as someone who made it because of people who were in my corner, someone who remains defiant, who overcame the odds and lived to spread beauty and promote justice.

ACKNOWLEDGMENTS

I want first to thank my family, who've been there for me from the beginning, my parents and grandparents, all my siblings. I also want to thank the community and Fifth African Baptist Church in St. Rose, which supported my mother spiritually and gave tangible support to my family.

Thank you to the people of New Orleans, the mothers and fathers and grandparents, the students and other young people, who were horrified by what happened to me and came together to be part of our struggle. Their Committee to Free Gary Tyler saw amazing work from Maureen Kelleher, Angie Celius, Sarah and John Dave, Lois Adams, Edna Montrell, Sandy Stimpson, and many others. I am grateful, too, to the people of Detroit, the epicenter of organizing support among unions, who educated workers in Michigan, Wisconsin, Illinois, Los Angeles, and Miami. In Los Angeles, Karen Pomer and Michael Letwin led the Red Tide in building widespread support for me.

My case awakened a lot of people. Black churches around the country during Sunday services told their parishioners about my ordeal and asked them to say a prayer on my behalf. I appreciate them all. I also want to thank all the groups around the country and internationally that supported me, with a special shout-out to Amnesty International, especially Karen Bagge and Birgit Duell, who reached across the Atlantic to visit me on more than one occasion. The organization gathered thousands of support letters and petitions from prominent people in government, law, academia, and more.

I was moved by the musicians and singers who composed songs to promote support for my case. These included the Neville Brothers family, Gil Scott-Heron and Brian Jackson, Anne Romaine, and Deff Generation, whose music educated the public about the injustices I faced. UB40 took up the baton of educating people throughout the world with their song about me. The Kumbuka African Drum & Dance Collective, led by Ausettua Amor Amenkum, were among the many local artists in New Orleans who donated their talents to build support for my freedom.

Thank you to Thurgood Marshall, the longtime soul of the Supreme Court, who wanted to hear my case when all the other justices refused to accept it; Louisiana Supreme Court Justice Pascal F. Calogero, Jr., the only state court judge who acknowledged the unfairness of my conviction; Ed Bradley of *60 Minutes*, who worked behind the scenes to get exposure for me; and Ernest Cojoe, bus driver of school bus 91, who refused to be pressured from telling the truth about what he knew and witnessed that October 7.

I am deeply grateful to Rosa Parks, who felt my mother's pain and assured her she would stand by her. Helen Halyard, an ardent supporter and strong advocate of my freedom, also became a close friend of my mother and family. It meant so much that Rubin "Hurricane" Carter repeatedly spoke out for justice for me.

Appreciation to local leaders in Louisiana like Dorothy Taylor, a councilwoman in New Orleans who was there for my mother; Wilma Irvin, the first African American and first woman on the city council in Kenner, who stood with my family; and Avery Alexander, the iconic civil rights leader of New Orleans, who spoke on my behalf and appeared before the pardon board twice to call for my release. Thanks to Marc Morial, New Orleans mayor, who spoke for me along with many members of the city council, and to State Senator Dennis Bagneris, who tried to convince Governor Edwin Edwards to accept the pardon board's recommendation.

A special thanks to several actors including Bill Cobbs, who visited and told me, "Young man, it's evident that you're strong. I want to encourage you to continue to fight, make your family proud, let the world know that injustices should always be met with resistance." Martin Sheen wrote to the pardon board. Mike Farrell, who became a strong supporter, joined Stephen Rohde to invite me to join Death Penalty Focus after my release. Much gratitude also to poet Deborah George, who believed in me and worked diligently to help the Drama Club do the impossible.

Words cannot express my respect and gratitude to Mary Howell, the archangel and champion who led my legal struggle along with Majeeda Snead, Pam Bayer, Sam Dalton, Katherine Mattes, Emily Ratner, and investigator Gary Eldredge. Many thanks also to my other A-team, George Kendall, Corrine Irish, Corine Williams, and Harmony Loube.

Enormous thanks to Bryan Stevenson, who took on the herculean task of challenging the cruel and unusual punishment of juvenile lifers and made it possible for me to win my freedom. Thanks also to Amy Singer at *The American Lawyer* and Bob Herbert at *The New York Times*, whose excellent reporting expanded the movement to win my release; and to Dave Zirin, sports reporter for *The Nation*, who mobilized world-renowned athletes to speak out for me.

ACKNOWLEDGMENTS

I will always be indebted to the men I met in prison who became my mentors and strongest advocates: Bockaloc, who felt that it was imperative for me to appeal to the public for support; Colonel Nyati Bolt, who always took the time to clear up issues that seemed murky; and Moja King, who encouraged me to persevere and never despair.

Several of these comrades have now passed: Herman Wallace became a very dear and honorable friend of mine and always led me to be true to myself and, despite the horrendous treatment I went through, to find the goodness in people and appeal to the humanity of those who could make a difference. RIP, Soldier. Albert Woodfox told me, "You're never free until you free your mind." I am grateful that he put life and limb on the line for me. Rest in peace, Fox. Clifford Doleman, one of the Three Amigos, was another comrade who was always there for me. You are missed, my brother.

Deepest thanks to Lawrence (Kenya) Jenkins, who I've known for a very long time and has always been supportive. He gave me sound advice and his best self, not only as a friend but as a committed comrade, no matter how difficult the challenges were. I wish him great endeavors and a chance to live his life as a free man. I'll never forget you, brother.

Special thanks also to Norris (Saboor) Henderson, comrade and family in and out of prison, who was steadfast in showing up for me, including the day I walked out of Angola; to Calvin Duncan, another comrade and family in and out of prison, who assured me he would always be in my corner; and to Wilbert Rideau, a dear friend and strong advocate, who was instrumental in educating me about prison politics.

I am grateful to John P. Whitley, former warden of Angola, who recognized my potential, making it possible for me to bring the message of redemption and change to the public through the Drama Club's plays and skits. Thanks also to Cathy Fontenot, who trusted me to take on the monumental task of directing the passion play at Angola; to Deputy Warden Leslie DuPont, who had an open-door policy and was always willing to assist me; and to Warden Darrel Vannoy, who gave me the time of day whenever I needed it.

I owe deep gratitude to Pam and Steve White, who paved the way for me to transition into a whole new life that had been waiting for so long, and who have been the pillars of that new life. I also want to thank the community of Pasadena, who welcomed me, got to know me, and became great supporters, bringing me into their homes as family; and Bob Zaugh, a longtime supporter, always on the move and working to make a difference and find opportunities for me.

Thank you to Paula and Barry Litt, who supported and closely orchestrated my smooth transition back into society with the help of the Liberty Hill Foundation.

ACKNOWLEDGMENTS

Since my release, my oldest sister, Ella, and my brother Jimmie Sims, who live nearby, have been adding regular care to four decades of supporting me while I was in Angola. I am deeply grateful to them. I'm also grateful to the mother of my son, who made sure he got to know the truth about what happened to me and who provided for him throughout his childhood and young adulthood.

My appreciation to Alison Hurst, former director of Safe Place for Youth, who became a dear supporter and gave me an opportunity to pursue my goals of working with young people to try to make a difference in their lives. Thank you also to Alyce Bonura and her sister Tekla Dennison Miller, for helping me acclimate to being back in society.

I have a studio for my quilting thanks to the generosity of many people, especially Ursula Diamond and Kay Gallin, donating to a GoFundMe started by Chandra and Keith McCormick. I was able to have an audience for my art because Robert Moreland sent photos of my quilts, taken by Lori Waselchuk, to the amazing people at the Library Street Collective in Detroit, including JJ and Anthony Curis, director Leah Rutt, and curator Allison Glenn. That audience has now grown thanks to Jesse Krimes, Russell Craig, and Kate Fowle of Right of Return Fellowships; Christine Messineo, director of Frieze Los Angeles and Frieze New York; and Kate Capshaw, who has generously celebrated me as a fellow artist.

I want to give special thanks to Charlotte Sheedy, my agent, who came out of retirement to represent this book after reading the first chapters, because she felt the importance of getting my story out to the public. Alessandra Bastagli and Rola Harb at One Signal Publishers were moved by this narrative and made clear their commitment to promote it to help debunk lies and speak truth to power. They and everyone at One Signal have been steadfast in their support and a pleasure to work with.

Last but not least, I would like to express my profound gratitude to Ellen Bravo, who made the effort to convince me that this was the time for me to tell my story, seeing how protective I was about trusting anyone to take on that task. I wanted my story to be told in its truest form and not embellished or falsely written. I humbly appreciate the time and sacrifice she made to listen to me and all the work she did to make it possible to create this book.

Space doesn't allow me to thank everyone I hold in my heart. Please know how deeply grateful I am to every one of the thousands of people who mobilized to free me, for the support and love that made it possible for me never to give up.

RESOURCE LIST

Amnesty International: A global movement of more than 10 million people in over 150 countries and territories who campaign to end abuses of human rights.
https://www.amnesty.org/

Anti-Recidivism Coalition: ARC works to end mass incarceration in California. To ensure our communities are safe, healthy, and whole, ARC empowers formerly and currently incarcerated people to thrive by providing a support network, comprehensive reentry services, and opportunities to advocate for policy change.
https://antirecidivism.org/

Critical Resistance: Building an international movement to abolish the prison-industrial complex by challenging the belief that caging and controlling people makes us safe.
https://criticalresistance.org/

Death Penalty Focus: Committed to the abolition of the death penalty through public education, grassroots and political organizing, media outreach, and domestic and international coalition building.
https://deathpenalty.org/

Equal Justice Initiative: Committed to ending mass incarceration and excessive punishment in the United States, to challenging racial and economic injustice, and to protecting basic human rights for the most vulnerable people in American society.
https://eji.org/

The Innocence Project: Working to free the innocent, prevent wrongful convictions, and create fair, compassionate, and equitable systems of justice for everyone.
https://innocenceproject.org/

Louisiana Parole Project: A nonprofit organization that helps formerly incarcerated men and women rebuild their lives through transitional housing, employment support, programming, and services, so that they can become fully productive members of their communities.
https://www.paroleproject.org/

NAACP Legal Defense Fund: A legal organization fighting for racial justice. Using the power of law, narrative, research, and people, we defend and advance the full dignity and citizenship of Black people in America.
https://www.naacpldf.org/

National Lawyers Guild: Our mission is to use law for the people, uniting lawyers, law students, legal workers, and jailhouse lawyers to function as an effective force in the service of the people by valuing human rights and ecosystems over property interests.
https://www.nlg.org/

Prison Policy Initiative: A nonprofit, nonpartisan initiative that produces cutting-edge research to expose the broader harm of mass criminalization and sparks advocacy campaigns to create a more just society.
https://www.prisonpolicy.org

Promise of Justice Initiative: Fights for the dignity, freedom, and autonomy of those targeted and touched by the criminal legal system and for an end to mass incarceration.
https://promiseofjustice.org/

Reprieve: An organization of investigators, lawyers, and campaigners fighting for justice, who defend people facing human rights abuses, often at the hands of powerful governments.
https://reprieve.org/us/

Right of Return Fellows: Established by artists, for artists as the first and only national initiative dedicated to supporting and mentoring formerly incarcerated creatives. Right of Return Fellows produce work that advances criminal and racial justice.
https://www.rightofreturnusa.com/

Sentencing Project: Advocates for effective and humane responses to crime that minimize imprisonment and criminalization of youth and adults by promoting racial, ethnic, economic, and gender justice.
https://www.sentencingproject.org/

Voice of the Experienced (VOTE): A grassroots organization founded and run by formerly incarcerated people, our families, and our allies, dedicated to restoring the full human and civil rights of those most impacted by the criminal (in)justice system.
https://www.voiceoftheexperienced.org/

NOTES

CHAPTER 1: THE DAY THE WORLD CHANGED

1 *I remember each detail*: The statements in this chapter are based on notes written by Gary Tyler while he was at Angola prison.

1 *We'd heard rumors there would be a fight*: Amnesty International, "United States of America: The Case of Gary Tyler, Louisiana," November 1, 1994, Index Number: AMR 51/089/1991, https://www.amnesty.org/en/documents/amr51/089/1994/en/.

7 *He was a Vietnam vet who had been wounded*: Shonna Riggs, "V.J. St. Pierre Running Against Snookie for Parish President," *St. Charles Herald Guide*, February 21, 2007.

14 *When the officers marched me out*: Bob Herbert, "They Beat Gary So Bad," *New York Times*, February 8, 2007, https://www.nytimes.com/2007/02/08/opinion/08herbert.html.

CHAPTER 2: AWAITING JUSTICE

23 *The attack on our bus happened at the same time*: Katie Zezima, "Louise Day Hicks Dies at 87; Led Fight on Busing in Boston," *New York Times*, October 23, 2003, https://www.nytimes.com/2003/10/23/us/louise-day-hicks-dies-at-87-led-fight-on-busing-in-boston.html.

23 *When this thing happened in St. Charles Parish, David Duke*: Adam Nossiter, "Legal Lynching in Louisiana: The Case That Refuses to Die," *The Nation*, March 12, 1990, reprinted on https://www.freegarytyler.com/1990/03/12/legal-lynching-in-louisiana-the-case-that-refuses-to-die/.

28 *It was well known in the community*: Danielle L. McGuire, "Black Women, Civil Rights and the Struggle for Bodily Integrity," National Civil Rights

Museum at the Lorraine Hotel, October 2017, https://www.civilrights museum.org/50-voices-for-50-years/posts/black-women-civil-rights-and -the-struggle-for-bodily-integrity.

29 *This was a few months after the incident with Joan Little*: Ashley Farmer, "Free Joan Little: Anti-rape Activism, Black Power, and the Freedom Movement," AAIHS, February 4, 2016, https://www.aaihs.org/free-joan-little/.

29 *The harassment against me was coming from*: Tyler Bridges, "The Duke Dilemma," *64 Parishes*, September 20, 2015, https:/64parishes.org/the-duke -dilemma.

CHAPTER 3: PRESUMED GUILTY

37 *The trial kicked off with jury selection:* Trial Transcript, *State of Louisiana vs. Gary Tyler*, No. 74-033, 29 Judicial District Court, Parish of St. Charles, Louisiana, Vols. 2 and 3.

38 *Black residents were only a quarter of the parish population*: USA Facts, "How Has the Racial and Ethnic Makeup of St. Charles Parish Changed?," https:// usafacts.org/data/topics/people-society/population-and-demographics /our-changing-population/state/louisiana/county/st-charles-parish/.

39 *One white deputy after another*: Trial Transcript, Vols. 4, 5, and 6.

39 *Deputy Mike Babin had to admit*: Trial Transcript, Vol. 5, 966.

39 *He also mentioned that the gun had been stolen*: Trial Transcript, Vol. 5, 975.

39 *"If something had been sticking out of the window"*: Trial Transcript, Vol. 5, 861.

39 *"It couldn't have been fired off of my bus"*: Trial Transcript, Vol. 5, 881.

40 *Cojoe described how a deputy held the particular seat*: Trial Transcript, Vol. 5, 898.

41 *When Williams asked whose peace*: Trial Transcript, Vol. 5, 996.

41 *If there had been anything like that*: Trial Transcript, Vol. 5, 999.

41 *The next morning, I watched Natalie Blanks raise her right hand*: Trial Transcript, Vol. 5, 1099.

42 *Then I had to listen to Herman Parrish*: Trial Transcript, Vol. 6, 1148–55.

42 *"Because I know he's innocent"*: Trial Transcript, Vol. 6, 58-Th.

42 *He said when V. J. St. Pierre questioned him at three in the morning*: Trial Transcript, Vol. 6, 108-Th.

42 *The seat was not torn*: Trial Transcript, Vol. 6, 110–11-Th.

43 *When my lawyer asked if Ulrich would have noticed*: Trial Transcript, Vol. 6, 133-Th.

43 *I interpreted that as, tell them everything*: Trial Transcript, Vol. 6, 134–52-Th, 159–89-Th.

44 *"Something was passed to me"*: Trial Transcript, Vol. 6, 165-Th.

Notes

44 *I told him, "You didn't ask"*: Trial Transcript, Vol. 6, 170-Th.
45 *The state had introduced a second person, Roland LaBranche*: Trial Transcript, Vol. 5, 1026.
45 *He told the jurors*: Trial Transcript, Vol. 6, 59-F.
45 *I heard the judge ask the jury*: Trial Transcript, Vol. 6, 66-F.
46 *It wasn't long*: Trial Transcript, Vol. 6, 67-F.

CHAPTER 4: WELCOME TO ANGOLA

48 *In the South, vigilante groups*: Kindaka Sanders, "The Watchman's Time to Kill: The Right to Vigilante Justice in the Jim Crow South," *Journal of Gender, Race & Justice*, University of Iowa, June 22, 20222, https://jgrj.law.uiowa.edu/sites/jgrj.law.uiowa.edu/files/2022-11/The%20Watchman%E2%80%99s%20Time%20To%20Kill-%20The%20Right%20To%20Vigilante%20Justice%20in%20the%20Jim%20Crow%20South%20.pdf.
49 *"I would like everyone to have a decent life"*: Trial Transcript, Vol. 6, 75-Tu.
49 *Then I listened as the judge announced the sentence*: Trial Transcript, Vol. 6, 77-Tu.
50 *It was Monday, December 15, 1975*: Listing of Personal Identification, Newly Committed Inmates, Gary Tyler, #C-127, December 15, 1975.
50 *No one had informed me of any upcoming dates*: Trial Transcript, Vol. 6, 77-Tu.
50 *There had once been a slave rebellion*: Maris Fessenden, "How a Nearly Successful Slave Rebellion Was Intentionally Lost to History," *Smithsonian*, January 8, 2016, https://www.smithsonianmag.com/smart-news/its-anniversary-1811-louisiana-slave-revolt-180957760/.
53 *I soon learned the mattress*: Abe Ahn, "Stark Photos of a Louisiana Prison That Was Once a Plantation," *Hyperallergic*, November 30, 2018, https://hyperallergic.com/473384/slavery-the-prison-industrial-complex-art-practice/.
54 *Some, like Jesse Washington and Joe Gleason, were former death row inmates*: Witherspoon v. Illinois, 391 U.S. 510 (1968), *Justia U.S. Supreme Court*, https://supreme.justia.com/cases/federal/us/391/510/.

CHAPTER 5: THE GUARDIANS

57 *The first guys I really got to know*: Bob Herbert, "One Man's Solitary State of Injustice," *New York Times*, May 24, 1988, reprinted in https://vachss.com/av_articles/colonel_bolt.html.
57 *Colonel Bolt was . . . an escapee from Chino*: Joy James, "George Jackson: Dragon Philosopher and Revolutionary Abolitionist," AAIHS, August 21, 2018, https://www.aaihs.org/george-jackson-dragon-philosopher-and-revolutionary-abolitionist/.

57 *I didn't know yet, but soon learned*: Laura Sullivan, "Doubts Arise About 1972 Angola Prison Murder," *All Things Considered*, NPR, October 27, 2008, https://www.npr.org/2008/10/27/96030547/doubts-arise-about-1972-angola-prison-murder.

58 *Then, in 1968, when I started sixth grade*: Ryan Arena, "Documentary Highlights First Students to Integrate in 1965," *St. Charles Herald Guide*, November 21, 2022, https://www.heraldguide.com/news/documentary-highlights-first-students-to-integrate-in-1965-2/.

60 *I knew about George Jackson's brother*: "The 50th Anniversary of the August 7th Marin County Courthouse Rebellion," *Freedom Archives*, 2020, https://freedomarchives.org/projects/the-50th-anniversary-of-the-august-7th-marin-county-courthouse-rebellion/.

60 *I already knew a little about Angela Davis*: "The History Behind Angela Davis' Arrest," Arthur Ashe Legacy at UCLA, August 18, 2016, https://arthurashe.ucla.edu/2016/08/18/the-history-behind-angela-davis-arrest/.

61 *That July, two thousand people marched*: Joe Allen, "Free Gary Tyler," *Counterpunch*, August 26, 2006, https://www.counterpunch.org/2006/08/26/free-gary-tyler/; "SCEF Calls for Massive Tyler Demonstration," *Southern Patriot*, April 1976, 8. Most issues of the *Southern Patriot* are in the Anne McCarty Braden Collection at the University of Louisville.

66 *One book that deeply affected me*: Dan T. Carter, *Scottsboro Boys: A Tragedy of the American South* (Baton Rouge: Louisiana State University Press, 1969).

66 *I was moved by reading about Malcolm X's experience*: Malcolm X, *The Autobiography of Malcolm X as Told to Alex Haley* (New York: Ballantine Books, 1992; reissue).

67 *On May 27, 1976, they came into my cell*: Louisiana State Penitentiary, Angola, Louisiana, Conduct Report, Gary Tyler, 84156.

69 *They had strangled Scully*: Letter from Attorney Mary Howell to Judge Lamonica, Division E Section 3 Criminal Court, Baton Rouge, Louisiana, re *State v Larry Lambert*, Docket No. 873165. Lambert was being tried for the murder of Clarence Williams (Scully).

70 *I remember seeing an interview with Rubin "Hurricane" Carter*: The Tomorrow Show, Episode #1.284, May 3, 1975, IMDb, https://www.imdb.com/title/tt22045670/.

CHAPTER 6: NOT GIVING UP ON LIFE

73 *In an affidavit in early March of 1976*: Transcript of an Interview with Natalie Blanks Conducted on February 5, 1976, in the Office of Jack Peebles, Attorney at Law, 9.

Notes

73 *She was sent to see the district attorney*: Transcript of Natalie Blanks interview, 18.

73 *In her own affidavit, Natalie's mother*: Affidavit of Elmira Blanks, Natalie's mother, November 20, 1976, 2.

74 *Natalie's mother also brought in her cousin*: Transcript of an Interview with Sylvia Taylor Conducted on March 15, 1976, in the Office of Jack Peebles, Attorney at Law, 1–6.

74 *In her deposition that same month*: Deposition of Loretta London Thomas in Orleans Parish, March 26, 1976, 1.

76 *Ruche Marino denied he'd ever heard*: Referenced in *State v. Tyler*, 342 So. 2d 574 (1977), *Justia U.S. Law*, https://law.justia.com/cases/louisiana/supreme-court/1977/342-so-2d-574-1.html.

76 *Then, on April 23, the judge rendered*: "Louisiana Youth Is Denied 2d Trial," *New York Times*, April 24, 1976, https://www.nytimes.com/1976/04/24/archives/louisiana-youth-is-denied-2d-trial-black-faces-electric-chair-on.html.

78 *On July 2, 1976, the U.S. Supreme Court*: *Roberts v. Louisiana*, 428 U.S, 325 (1976), *Justia U.S. Supreme Court*, July 2, 1976, https://supreme.justia.com/cases/federal/us/428/325/#.

78 *"The death penalty would never be mandatory"*: "State Seeks Review of Death Law Ruling," *New Orleans States-Item*, September 3, 1976.

79 *It turned out a Norwegian tanker*: Liz Skelton, "George Prince Ferry Disaster," *64 Parishes*, March 22, 2021, last updated June 15, 2021, https:/64parishes.org/entry/george-prince-ferry-disaster.

80 *I was determined not to*: *State v. Tyler*, 342 So. 2d 574 (1977).

80 *On March 8, 1977, deputies flew me*: Gary Tyler notes.

82 *"In the state of Louisiana when you get life"*: Jessica Schulberg, "Louisiana Passes a Bill That Could Free Some '10/6 Lifers,'" *HuffPost*, May 30, 2022, https://www.huffpost.com/entry/louisiana-lawmakers-pass-bill-ten-six-lifers_n_62900f1fe4b0edd2d0215901.

CHAPTER 7: STILL FIGHTING TO SURVIVE

83 *They put me back on death row until March 25*: Gary Tyler notes.

84 *Then I had to go to Angola's D.B. Court*: Conduct Report, Gary Tyler, #84156.

85 *Over and over again, they used that "original reason for lockdown"*: Conduct Report, Gary Tyler, #84156.

87 *Camp J was known as a death camp*: Grace Toohey, "Angola Closes Its Notorious Camp J, 'A Microcosm of a Lot of Things That Are Wrong,'" *The Advocate*, May 13, 2018, https://www.theadvocate.com/baton_rouge/news

/crime_police/angola-closes-its-notorious-camp-j-a-microcosm-of-a-lot-of-things-that-are/article_b39f1e82-4d84-11e8-bbc2-1ff70a3227e7.html.
- 88 *Robert King, who we called Moja*: See Albert Woodfox, *Solitary: Unbroken by Four Decades in Confinement* (New York: Grove Atlantic, 2019).
- 90 *He used to put on his shorts*: Woody Strode, Wikipedia, last edited November 30, 2024, https://en.wikipedia.org/wiki/Woody_Strode.
- 92 *The free men told me to get my stuff*: Conduct Report, Gary Tyler, #84156.
- 95 *I didn't read romance novels*: Harry Haywood, *Black Bolshevik: Autobiography of an Afro-American Communist* (Minneapolis: University of Minnesota Press, 1978).
- 95 *I read Louis Tackwood*: Louis Tackwood, *The Glass House Tapes* (New York: Avon Books, 1973).
- 95 *The power structure came up with Black Codes*: "The History of Slave Patrols, Black Codes, and Vagrancy Laws," *Facing History & Ourselves*, updated April 30, 2021, https://www.facinghistory.org/resource-library/history-slave-patrols-black-codes-vagrancy-laws.
- 96 *It included one big exception*: Daniele Selby, "How the 13th Amendment Kept Slavery Alive: Perspectives from the Prison Where Slavery Never Ended," *Innocence Project*, September 27, 2021, https://innocenceproject.org/news/how-the-13th-amendment-kept-slavery-alive-perspectives-from-the-prison-where-slavery-never-ended/.
- 96 *The number wasn't much different*: James Ridgeway, "God's Own Warden," *Mother Jones*, July 2011, https://www.motherjones.com/politics/2011/07/burl-cain-angola-prison/.
- 96 *Because of a lawsuit filed by Big John Fulford*: *Fulford v. Phelps*, casetext, November 20, 1978, https://casetext.com/case/fulford-v-phelps.
- 98 *When the special board took place*: Gary Tyler notes.
- 99 *After a few months, a guy named James Singerton*: Gary Tyler notes.
- 99 *In May 1985, I finally got classified out of the cell block*: Gary Tyler notes.

CHAPTER 8: LEARNING TO TONE IT DOWN
- 100 *One case that really disturbed me*: Jay Workman, "Tarter Acquitted of Slaying," *Morning Advocate*, Baton Rouge, Louisiana, July 15, 1983.
- 100 *Even more enraging was reading about a white kid*: Tim Talley, "New Probe Ordered in Ascension Shooting," *Morning Advocate*, August 28, 1985.
- 101 *The judge thought Acaldo*: Associated Press, "Killer Given Suspended Sentence," *New Orleans Times-Picayune/States-Item*, August 16, 1985.
- 103 *In order for me to make the move*: Gary Tyler notes.
- 104 *I was influenced by the Seven Principles*: Nguzo Saba, Us Organization,

November 25, 1999, https://www.us-organization.org/nguzosaba/Nguzo Saba.html.

106 *Five guards came and locked me up*: Conduct Report, Gary Tyler #84156.

107 *Not long after this, I was in the* Angolite *office*: For more on Wilbert Rideau, see wilbertrideau.com.

CHAPTER 9: FIGHTING FOR THE RIGHT TO EDUCATION

111 *He sent me a notice that I was not eligible*: Gary Tyler notes. Letter to Mary Howell from Scott Tycer, former classifications officer at Angola, written November 30, 1991, confirming that "education programs available to inmates at Angola were available [only] to those inmates housed in the Main Prison complex."

112 *No surprise that the majority of us on death row*: Ed Pilkington, "Louisiana's Death Row Inmates Make Rare Mass Petition for Commutation," *Guardian*, August 3, 2023, https://www.theguardian.com/us-news/2023/aug/03/louisiana-death-row-inmates-petition-john-bel-edwards.

112 *My anguish over the policy*: Kimberly Sambol-Tosco, "The Slave Experience: Education, Arts, & Culture," PBS, 2004, https://www.thirteen.org/wnet/slavery/experience/education/docs1.html.

112 *Vocational school was also off the list*: Scott Tycer letter to Attorney Mary Howell.

112 *we were a disproportionate percentage of those locked up*: "Criminal Justice Fact Sheet," NAACP, https://naacp.org/resources/criminal-justice-fact-sheet.

113 *In 1979, Mary Howell*: "Civil Rights Attorney Mary Howell Kicks Off St. Peter Claver Club Speaker Series," Jesuit High School of New Orleans, October 3, 2019, https://www.jesuitnola.org/2019/10/03/civil-rights-attorney-mary-howell-kicks-off-st-peter-claver-club-speaker-series/.

113 *But on March 12 of that year*: Gary Tyler notes.

114 *Willie James Howard was fifteen*: "15-Year-Old Boy Lynched in Florida for Sending Love Note," Equal Justice Initiative, *A History of Racial Injustice*, January 2, 1944, https://calendar.eji.org/racial-injustice/jan/2.

114 *George Stinney, a fourteen-year-old Black kid*: Hayley Bedard, "Remembering the Execution of 14-Year-Old George Stinney 80 Years Later," Death Penalty Focus, posted June 14, 2024, updated September 25, 2024, https://deathpenaltyinfo.org/remembering-the-execution-of-14-year-old-george-stinney-80-years-later.

114 *I learned that in the twenties and thirties*: Rita Modak, "Police Unions Are Anti-Labor," *Harvard Political Review*, November 27, 2024, https://harvardpolitics.com/police-unions-are-anti-labor/.

114 *In 1984, the institution changed its policy*: Gary Tyler notes.

115 *In May 1986, having spent time in the Main Prison*: Gary Tyler notes.
115 *He was one of the people incarcerated in Cuba*: Anthony Capote, "Crisis In Context: What the Mariel Boatlift Can Teach Us about the Current Trends in Immigration," Immigration Research Initiative, May 8, 2024, https://immresearch.org/publications/crisis-in-context-what-the-mariel-boatlift-can-teach-us-about-the-current-trends-in-immigration/.
116 *In September 1987, I applied again for the GED program*: Gary Tyler notes.
116 *I immediately wrote a letter to Mr. Tilghman Moore*: Gary Tyler notes.
117 *I felt linked to a long line of Black men*: "A Guide to Working in the Trades as a Person of Color," *Service Direct*, March 18, 2024, https://servicedirect.com/resources/poc-in-the-trades/.
117 *In October of 1988, I wrote again*: Gary Tyler notes.
117 *I finished my GED*: Gary Tyler notes.
117 *Against all odds, on October 27, 1992, I got the diploma*: Gary Tyler notes.
117 *One of the most important lessons of my life*: Dan Rather, Alex Van Amson, and Team Steady, "Truth and Reconciliation, A Look Back: February 11, 1990," *Steady Substack*, February 21, 2021, https://steady.substack.com/p/truth-and-reconciliation.

CHAPTER 10: MAKING CHANGE FROM THE INSIDE

121 *On top of that, we had to put up with horrible medical care*: Jessica Pishko, "At Angola Prison, 'People Are Suffering, People Are Dying,'" *The Appeal*, October 12, 2018, https://theappeal.org/at-angola-prison-people-are-suffering-people-are-dying/.
123 *Back in 1971, before I got to Angola, a guy named Hayes Williams*: Referenced in Hayes Williams and Arthur Mitchell, *Plaintiffs-appellants, v. David C. Treen, Governor of the State of Louisiana et al, defendants-appellees*, 671 F2d 892 (Fifth Circuit 1982), March 31, 1982, in *Justia U.S. Law*, https://law.justia.com/cases/federal/appellate-courts/F2/671/892/442429/.
124 *But conditions overall were still horrible*: John Vodicka, "Prison Plantation," *Facing South*, December 1, 1978, https://www.facingsouth.org/1978/12/prison-plantation.
125 *The major work stoppage when I was there*: "Convicts Stage Protest at Louisiana Prison," UPI, July 23, 1991, https://www.upi.com/Archives/1991/07/23/Convicts-stage-protest-at-Louisiana-prison/6586680241600/.
125 *The Loyola Death Penalty Resource Center in New Orleans challenged*: Death Penalty Information Center, "Botched Executions," last updated February 28, 2024, https://deathpenaltyinfo.org/executions/botched-executions.
125 *His experience reminded me*: Vanessa Tolino, "Louisiana State Penitentiary

at Angola," *64 Parishes*, July 30, 2013, last updated December 30, 2022, https:/64parishes.org/entry/louisiana-state-penitentiary-at-angola.

125 *The self-mutilation attracted a lot of media*: 2023 Louisiana Laws Revised Statutes Title 14—Criminal Law 14:404. Self-Mutilation by a prisoner, in *Justia U.S. Law*, https://law.justia.com/codes/louisiana/revised-statutes/title-14/rs-14-404/#; WAFB Staff, "Attorney Challenges La. Law That Punishes Inmates for Self-Harming," WAFB9, October 12, 2023, https://www.wafb.com/2023/10/12/attorney-challenges-la-law-that-punishes-inmates-self-harming/.

126 *Over the years I also heard talk about the rebellion at Attica*: Amy Goodman, "Former Attica Prisoner Describes Racist Brutality That Sparked Deadly Uprising," *Democracy Now!*, September 13, 2021, as published in *Truthout*, https://truthout.org/video/former-attica-prisoner-describes-racist-brutality-that-sparked-deadly-uprising/; Randall Berlage, "State Prison Inmates Who Took 17 Guards Hostage Began . . . ," UPI, January 10, 1983, https://www.upi.com/Archives/1983/01/10/State-prison-inmates-who-took-17-guards-hostage-began/5202411022800/; Julia Tanenbaum and Jake Hawkings, "Prisoner Uprisings from San Quentin to Attica," *Rebel in the Golden Gulag Archives*, UCLA Department of Information Studies.

126 *We were already members of CURE*: https://www.curenational.org/.

126 *The Angola Special Civics Project began*: Lydia Pelot-Hobbs, "Organizing for Freedom: The Angola Special Civics Project, 1987–1992," Master's Thesis, *ScholarWorks* at *UNO*, August 2011, https://scholarworks.uno.edu/td/349.

127 *Louisiana statute 15:574 said you couldn't get paroled*: Louisiana State Legislature, RS 15:574.2, https://legis.la.gov/Legis/law.aspx?d=79324.

127 *Many had been sentenced to life under the 10/6 law*: Jessica Shulberg, "Louisiana Passes a Law That Could Free Some '10/6 Lifers,'" *HuffPost*, March 30, 2022, https://www.huffpost.com/entry/louisiana-lawmakers-pass-bill-ten-six-lifers_n_62900f1fe4b0edd2d0215901.

127 *Naomi Farve and Ted Quant*: On Nancy Farve, see "This Session Let's Strengthen Our Collective Voice," *Voice of the Experienced* blog, February 26, 2020, https://voiceoftheexperienced.blog/2020/02/this-session-lets-strengthen-our-collective-voice/. On Ted Quant, see Pamela Yates, "An Interview with Social Justice Advocate Ted Quant, Featured in Skylight's Film *Resurgence*," skylight.is, February 28, 2021, https://skylight.is/2021/02/28/an-interview-with-social-justice-advocate-ted-quant-featured-in-skylights-film-resurgence/.

128 *Buddy Roemer was elected as a Democrat*: Tyler Bridges, "Buddy Roemer,

Reform Governor Who Switched Parties and Lost Re-Election Bid, Dies at 77," *Advocate*, May 17, 2021, https://www.theadvocate.com/baton_rouge/news/buddy-roemer-reform-governor-who-switched-parties-and-lost-re-election-bid-dies-at-77/article_4e8cd89e-3676-11eb-b2fc-eb5c23580375.html.

129 *I recall several key events held by ASCP*: Pelot-Hobbs, "Organizing for Freedom," 53–54.

129 *The stated reason for his removal*: Associated Press, "Louisiana Warden Dismissed Over Security," *New York Times*, October 15, 1989, https://www.nytimes.com/1989/10/15/us/louisiana-warden-dismissed-over-security.html.

129 *In July 1989, we were surprised when Governor Roemer appointed Larry Smith*: Angola Museum Instagram, "Black History Month: Warden Larry Smith," https://www.instagram.com/angolamuseum/p/CZ2SKXlOdWx/.

130 *Larry Smith set up the Inmate Welfare Fund Board*: Tolino, "Louisiana State Penitentiary at Angola."

131 *A powerlifting team came into existence*: Gary Tyler notes.

132 *Among other things, he put restraints on* The Angolite: Wilbert Rideau, *In the Place of Justice: A Story of Punishment and Redemption* (New York: Penguin Random House, 2010), 268–70, 279–80.

CHAPTER 11: WHAT KEPT ME GOING

134 *How could I have hidden it if I had tight clothes*: See Amy Singer, "So Why Is He Still in Prison?," *American Lawyer*, June 1991, 65–71.

134 *As one of my lawyers, Mary Howell, later said*: Singer, "So Why Is He Still in Prison?," 66.

134 *At a 1977 state hearing, Williams described his preparation*: Singer, "So Why Is He Still in Prison?," 67–68.

135 *But incredibly, he claimed he couldn't remember*: Singer, "So Why Is He Still in Prison?," 70.

135 *It hurt like hell when I heard*: State of Louisiana v. Gary Tyler, 342 So. 2d 574 (1977), *Justia U.S. Law*, January 24, 1977, Rehearing denied February 25, 1977, https://law.justia.com/cases/louisiana/supreme-court/1977/342-so-2d-574-1.html.

135 *We got another denial, although this time*: State Ex Rel. Tyler v. Phelps, Supreme Court of Louisiana, January 13, 1978, CaseMine, https://www.casemine.com/judgement/us/59149447add7b049345b9993.

135 *And on July 24, that court said the words*: Tyler v. Phelps, United States Court of Appeals, Fifth Circuit, July 24, 1980, CaseMine, https://www.casemine.com/judgement/us/5914c4bbadd7b049347cf646.

Notes

136 *That same year, 1980, the legal team got a big boost*: Affidavit by William E. Rittenberg, Exhibit 1, Petition of Pardon in the Matter of Gary Tyler, 1989, 22.

137 *On April 27, 1981, my case was back*: Gary Tyler, Petitioner-appellant, v. C. Paul Phelps, Director, Department of Corrections and Attorney-General of the State of Louisiana, William Guste, Jr., Respondents-appellees, 643 F.2d 1095 (5th Cir. 1981), April 27, 1981, *Justia U.S. Law*, https://law.justia.com/cases/federal/appellate-courts/F2/643/1095/454296/.

137 *What really stung was a concurring opinion*: Tyler v. Phelps, 643 F.2d 1095.

137 *The decision set me back*: Singer, "So Why Is He Still in Prison?," 70.

139 *I got a boost in 1977 when CBS*: CBS News report on Gary Tyler, April 21, 1977, https://m.youtube.com/watch?v=zkrDDdUbgKo.

140 *Rosa Parks spoke at a big event*: Library Street Collective, "Gary Tyler, We Are the Willing," Curated by Allison Glenn, July 8, 2023–September 13, 2023, Press Release, https://lscgallery.com/exhibitions/we-are-the-willing.

140 *Local people like Marie Galatas*: "Reverend Marie Galatas Ortiz," New Orleans Historical, https://neworleanshistorical.org/items/show/1624.

140 *I learned that he yelled for his friend*: Clancy DuBos, "Man Guilty in Death of 16-Year-Old Orleanian," *Times-Picayune*, June 21, 1978.

140 *This white guy, the killer of a Black man*: Singer, "So Why Is He Still in Prison?," 71.

140 *A year later, Tom Henehan, an activist in New York*: David North, "Tom Henehan: A Revolutionary Life," World Socialist Web Site, October 16, 2022, https://www.wsws.org/en/articles/2022/10/17/hene-o17.html.

141 *In 1977, a dozen or more supporters*: Gary Tyler notes.

141 *Soon, he wrote a song about me*: Gil Scott-Heron and Brian Jackson, "Angola, Louisiana," genius.com, https://genius.com/Gil-scott-heron-and-brian-jackson-angola-louisiana-lyrics.

141 *Then, in 1980, British reggae band UB40*: UB40, "Tyler," genius.com, https://genius.com/Ub40-tyler-lyrics.

141 *They told representatives of the National Black Caucus of State Legislators*: Harry Amana, "U.S. Political Prisoners Interviewed," *Guardian*, August 22, 1979.

141 *A few years later, the Russian newspaper* Pravda: Wilbert Rideau and Ron Wikberg, "The Long Road Back," *Angolite*, January/February 1990, 21.

142 *In the early 1990s, Amnesty International*: Amnesty International, United States, The Case of Gary Tyler, Louisiana, November 1994, https://www.amnesty.org/en/wp-content/uploads/2021/06/amr510891994en.pdf.

142 *And in September 2007, marchers protesting the racist charges against the Jena 6*: Malik Miah, "Race and Class: What the Jena 6 Case Shows," Against

the Current, November/December 2007, https://againstthecurrent.org/atc131/p1168/. The Jena 6, Black high school students, were charged as adults with attempted murder after a fight broke out with white students angry that a Black youth had sat under the "white tree" in their schoolyard, which some then decorated with three nooses.

142 *That same year, a reporter from* The New York Times: Bob Herbert, "A Death in Destrahan," *New York Times*, February 1, 2007, https://www.nytimes.com/2007/02/01/opinion/01herbert.html; "Gary Tyler's Lost Decades," *New York Times*, February 5, 2007, https://www.nytimes.com/2007/02/05/opinion/05herbert.html; and "They Beat Gary So Bad," *New York Times*, February 8, 2007, https://www.nytimes.com/2007/02/08/opinion/08herbert.html.

142 *That coverage led to a story on* Democracy Now!: Amy Goodman, "The Case of Gary Tyler: Despite Witness Recantations and No Physical Evidence, Louisiana Prisoner Remains Jailed after 32 Years," *Democracy Now!*, March 1, 2007, https://www.democracynow.org/2007/3/1/the_case_of_gary_tyler_despite.

143 *Once I was arrested, my parents and siblings*: Bob Nirkind, "Gary Tyler Family Victimized," *Fifth Estate*, #274, July 1976, https://www.fifthestate.org/archive/274-july-1976/gary-tyler-family-victimized/.

143 *Police stopped a number of them*: Associated Press, "Two Klansmen Seized in Destrehan Area," *Shreveport Times*, October 10, 1974, https://www.newspapers.com/newspage/217265425/.

144 *On January 21, 1977, at 10:00 a.m.*: Nirkind, "Gary Tyler Family Victimized."

147 *One example was a white nurse*: James Minton, "Teen Puts Life in Hands of Convicts," *Advocate*, May 23, 1995.

147 *I wanted to be a match*: Associated Press, "Prisoners Mourn Death of Boy They Tried to Help," *New Orleans Times-Picayune*, October 22, 1995.

147 *David Duke got a lot of votes in that parish*: Jeremy Alford, "Much of David Duke's '91 Campaign Is Now in Louisiana Mainstream," *New York Times*, December 31, 2014, https://www.nytimes.com/2015/01/01/us/politics/much-of-david-dukes-91-campaign-is-now-in-louisiana-mainstream.html.

CHAPTER 12: PARDON ME

149 *A year earlier, when they had filed*: Singer, "So Why Is He Still in Prison?," 65.

149 *Among my biggest supporters*: "Former Death Row Inmate Gary Tyler Starts a New Life in Pasadena," *Pasadena Weekly*, June 29, 2017, https://www.pasadenaweekly.com/news/feature-stories/former-death-row

-inmate-gary-tyler-starts-a-new-life-in-pasadena/article_5b51c9c6-2847-5ac6-bfd7-9f2a1dbe9fe0.html.

149 *Larry's statement was detailed*: Singer, "So Why Is He Still in Prison?," 69.
150 *Michael Campbell, who shared that bus seat*: Affidavit of Michael R. Campbell, State of Louisiana, County of Bell, November 12, 1989.
151 *Mary Howell's team got an affidavit*: Singer, "So Why Is He Still in Prison?," 70.
151 *That firing range in Kenner*: Nossiter, "Legal Lynching in Louisiana."
151 *They located a former colleague of his*: Singer, "So Why Is He Still in Prison?," 70.
152 *Kenneth Gaillot, the firearms examiner*: Trial transcript, Vol. 6, 12–20.
152 *In April 1962, along with two others*: "Segregation Figures Are Excommunicated," *New Orleans Times-Picayune*, November 27, 2011.
152 *The bullet the police claimed killed Timothy Weber*: Mary Howell, "Reply on Behalf of Gary Tyler to State's Memorandum," sent to Louisiana Board of Pardons, 1989, 10.
152 *In early 1989, we found out*: "Report of the Crime Lab," Southeastern Louisiana Criminalistics Laboratory, December 5, 1974.
152 *The team brought in another group of lawyers*: "Clive Stafford Smith," Reprieve, https://reprieve.org/uk/person/clive-stafford-smith/.
152 *In 1988, Mary Howell decided to go that route*: Petition for Pardon, In the Matter of Gary Tyler, 1989.
153 *The petition for pardon covered all the major problems*: Petition for Pardon, In the Matter of Gary Tyler, 1989, 1–19.
153 *She ended her argument by saying*: Petition for Pardon, In the Matter of Gary Tyler, 1989, 18.
153 *And she made the important point of what a "pardon" would mean*: Petition for Pardon, In the Matter of Gary Tyler, 1989, 19.
154 *A lot of people wrote letters*: "Avery Alexander," Wikipedia, last modified July 25, 2024, https://en.wikipedia.org/wiki/Avery_Alexander; "Dorothy Mae Taylor," Historic New Orleans Collection, https://www.hnoc.org/virtual/voices-progress/dorothy-mae-taylor.
154 *On May 4, 1989, Yvonne Campbell*: Letter from Yvonne Campbell to Gary Tyler, Mary 4, 1989.
154 *I wrote back May 12*: Letter from Gary Tyler to Yvonne Campbell, May 12, 1989.
154 *The state tried to trash*: State's Response in Opposition to the Petition for Pardon of Gary Tyler, 1989, 2.
154 *But in early November of 1989*: Singer, "So Why Is He Still in Prison?," 71.
155 *But in January of the following year*: Associated Press, "Louisiana Governor

Refuses to Pardon Black in '74 Killing," *New York Times*, January 25, 1990, https://www.nytimes.com/1990/01/25/us/louisiana-governor-refuses-to-pardon-black-in-74-killing.html.

155 *The truth was, Roemer was running for re-election against David Duke*: Singer, "So Why Is He Still in Prison?," 71.

155 *My legal team tried again two years later*: Petition of Pardon, In the Matter of Gary Tyler, October 30, 1991.

155 *In their response, the attorney general*: State's Response in Opposition to the Petition for Pardon of Gary Tyler, 30.

155 *This time the decision of the Louisiana Board of Pardons*: Letter to Gary Tyler from Yvonne G. Campbell, December 18, 1991.

155 *But four days before he left office*: "Roemer Denies Pardons to Prominent Convicts," *New Orleans Times-Picayune*, January 26, 1990.

156 *The third pardon attempt was with Governor Edwin Edwards*: Presentation on Behalf of Gary Tyler, Louisiana State Pardon Board, State of Louisiana, In re Request for Clemency for Gary Tyler, DOC/File.# 84156, 1995.

156 *There was a support letter from former Angola warden John Whitley*: Presentation on Behalf of Gary Tyler, 1995, 34.

156 *And there was an excellent psychological evaluation*: Presentation on Behalf of Gary Tyler, 1995, 14–19.

156 *The recommendation was again favorable*: Letter to Gary Tyler from Cynthia F. Fayard, June 19, 1995.

156 *When he was corrected, he said*: Gary Tyler notes.

157 *But when a Black state senator*: Conversation between Gary Tyler and Dennis Bagneris, December 12, 2024.

157 *Later we learned from* The Morning Advocate: Advocate Staff, "Excerpts of Taped Conversations Introduced at Cascade Trial," *Morning Advocate*, October 1, 2000.

157 *Yet I found out he wrote a letter of support*: Gary Tyler notes.

157 *They talked to groups like the Innocence Project*: https://innocenceproject.org/.

157 *Deputy Warden Darrel Vannoy over at Angola*: Gary Tyler notes.

158 *We found out that Governor Haley Barbour*: "Governor Haley Barbour: EXECUTIVE ORDERS ISSUED DURING FIRST TERM 2004–2008," https://www.sos.ms.gov/content/executiveorders/ExecutiveOrders/barbour.exec.orders.index.2004-08.pdf.

158 *In early 2006, Deputy Warden Leslie DuPont talked to me*: Gary Tyler notes.

159 *George Kendall was working with Wilbert Rideau*: Rick Bragg, "Prison Journalist's Conviction for 1961 Murder Is Overturned," *New York Times*, December 23, 2000, https://www.nytimes.com/2000/12/23/us/prison-journalist-s-conviction-for-1961-murder-is-overturned.html.

159 *In May 2006, more than two dozen world-class athletes*: Dave Zirin, "Gary Tyler's Quest for Justice," *The Nation*, April 2, 2007, https://www.thenation.com/article/archive/gary-tylers-quest-justice/.

159 *On February 12, 2007, Amnesty International*: Amnesty International, "Serious Miscarriage of Justice in Louisiana Must Be Rectified," Press Release, February 12, 2007, https://www.amnesty.org/en/wp-content/uploads/2021/07/amr510262007en.pdf.

CHAPTER 13: QUALIFIED TO DO ANYTHING WITH NOTHING

161 *When Ronald Little first asked me to join*: Gary Tyler notes.

161 *Herman invited me into his office*: Gary Tyler notes.

163 *Our first breakthrough was a play*: Plays referenced in this chapter with the permission of the Angola Drama Club.

164 *We performed the play in the Visiting Shed*: Gary Tyler notes.

164 *The following year we wrote* Just Us: Gary Tyler notes.

164 *In August of 1988, we faced another change in leadership*: Gary Tyler notes.

164 *Kenya did something that pissed Wells off*: Gary Tyler notes.

165 *In June of 1990, we invited a group of professors*: Laurie Smith Anderson, "Budding Playwrights at Angola Get Tips from Pros," *Morning Advocate*, November 10, 1991.

165 *I was at the podium reciting Alice Walker's poem*: Quoted in K. Narayana Chandran, "'First, They Said': Alice Walker's Poem for All Seasons (Alas!)," Project Muse, https://muse.jhu.edu/article/379741/summary.

165 *She returned for a second workshop*: Gary Tyler notes.

166 *Barry Kyle taught us how to make violence on stage*: Anderson, "Budding Playwrights."

166 *On the ninth anniversary of the Drama Club*: Gary Tyler notes.

166 *That night, Angola warden John Whitley sat*: *Angolite*, January/February 1992, referenced in Gary Tyler notes.

166 *On January 15, 1992, Warden Whitley appeared before the Classification Board*: Gary Tyler notes.

167 *A photographer named Lori Waselchuk*: Lori Waselchuk photos in Anderson, "Budding Playwrights."

168 *In November 1994, Reader's Digest*: Robert James Bidinotto, "Must Our Prisons Be Resorts?," *Reader's Digest*, November 1994, 65–71.

168 *That made the newspaper*: James Minton, "Toy Gun Costs Jobs, Discipline at Penitentiary," *Morning Advocate*, August 27, 1993.

171 *I didn't see Fox or Hooks again until 1988*: Gary Tyler notes.

171 *I was selected to go as an orderly*: Gary Tyler notes.

172 *After Jerry Wells died of cancer*: Gary Tyler notes.

Notes

172 *Directors of films that had prison scenes*: James Ridgeway, "God's Own Warden," *Mother Jones*, July–August 2011, https://www.motherjones.com/politics/2011/07/burl-cain-angola-prison/.

172 *It was common knowledge that Cain made private deals*: Ridgeway, "God's Own Warden."

172 *Cain never went to jail*: David M. Reutter, "Controversy Surrounds Angola Prison Warden's Retirement, Indictment of Family Members," *Prison Legal News*, January 8, 2018, https://www.prisonlegalnews.org/news/2018/jan/8/controversy-surrounds-angola-prison-wardens-retirement-indictment-family-members/.

172 *In 1997, a crew came to Angola*: Gary Tyler notes.

173 *On August 23, 2001, I was called from work*: Gary Tyler notes.

CHAPTER 14: PROMISES KEPT

175 *The vast majority of prisoners at Angola*: Ridgeway, "God's Own Warden," cites Deputy Warden Cathy Fontenot as saying 90 percent of Angola inmates die there.

175 *Prisoners were dying*: Ginny Shubert, "Mass Incarceration, Housing Instability and HIV/AIDS: Research Findings and Policy Recommendations," National Minority AIDS Council, February 6, 2013, https://www.nmac.org/wp-content/uploads/2013/02/Incarceration-Report-FINAL_2-6-13_Two.pdf.

175 *In fall of 1993, when I was thirty-five*: Gary Tyler notes.

176 *Nurse Hager and Mr. Crawford were part of a national program*: Gary Tyler notes.

176 *I still have the clip*: Barbara Schlichtman, "Peer Plan Curbs AIDS at Angola," *Sunday Advocate*, October 9, 1994.

176 *That network held a follow-up conference*: Gary Tyler notes.

176 *They came back in March 1997*: Anne Seditz, "Fixin' to Die," National Prison Hospice Association, https://npha.org/npha-articles/view-from-the-inside/fixin-to-die/; Gary Tyler notes.

177 *In October 1997, we underwent two weeks*: Gary Tyler notes.

177 *I certainly felt challenged*: Gary Tyler notes.

178 *In late November of 1998, my two worlds*: Gary Tyler notes.

178 *My next patient, Leroy Rayford*: Gary Tyler notes.

179 *Melvin Lewis was a good friend*: Gary Tyler notes.

179 *After the hospice program began*: Rideau, *In the Place of Justice*, 272.

179 *Charlie Hamilton was an inmate*: Gary Tyler notes.

180 *Afterward someone said, "Why not keep making quilts"*: Lauren Stroh, "The

Prison Rodeo at the Heart of Legal Enslavement," *The Nation*, November 12, 2024, https://www.thenation.com/article/society/angola-prison-rodeo/.

181   *And then in August of 2002, Warden Linda Miller*: Gary Tyler notes.
183   *One major rodeo event called "Guts and Glory"*: Stroh, "The Prison Rodeo."
185   *On April 22, 2004, Hospice Coordinator Tillman called us*: Gary Tyler notes.
186   *Less than six months later, I received a call*: Gary Tyler notes.
187   *In May 2007, we had an opportunity to meet*: Gary Tyler notes.
187   *Thanks to Albert Woodfox, Herman Wallace, and others*: See Woodfox, *Solitary*.
188   *In September 2006, I was asked*: Gary Tyler notes.

CHAPTER 15: CAST THE FIRST STONE

189   *The idea for prisoners to perform a passion play*: Campbell Robertson, "In Prison, Play with Trial at Its Heart Resonates," *New York Times*, May 5, 2012, https://www.nytimes.com/2012/05/06/us/in-prison-play-with-trial-at-its-heart-resonates.html.
189   *Fontenot called a meeting*: Gary Tyler notes.
190   *I had done a play at her request*: Gary Tyler notes.
191   *Once, Cain called all the club leaders*: Daniel Bergner, *God of the Rodeo: The Search for Hope, Faith and a Six-Second Ride in Louisiana's Angola Prison* (New York: Random House, 1999) https://www.danielbergner.com/god-of-the-rodeo.
198   *In April of 2012, Susan Lofthus*: Robertson, "In Prison, Play with Trial at Its Heart Resonates."
201   *Jonathan named his documentary:* Quotes that follow are all from *Cast the First Stone*.

CHAPTER 16: THE LONG ARC

204   *In 2002, the U.S. Supreme Court issued a ruling*: Brian Stull, "The Supreme Court Decision to Protect People with an Intellectual Disability from Execution Was Long Overdue," ACLU, April 3, 2017, https://www.aclu.org/news/capital-punishment/supreme-court-decision-protect-people-intellectual-disability-execution-was.
204   *A watershed moment for me came three years later*: Joshua Rovner, "Juvenile Life Without Parole: An Overview," The Sentencing Project, April 7, 2023, https://www.sentencingproject.org/policy-brief/juvenile-life-without-parole-an-overview/.
205   *Cases on juvenile sentencing*: Joshua Rovner, "Juvenile Life Without Parole."

205 *In 2010, the Supreme Court ruled in* Graham v. Florida: *Graham v. Florida*, 560 U.S. 48 (2010), *Justia U.S. Law,* May 17, 2010, https://supreme.justia.com/cases/federal/us/560/48/.

205 *Next up was a case known as* Miller v. Alabama: *Miller v. Alabama*, 567 U.S. 460 (2012), *Justia U.S. Law,* June 25, 2012, https://supreme.justia.com/cases/federal/us/567/460/.

205 *The papers mentioned my case*: Rovner, "Juvenile Life Without Parole."

205 *The chief lawyer for the case was Bryan Stevenson*: "Graham v. Florida," Equal Justice Initiative, May 2010, https://eji.org/cases/graham-v-florida/.

207 *But soon state authorities declared that* Miller: Gary Tyler notes.

211 *In 2013, the district attorney out of St. Charles Parish*: Gary Tyler notes.

211 *This was a guy who stooped to playing the prisoners*: Gary Tyler notes.

212 *In the summer of 2013, I had my visit with DA*: Gary Tyler notes.

214 *In September of 2013, the Louisiana Supreme Court ruled*: Referenced in *Montgomery v. Louisiana*, 577 U.S. 190 (2016), *Justia U.S. Law,* https://supreme.justia.com/cases/federal/us/577/190/.

CHAPTER 17: FREE AT LAST

215 *George Toca, another Angola inmate, had been sentenced to life without parole*: Helen Freund, "Imprisoned for 30 Years, Angola Inmate to Be Released After New Orleans DA Cuts a Deal," NOLA, January 30, 2015, https://www.nola.com/news/crime_police/imprisoned-for-30-years-angola-inmate-to-be-released-after-new-orleans-da-cuts-deal/article_496cef7e-3ffe-5c1a-b7f4-605cd6ba3a45.html.

216 *It appeared the next case would be Henry Montgomery's*: Associated Press, "An Inmate Whose Story Was Key to the Debate over Juvenile Life Sentences Gets Parole," NPR, November 17, 2021, https://www.npr.org/2021/11/17/1056554393/henry-montgomery-parole-juvenile-life-sentence.

216 *The decision in* Montgomery v. Louisiana: *Montgomery v. Louisiana* 577 U.S. 190 (2016).

218 *Herman Wallace only got out when he was terminally ill*: "Herman Wallace, 'Angola 3' Inmate, Dies Days After Release from Solitary," *Guardian,* October 4, 2013, https://www.theguardian.com/world/2013/oct/04/herman-wallace-angola-three-dies-solitary-confinement.

221 *Darrel Vannoy was now the head warden*: WAFB Staff, "Interim Warden to Take over Permanently at Angola," WAFB9, July 14, 2016, https://www.wafb.com/story/32441382/interim-warden-to-take-over-permanently-at-angola/.

CHAPTER 18: STITCHING A LIFE TOGETHER

225 *Norris had started an organization called VOTE*: https://www.voiceofthe experienced.org/.

232 *The group was also honoring Albert Woodfox and John Thompson*: Sam Roberts, "John Thompson, Cleared After 14 Years on Death Row, Dies at 55," *New York Times*, October 4, 2017, https://www.nytimes.com/2017/10/04/obituaries/john-thompson-cleared-after-14-years-on-death-row-dies-at-55.html.

232 *In July, I joined a rally and press conference*: "Do They Deserve Death? Diverse Coalition Kicks Off 'Yes-on-62' Campaign," *Angelus*, July 20, 2016, https://angelusnews.com/local/la-catholics/do-they-deserve-death-diverse-coalition-kicks-off-yes-on-62-campaign/.

232 *In September 2016, I was a keynote speaker*: Susan Burton, Ford Foundation, https://www.fordfoundation.org/news-and-stories/big-ideas/the-future-is-hers/susan-burton/.

234 *In December of 2016, Bob brought me to Safe Place for Youth*: https://www.safeplaceforyouth.org/.

234 *Then Alison approached me about being part of a group*: Campbell Robertson, "A Lynching Memorial Is Opening. The Country Has Never Seen Anything Like It," *New York Times*, April 25, 2018, https://www.nytimes.com/2018/04/25/us/lynching-memorial-alabama.html.

235 *That same year, I was honored that a short film about me*: "The Winners of Our 2017 Speak Truth to Power Video Contest," Robert F. Kennedy Human Rights, Press Release, April 17, 2018, https://rfkhumanrights.org/press/the-winners-of-our-2017-speak-truth-to-power-video-contest/.

235 *Then in 2020 a group called Art Matters*: "Gary Tyler," Art Matters, 2020, https://www.artmattersfoundation.org/grantees/gary-tyler.

235 *She got a grant from the Open Society Foundation*: "Grace Before Dying: An Examination of Human Dignity and Transformation," St. Patrick–St. Anthony Church, 2015, https://spsact.org/grace-before-dying/.

236 *Robert sent those photographs*: Library Street Collective, https://lscgallery.com/.

237 *To my surprise, the Library Street Collective invited me*: "Gary Tyler: We Are the Willing," curated by Allison Glenn, July 8, 2023–September 13, 2023, Library Street Collective, https://lscgallery.com/exhibitions/we-are-the-willing.

238 *In February of 2024, I was presented*: Nicole Fell, "Gary Tyler, Artist Wrongfully Imprisoned for 41 Years, Awarded 2024 L.A. Impact Prize," *Hollywood*

Notes

239 *Reporter*, February 15, 2024, https://www.hollywoodreporter.com/life style/arts/gary-tyler-2024-frieze-la-impact-prize-exclusive-1235825452/.

239 *In 2024, I was one of six formerly incarcerated artists*: News Desk, "Center for Art & Advocacy Announces 2024 Right of Return Fellows," *Art Forum*, February 12, 2024, https://www.artforum.com/news/center-for-art-advocacy-announces-2024-right-of-return-fellows-549255/.

239 *That December, I was invited to show my work*: Library Street Collective, Instagram, December 7, 2024, https://www.instagram.com/librarystreet collective/p/DDTF5QmvVPa/?img_index=1.

239 *I was also invited to speak at the World Economic Forum*: Nel-Olivia Waga, "A Cultural Awakening at the World Economic Forum's Annual Meeting 2025 in Davos," *Forbes*, January 15, 2025, https://www.forbes.com/sites/neloliviawaga/2025/01/15/a-cultural-awakening-at-the-world-economic-forums-annual-meeting-2025-in-davos/.

240 *In 2022, COVID also took*: Alex Traub, "Albert Woodfox, Survivor of 42 Years in Solitary Confinement, Dies at 75," *New York Times*, August 4, 2022, https://www.nytimes.com/2022/08/05/us/albert-woodfox-dead.html.

240 *Whenever I went back, I also got to see friends*: https://www.paroleproject.org/.

240 *They called him No Hum Bow*: Matthew Hinton, "No Hum Bow: Wrongly Convicted and Never Wanting Revenge, Mardi Gras Indians Chief Joe Jenkins Chose Love," *Very Local*, August 25, 2020, https://www.verylocal.com/no-hum-bow-wrongly-convicted-and-never-wanting-revenge-mardi-gras-indians-chief-joe-jenkins-chose-love/6653/.

240 *When I got out, I had a long talk with David Deniger*: David Deniger, producer, IMDb, https://www.imdb.com/name/nm3088217/.

EPILOGUE: REFLECTIONS

245 *In May of 2024, I received an Honorary Doctor of Fine Arts*: "Massart Announces Honorary Degree Recipients and Commencement Speaker for Class of 2024," https://massart.edu/massart-announces-honorary-degree-recipients-and-commencement-speaker-for-class-of-2024/.

ABOUT THE AUTHORS

Gary Tyler is an artist and a spokesperson for justice. During his years in prison, Tyler galvanized a movement that grew to have national and international support, one of the precursors to today's abolition and Black Lives Matter movements. Upon his release, he became involved in the fight to end the death penalty. Tyler was recently awarded a Right of Return Fellowship and the 2024 Frieze Los Angeles Impact Prize, which recognizes artists who use their talents and abilities to address social justice issues. He holds an honorary doctorate of fine arts from MassArt. *Stitching Freedom* is his first book.

Ellen Bravo's connection to Gary Tyler began in July 1976, when she marched with two thousand others in New Orleans demanding his freedom. A longtime activist, Bravo has written three nonfiction books about working women and two novels, *Again and Again*, about date rape and politics, and *Standing Up: Tales of Struggle*, about love and organizing. Among Bravo's many commendations are the Ford Foundation's Visionary Award and a Trailblazer award from the Ms. Foundation.

One Signal Publishers, an imprint of Simon & Schuster, fosters an open environment where ideas flourish, bestselling authors soar to new heights, and tomorrow's finest voices are discovered and nurtured. Since its launch in 2002, Atria has published hundreds of bestsellers and extraordinary books, which would not have been possible without the invaluable support and expertise of its team and publishing partners. Thank you to the Atria Books colleagues who collaborated on *Stitching Freedom,* as well as to the hundreds of professionals in the Simon & Schuster advertising, audio, communications, design, ebook, finance, human resources, legal, marketing, operations, production, sales, supply chain, subsidiary rights, and warehouse departments who help Atria bring great books to light.

EDITORIAL
Alessandra Bastagli
Rola Harb

JACKET DESIGN
James Iacobelli
Claire Sullivan

MARKETING
Jolena Podolsky
Morgan Pager
Erin Kibby
Annie Probert

MANAGING EDITORIAL
Paige Lytle
Shelby Pumphrey
Lacee Burr
Sofia Echeverry

PRODUCTION
Kathleen Rizzo
Beth Maglione
Rick Willett
Davina Mock-Maniscalco

PUBLICITY
Shida Carr
Molly Burgoyne

PUBLISHING OFFICE
Suzanne Donahue
Abby Velasco

SUBSIDIARY RIGHTS
Nicole Bond
Sara Bowne
Rebecca Justiniano